Idle Fictions

Frontispiece: Poster by Batty, "Return of Persephone"

(Reproduced by permission of the Victoria and Albert Museum: Crown copyright)

Idle Fictions

The Hispanic Vanguard Novel, 1926–1934

Gustavo Pérez Firmat

There were several ways of understanding her:
there was what she said, and there was what she
meant, and there was something between the two,
that was neither.

Henry James, *The Europeans*

DUKE UNIVERSITY PRESS   DURHAM, N.C.   1982

This publication has been assisted by a grant
from the Andrew W. Mellon Foundation.

© 1982, Duke University Press

Printed in the United States of
America on acid-free paper

Library of Congress Cataloging in Publication Data

Pérez Firmat, Gustavo, 1949–
  Idle fictions.

    Bibliography: p.
    Includes index.
    1. Spanish fiction—20th century—History and
criticism. 2. Spanish American fiction—20th
century—History and criticism. I. Title.
PQ6144.P475   1982   863'.63'09   82–12773
ISBN 0–8223–0528–3

A mis padres

Acknowledgments

I would like to thank the Duke University Research Council for its generous support of the publication of this book and for a Faculty Travel Grant that allowed me, some summers ago, to spend several painful but productive weeks at the Hemeroteca Municipal in Madrid.

Part of chapter 6 was originally published in the *Romanic Review* as "*Locura y muerte de Nadie*: Two Novels by Jarnés." I thank the editors for permission to reprint.

Contents

Introduction

This book began several years ago as an experiment. I wanted to study the Hispanic vanguard novel, an interesting but little-read body of fiction produced in Spain and Spanish America during the third and fourth decades of this century, but to do so in a way that avoided—or at least deferred—the circularity typical of most generic studies, and which might be summarized thus: in order to describe a class, one must first delimit a corpus of works, but the delimitation of a corpus requires a prior definition of the class, which in turn presupposes the existence of a corpus, and so on. My approach to this dilemma was to adopt a strictly historicist stance: instead of starting with a noninductive delimitative leap, I would let the genre circumscribe itself. My corpus would contain those works that, at the time of their publication, were included in the genre, and my characterization of the genre would be that given in the critical discourse contemporary with the novels. My task was not to contrive a retrospective definition of the vanguard novel but simply to reconstruct (a favorite word) the definition already embedded in the critical literature of the period, a definition I would then apply to the novels. The way to bolt the hermeneutic circle, I thought, was simply to ask a different set of questions—not: What is the vanguard novel? What works belong to the genre?—but: What was the vanguard novel thought to be? What works were thought to belong to the genre? Instead of developing my own criteria, I was to act as organizer and relayer of a generic conception already present in the critical discussion of the period that concerned me.[1]

I soon realized, however, that my reception study would inevitably become, to some extent, a deception study, since no amount of historicist fact-finding was going to permit me to see these novels with eyes other than my own. Regardless of the breadth and specificity of the documentation, my characterization of the vanguard novel and, more particularly, my readings of the novels, would be shaped by that noninductive interpretive arbitrariness I had sought to exclude. To believe that I could read those texts now as they were read fifty years ago, to believe, in other words, that I could occupy a value-free, neutral post of observation from which to assemble and evaluate information, would have been to fall victim to the postulate of the privileged observer.[2] And although it seems clear to me now that the privileged observer is an unnecessary critical fiction, in its primitive version this book was to have resulted from just such a perspective. A related difficulty was that the more I endeavored to apply the criteria unearthed by the reception study, the more constraining my premises became. By so narrowing the scope of the readings, I was, in effect, short-circuiting my access to these novels, and thereby not allowing myself to say a good many things I wanted to. It was not long before I abandoned my initial assumptions, and soon after the book took its present shape.

Two things remain, nevertheless, from the original project. First, I have used, as a point of departure, a corpus circumscribed according to historicist criteria (thus, I consider only those novels that were placed in the genre by their contemporaries); this seems to me still the only sensible approach to the problem of corpus delimitation. Second, the book as a whole breaks down into two parts. Part One (chaps. 1 and 2) consists of a reception study of the vanguard novel for the years between 1926 and 1934.[3] Part Two (chaps. 3 through 6) develops a reading of some of the novels singled out in the reception study. What is new, besides the unembarrassed acknowledgment of my intervention, is that the second part does not simply instantiate the criteria elicited from the metalanguage contemporary with the novels. Both parts are now locked in an "interpreting relationship" in which fiction and criticism mutually illuminate and condition each other.[4] Even if my order of presentation implies a certain determining structure, I intend no such role for the criticism; in fact, were it mechanically and rhetorically possible, the book could also be read backwards, novels-first. One of the authors I will be discussing, Benjamín Jarnés, with his customary flair for the abstruse metaphor and the recondite image, once compared fiction and commentary to the chicken and the egg. My two-way contextualist study sets out to corroborate the metaphor by demonstrating the interdependence of vanguard fiction and its accompanying body of commentary. As in Jarnés' comparison, the question of priority, of which came first, remains open. (The reader should recognize, however, that this interdependence widens the hermeneutic circle to embrace not only the connection between my discourse and my subject but also that between my subject's two parts. The original dilemma persists, deliberately, as a double bind.)

If one purpose of this book, therefore, is to examine Hispanic vanguard fiction under its two aspects—as an ongoing critical debate that sought to redefine the novel and as a group of novels that ostensibly embodied the new definition—a second purpose is to show the difficulty of maintaining this distinction. Both discourses permit the same hermeneutical operations (indeed, I will in parts be reading the criticism as fiction and the fiction as criticism); and these operations yield, on both levels, comparable results. I should say, then, that my aim has been to undertake a study of the relationship between language and metalanguage, or fiction and criticism, for about a ten-year period in the history of the modern Hispanic novel—a study effected through the good offices of a third language: my own. It is to this triplication of linguistic levels that my epigraph alludes. *Idle Fictions* is thus a book about boundaries, and for this reason—as well as for several others, as we will see—appears under the aegis of an art-deco Hermes, caught between the street and the subway.

Part One: Criticism

1. The Vanguard Novel as a Discursive Category

i. A Critical Text

"La novela, con sus características actuales, es un género de ayer." ("The novel, with its present characteristics, is yesterday's genre.") Lifted from its immediate context, this observation, made by Jaime Torres Bodet in 1928, displays a puzzling inconsistency.[1] To refer to the novel's present characteristics, while at the same time asserting its obsolescence, is to open a perplexing gap between the genre's viability and its survival, a gap made more visible by the causal force of the preposition *con*: one is tempted to read Torres Bodet as affirming that, precisely because of its present form, the novel is a thing of the past. One is thus confronted with a genre that is viable but has not survived; or, more simply, with a genre that is and is not viable, that has and has not survived. The problem stems from Torres Bodet's uncertainty in situating the novel temporally. Although the prepositional phrase, "con sus características actuales," lodges it in the present, with the predicate that follows, "un género de ayer," it recedes into the past. Where then does the novel belong? One cannot, it seems, have it both ways. Either the prepositional phrase, or the predicate, must be given precedence. Either the novel is "actual," or it is obsolete.

One could defend the coherence of the statement by arguing that it alludes to the fact that by 1928 the nineteenth-century form of the novel had become obsolete and a new fictional genre had taken its place. Torres Bodet would merely be echoing the commonplace that, in the Modern period, the novel changed. But this explanation leads back to the original inconsistency, for the passage, even as it concedes the obsolescence of the old genre, forecloses the possibility of its replacement. Although it leaves room—implicitly—for a "género de hoy," it does not allow for its instantiation in a set of norms. The "características actuales" *remain* those of the outmoded form. Indeed the paradox lies here: the traditional novel is dead but its structures are still in place; the edifice has been gutted but not demolished. It is as if two opposed constitutive forces met in the quotation: one which would end the viability of the traditional novel, thus freeing the way for a successor; another which would extend it, and thus suppress or protract the emergence of a new genre. The former generates the predicate; the latter generates the prepositional phrase. Their confluence obscures Torres Bodet's meaning. Tugged in contrary directions, the sentence becomes the site of a struggle where conflicting forces vie for precedence, a reflection of Jeffrey Mehlman's recent characterization of a text—"less a monument than a battlefield."[2]

If one pursued this line of argument, one would argue that this sentence exhibits in a particularly lucid way the stresses that constitute critical discourse about the vanguard novel. Like Torres Bodet's sentence, the criticism of this time shelters antinomies. It splits its allegiance between the old and the new fiction, refusing to relinquish either one. The interpretive task would then be to account for the conflict by identifying the warring factions and documenting its dispersive effect.

The hitch is that the argument seems to crumble once the passage is reinserted into its context. The inconsistencies vanish, and a different, unambiguous sense materializes. "Un género de ayer," it turns out, does not mean a genre of the past, an obsolete genre, but rather "a recent genre." Torres Bodet is tracing the genealogy of the novel and pauses to remark on the recency of the form: "The novel already knows its masters; it has learned to love them and begins to feel the need to choose them. In the beginning—one must not forget that the novel, with its present characteristics, is yesterday's genre—to say 'novel' was, implicitly, to allude to Balzac" (p. 12). The battlefield, it appears, was really a monument after all—or was it? Interestingly, if one examines the rest of Torres Bodet's essay, one discovers that it too is beset by inconsistencies, for the same hesitation that we found in the quotation can be observed throughout his discussion. At times he speaks of the traditional novel as a dead genre that has been replaced by the contemporary or modern novel. At other times, however, the traditional novelistic canons are perceived as still in force, the contemporary novel figuring as an unrealized project. With respect to the traditional novel, his temporal register wavers uneasily between past and present; with respect to the contemporary novel, between present and future. He recognizes, for instance, that "the only thing that has entered, not a period of decadence but a period of clear neglect, is the naturalistic novel, the novel intended for the consumption of young ladies and shopgirls," adding that "it has fallen into disuse because, not being a pure literary form, it could not compete with the cinematographer" (p. 10). In these passages the nineteenth-century novel has been supplanted by a newer genre. It belongs to the past, as is indicated by the use of the past indefinite and the preterit ("has entered . . . a period of clear neglect"; "has fallen into disuse"; "it could not compete"). The obsolescence of this kind of fiction is underscored by the contemporary novel's accomplishments, which have already become history: "This is what the contemporary novel has tried to do . . ." (p. 10). But a few paragraphs later he remarks: "Will the novel change directions? We hope so. Why should change mean decadence? Is it that the novel had reached maturity? Did it have nothing left to do but die?" (p. 11). And again: "The best quality of the modern novelist will lie in his scrupulous fidelity to memory" (p. 14). In the interval between the first and second set of quotations the temporal register has modulated from past to present and from present to future. The traditional novel, formerly consigned to the past, is once again in the present. A change in generic orientation has not yet taken place ("Will the novel change directions?"). The contemporary novel, which had been firmly entrenched in the present, is now pushed forward into the future. It exists only as promise or expectation. Where then does the novel belong? One cannot, it seems, have it both ways. The contemporary novel is either a reality or a project. The traditional novel is either obsolete or it is "actual."

One might say that the true temporal register of the essay is the present progressive, the tense of crisis, the tense that subsists in the transformation of a future into a present and of a present into a past. Pertinently, Torres Bodet also places the modern novel in this time-frame: "The novelistic aptitudes that in Walter Scott, in Balzac, in Dickens, involved creation, imagination, *are rapidly becoming* an aptitude for definition, a subtlety of exegesis, a real analytical magic" (pp. 13-14; my italics). It is precisely this temporal flux, this rapid becoming, that Torres Bodet's own analysis evokes. Although the essay is framed as a rebuttal of Ortega's argument that the novel has entered a period of crisis, it only provides further corroboration of this view. To judge by Torres Bodet's vacillations, by his inability to *place* the alternative generic options, the novel is a vexed form indeed. Even if its author does not seem aware of it, what "Reflexiones" reflects is this same crisis translated into the language of commentary.

We are thus led back to the previous analysis, which no longer appears unmotivated. The essay does exhibit a peculiar inconsistency. It does adopt an equivocal stance toward the novel. It is in fact a battlefield, not a monument. And placed against the backdrop of the entire piece, the sentence with which I began admits the original reading. Its ambiguity is a symptom of the instability of the whole essay, which displays a certain determination *not* to make sense about the novel. As a general rule "Reflexiones" tends to undermine its own discussion, rendering it equivocal or incoherent. By repeatedly moving the temporal frame of reference, it turns back on itself, it evinces an unmistakeable tilt toward the ambiguous. How else to explain the fact that the quotation occurs in the second sentence of a section entitled "Realidad y memoria"? Like the quotation, this phrase has a different intended meaning, but the fit is too close to be overlooked. *Realidad:* "con sus características actuales." *Memoria*: "es un género de ayer." The novel is both present and past, reality and memory. The ambiguity persists.

It is important to realize that Torres Bodet's essay is not unusual in its contradictions. I should like to claim that it does nothing more than embody the essential structure of eclecticism, and that as such it is entirely typical of Hispanic discourse about the novel during this time. Consider, for example, the following assertion: "Carefully considered, the novel today possesses a breadth unmatched by any other literary genre; it is a total genre, with a place for the simple stringing together of events as well as for the most complicated analysis of ideas, for physical exaltation as well as for dramatic contrast." Or consider this definition of the novel: "A free genre, undisciplined and open to every adventure and adventurer . . . This explains the actual coexistence of antagonic forms and the impossibility of tracing a straight and clear line of development."[3] The first statement, like the quotation from "Reflexiones," counterpoises the traditional and the contemporary novel: the type of fiction built on plot and dramatic effects and the type that is morose and lyrical (Torres Bodet points out that the two strains in the contemporary novel are the "psychological" and the "lyrical" [p. 97]). The second statement, similarly, acknowledges the coexistence of "antagonic" forms but smooths over the intimation of strife with an appeal to the genre's unlimited capaciousness. The difficulty with these positions, however, is that the phrase "total genre" or "free genre" is a contradiction in terms. To conceive of the novel as a "total genre" is to posit the existence of a kind of all kinds—the kind of kind that is hardly a kind at all. A genre, by definition, must restrict admission; the moment the novel becomes "free" it stops being a genre. And from the practical standpoint the problem is that, as we shall see, the traditional and the modern novel are usually defined in such a way as to preempt their cohabitation under the same rubric, an incompatibility already insinuated in Guillermo de Torre's reference to "antagonic forms." Thus, the varying definitions of the novel that one finds scattered in the critical literature of this time cannot be brought together without contradiction under the banner of eclecticism. Placed in a narrow enough context, generic eclecticism is ultimately reducible to an antinomy like that embodied in Torres Bodet's observation. The only difference is that "Reflexiones," in attempting to compress a panorama of the current state of the novel into just a few pages, condenses contradictions that a broader perspective tends to dilute.

At this point, in the midst of the problematic of obsolescence and substitution, the vanguard novel enters the argument. For in the ongoing discussion of the novel during the decade preceding the Spanish Civil War, the vanguard novel will figure prominently as the new, up-to-date genre to juxtapose against the canonic form. It will be the "género de hoy" out to replace the "género de ayer." If Hispanic discourse about the novel during the late twenties and early thirties is beset by inconsistency and dissension, a major cause is the advent of an experimental form of fiction at odds with the normative definitions of the genre. The appearance of the vanguard novel will precipitate a class struggle, not between social groups but between literary classes. The pun is relevant because the place of the vanguard novel in the critical discourse of the 1920s and 30s cannot be understood without taking into account the genre's incompatibility with the dominant novel-form and the struggle for precedence to which this incompatibility gave rise. By studying the critical reaction to the vanguard novel we will thus be laying the groundwork for further discussion of the problematic inherent in Torres Bodet's essay.

ii. The Reception of the Vanguard Novel

Four principal moments articulate the history of the vanguard novel between 1926 and 1934. Three of them arise from editorial ventures: the first moment corresponds to the founding of the series "Nova novorum" of the *Revista de Occidente*. Three of the titles published under this imprint were works of fiction—*Víspera del gozo* by Pedro Salinas, *El profesor inútil* by Benjamín Jarnés, and *Pájaro pinto* by Antonio Espina—and they provided the initial stimulus and occasion for a general awareness of the new fictional form.[4] The second moment belongs to the "Contemporáneos," a group of young Mexican writers who collaborated in the magazine of the same name and who wrote several novels that were classed with those of the "Nova novorum" as manifestations of the same revisionary impulse.[5] The third moment comprehends those works published by the Colección Valores Actuales of the Ediciones Ulises. This collection, which was established in 1930 and disappeared the following year,[6] served as an outlet for a new installment of vanguard novels, some by already known figures (Benjamín Jarnés, Francisco Ayala) and others by lesser lights (Corpus Barga, Rosa Chacel, Felipe Ximénez de Sandoval, etc.). The fourth moment subsumes three works that came out in 1934 when the vanguard fashion had all but run its course: Antonio de Obregón's *Hermes en la vía pública*, Ricardo Gullón's *Fin de semana* (aptly titled), and the second edition of *El profesor inútil* by Jarnés. By studying their reception, we will be able to follow the falling fortunes and witness the rapid demise of the genre as the decade of the 1930s progressed. One of the ironies of this demise is that *El profesor inútil*, the same work that only a few years earlier had helped launch the genre, surfaces again in the waning moment. In vanguard fiction beginning and end, timeliness and belatedness, join to form a neat, self-contained circle, a closed world whose dimensions I will be tracing. The two editions of *El profesor inútil*—the first a prelude, the second a swan song—furnish only the first of several illustrations of this phenomenon.

There are, of course, some writers and works not adequately covered by this scheme, but I do not intend to record the critical reaction to all vanguard novels. I aim rather to document the existence of the *genre*, to reconstruct the process of inscription of a new and problematic class; and this aim can best be met by concentrating on the four moments when the genre achieved the highest visibility. Since I am interested not in a generation of authors but in a "generation" of books, my scheme privileges the class over the work, and the work over the author. For this reason also, I have made no attempt to do justice to the novelistic careers of writers like Max Aub or Francisco Ayala, in whose total output the vanguard moment represents but a brief flirtation.[7] I have tried though, albeit briefly in some instances, to say something of those of their works that became part of the debate surrounding vanguard fiction.

In essence, this debate began in the summer of 1926 with the publication of *Víspera del gozo*, the inaugural work in the series "Nova novorum." *Víspera del gozo* was quickly and, for the most part, favorably reviewed by many of the important critics of the day—Azorín, Fernando Vela, Eugenio D'Ors, Ernesto Giménez Caballero, Enrique Diez-Canedo, Corpus Barga, and others. Salinas, who had already published a book of poems, *Presagios*, a version of the *Cantar de Mio Cid*, and a translation of the first two volumes of *A la recherche du temps perdu*, was well-known to his reviewers and did not really fit the rubric under which his book appeared. Indeed, because his translation of Proust had recently been published (*Por el camino de Swann*, 1920; *A la sombra de las muchachas en flor*, 1922), one of the topics discussed by most reviewers was the possible (and plausible) influence of Proust on the stories that made up *Víspera del gozo*. According to some, the Proustian imprint was unmistakeable and even embarrassing. According to others, it did not exist. For Ernesto Giménez Caballero Salinas' stories amount to little more than pallid imitations of their French model.[8] In order to expose Salinas' Gallic sensibility, Giménez translates into French a passage from *Víspera del gozo*, and asks: "Can it be said that the following paragraph embodies the genuine sensibility of our race?"[9] (As we will soon see, this is only one of the first of many similar impeachments of the *hispanidad* of the genre, which was often criticized for being foreign-born and thus incompatible with the Hispanic temperament.) Similarly, Corpus Barga goes as far as likening *Víspera del gozo* to Salinas' version of the *Cid*, since both works should be considered translations, "remedos." Salinas is simply doing for the French prose of his day what he has already done for the medieval Spanish of the *Cid*.[10] Barga differs from Giménez Caballero, however, in that for him the prevalent model is not Proust but Giraudoux—an epigonism that in his view aligns Salinas with Paul Morand, Pierre Girard, and Benjamín Jarnés.

Azorín and Fernando Vela, among others, defend Salinas from charges of derivativeness. According to Azorín, the technique of Salinas and Proust could not be more different. Proust approaches reality frontally, directly, as with a microscope, in order to recover and magnify the seemingly negligible detail. His procedure is classical in that he offers a direct transcription of what he has experienced. Salinas, on the contrary, works obliquely: his stories do not portray "reality." His approach is to fragment and deflect, as if he were seeing the world reflected in multiple mirrors (we will see a bit later that Azorín was subsequently to find a more elaborate metaphor for this procedure). Thus: "Where is the resemblance between one art and the other? Where is the parity of one technique and the other? In one of the two novelists we find the species of things directly seen; in the other one, the reflections of the species. And that is all."[11] For Vela, also, Salinas contrasts sharply with Proust. Following Ortega he argues that Proust is a late representative of the nineteenth-century novel, and that his originality resides in the obsessiveness with which he has applied the fictional procedures of the previous century, all with a view to providing a more exhaustive and dramatic transcription of his experience.[12] In Salinas, however, fictional technique loses its instrumentality, turns into an end in itself, with the result that his art becomes—Vela is still echoing the Ortegan argument—intranscendent, playful, gratuitous. Vela thus reads *Víspera del gozo* as an example of "the dehumanized art of today," an art that produces in the reader "a purely artistic delight."[13] The only human element in the book is the recurring motif of unfulfilled expectations; yet even this Romantic preoccupation is given a Modern treatment, since Salinas' attitude toward limitation is not despair or disillusionment but a healthy and cheerful acceptance of life as it is. If the flesh-and-blood woman— "Aurora de verdad," as in one of the stories—does not live up to the dream vision, the dream gives way. In effect, Vela has taken Azorín's argument one step further, for to Azorín's claim that Salinas renders life obliquely, Vela replies that Salinas' achievement consists in not rendering life at all, directly or indirectly, but in dissolving it in the free play of artistic forms. Herein would lie the pleasure, the *gozo* of his text.[14]

The other important question addressed by most reviewers was that of the genre of the book. At least superficially, because of their brevity and condensed action, the pieces in Salinas' collection are short stories. Many reviewers, however, felt uncomfortable with this designation, and some of them opted for less precise labels like "narración" or "relato" (the latter used as a translation of the French *récit*). Azorín ("El arte de Pedro Salinas") calls the book "an aggregate of novelistic visions of the world," insisting that these "fragments" are neither stories nor novelettes. They are simply the "fruits" of Salinas' observation and analysis of reality. Corpus Barga ("La originalidad y el valor") likewise thinks that these pieces are not stories but "elements of stories," "conflicts so simple and brief that they are barely real." According to Gómez de Baquero ("Las prosas líricas de Salinas"), their resistance to classification, of far more importance than the supposed Proustian influence, testifies to recent developments in the novel. To him these "proses" are not stories or novels, even if they do contain "a slight novelistic outline, a narrative germ." The proper generic umbrella under which to place them is "lyric poetry in prose," since they contain the two essential ingredients of the lyric—rich imagery and emotional depth. *Víspera del gozo* thus exemplifies the contemporary phenomenon of the "transformation of the novelistic into the lyrical." This transformation is not without serious consequences, however, for although the novel—which originally was narration or history—has in recent times enriched itself with lyrical, didactic, dramatic, and psychological elements, this broadening of scope has involved a blurring of the novel's properly narrative function, with the result that the genre has been drifting farther and farther away from its true nature—"de su propia naturaleza narrativa." Gómez de Baquero's name for this phenomenon is *desnaturalización*: because the novel has accommodated so many other kinds of discourse, it has been "denaturalized." What began as the expansion of a province into a continent has resulted in the obliteration of boundaries altogether.[15]

Although the notion of denaturalization will play a crucial role in my account, for now I want only to note vanguard fiction's uncertain generic standing: from the beginning vanguard fiction was seen as something of a *rara avis*, a pigeon without a pigeonhole. It contained novelistic or fictional matter but did not fit the definition of the novel or story; it contained lyrical and essayistic matter but was neither poetry nor essay. Paradoxically, we have here a class—a group of novels perceived jointly, of which *Víspera del gozo* is one of the earliest examples—whose class standing is constantly being put into question. Just as the eclectic conception of the novel posits a kind of all kinds, much of the criticism of vanguard fiction posits a genre without genre, a collection of similar works that fits under no particular rubric. In this view the only thing that defines these works is their uniform recalcitrance to generic definition. One should not overlook that the two positions are closely connected: what produces the stretching of boundaries under eclecticism is the desire to classify such works as *Víspera del gozo* as novels; inversely, the accusation of denaturalization originates in a desire to keep the novel's borders tidy and secure. Those who would naturalize vanguard fiction seek to broaden the genre; those who would protect the genre from amorphousness seek to proscribe vanguard fiction.

A few months after the publication of *Víspera del gozo*, *El professor inútil* appeared. Like *Víspera del gozo*, it was a brief volume containing several distinct narrations. Because of the similarities between the two books, and because both appeared within months of each other in the same collection, comparisons were inevitable, and some of the same questions of influence and taxonomy were raised with respect to Jarnés' work. Giménez Caballero, who did not like *El profesor inútil* any better than *Víspera del gozo*, came to the book looking for "the novel of the present literary generation in Spain" but did not find it.[16] He found instead a pretty text ornamented with an abundance of metaphors—a sure sign of creative sterility. Gómez de Baquero held the opposite view; in Jarnés he saw a writer with a natural gift for narration.[17] For him what distinguishes the "lyrical prose" of Salinas from the "novelistic poems" of Jarnés is precisely this: Jarnés possesses novelistic gifts that Salinas, primarily a poet, lacks. Thus, while Salinas is the better stylist, Jarnés is the more promising novelist—an intuition that the subsequent output of both writers would soon bear out. *Víspera del gozo* and *El profesor inútil*, however, "belong to the same genre and to a similar tendency." A similar opinion is expressed by Juan G. Olmedilla; although Salinas and Jarnés belong to the same "team," they play different positions: Jarnés occupies the left wing and Salinas the right; that is, Salinas is more intimate, more subjective, while Jarnés is more open to the world, more interested in sensation than in emotion.[18] (Not coincidentally, Azorín's review of *El profesor inútil* had been titled "Un librito de sensaciones.")[19]

Opinions vary, however, as to the complexion of this "genre," "tendency," or "team." For Rafael Laffón the signal characteristic of these works is lack of plot. In *El profesor inútil*, the action appears "laminated, pulverized, atomized, impalpable"—a phenomenon underscored by the fact that the novel opens as the professor is beginning his vacation. Therefore, as Laffón notes, "A vacation action: a parenthesis of action or action contradicted." And the underlying reason for the elision of plot is that readers are no longer interested in adventure, at least not in reading about it. *El profesor inútil* thus attempts to weave "the unexplored fabric of the pure speculative novel," a goal not entirely realized because of Jarnés' inexperience.[20] Francisco Ayala probes a bit deeper by identifying other characteristics besides a tenuous plotline: the book is "lyrical;" it focuses on the psychology of the protagonist; it indulges description; and it is unified by the presence in each vignette of the same central character, who bears some resemblance to Julien Sorel (years later Jarnés was to write *Lo rojo y lo azul*, a "tribute" to Stendhal, and name the protagonist Julio). But these features do not a novel make, nor even a "cuerpo de novela," according to Ayala, for the professor's passivity renders him an unfit protagonist. Thus *El profesor inútil* falls outside the novel, though it is not clear in what genre Ayala would include it.[21] A similar evasiveness is shown by Esteban Salazar y Chapela, whose views I will discuss in more detail in a moment, and for whom Jarnés has initiated "a new discursive genre."[22] He does not, however, specify what this genre might be.

For several of these critics the difficulty of classification was related to the work's filiation with Ortegan aesthetics. The consensus was that Jarnés was putting into practice or working out the consequences of the theses of *Ideas sobre la novela* and *La deshumanización del arte*, which had appeared in book form only the year before. Thus Eduardo Mallea thought the book nourished by Ortegan theorizing on dehumanized art: "*El profesor inútil*—

optimistic, digressive—is spiritually very similar to those young professors of the *Revista de Occidente* who, seen from a distance, do not conceal from us the expertise with which they have constructed the scaffolding of their works, a scaffolding that is already an almost perfect architecture. The well-digested morsel of current theories of dehumanized art—a nutritious and frugal repast—is, after long hours of wise labor, put by them to its best use."[23] Similarly Ayala explains the book's psychologism by reference to *Ideas sobre la novela*; and for Rafael Laffón its generic ambiguities stem from "the difficulty of the genre," which arises in turn from the depletion of the novel's resources. He concludes his review in *Mediodía* by echoing the *caveat* with which Ortega concludes *Ideas sobre la novela*: "What cannot be doubted is that the author of *El profesor inútil* has profited from that initial fear that Ortega y Gasset mentions in order to guide young novelists, perhaps, toward lasting success."

The third book published by "Nova novorum" was Antonio Espina's *Pájaro pinto*, also a collection of several pieces of varying lengths, though lacking the uniformity of *Víspera del gozo* or *El profesor inútil*. While still considered a manifestation of "the new prose," *Pájaro pinto* was seen to depart from the pattern established by Salinas and Jarnés. Although it was thought to share with these works certain features (fragmentarism, filmic techniques[24]), in the opinion of some reviewers it was a more human achievement. According to Esteban Salazar y Chapela, for instance, who reviewed *El profesor inútil* and *Pájaro pinto* together for *Revista de Occidente* ("Literatura plana y literatura del espacio"), Jarnés' book is an example of "flat literature"—the kind of literature that reproduces the world only in one dimension (*Víspera del gozo* he regarded as "pseudoflat"). *Pájaro pinto*, on the contrary, portrays objects in relief, corporeally, as they endure through time; it thus introduces depth and duration, the third and fourth dimensions that had been absent from *El profesor inútil*. Since two-dimensional literature is lyrical while spatial literature is dramatic, only in Espina's work does one find human conflict, and for this reason he is a better novelist than either Salinas or Jarnés. Significantly, Salazar y Chapela does not resort to foreign models in his discussion of literary influences; he places *Pájaro pinto* in the tradition of Quevedo, Larra, and Unamuno, with whom Espina shares a pessimistic outlook on life. The difference is that Espina's bitterness (*agrura*) has a clownish, Chaplinesque quality: if Larra is Espina's *papá*, Charlot must be his *hermanito*. In contrast, the kind of fiction cultivated by Salinas and Jarnés is superficial, frivolous, of foreign provenance, and not in consonance with the tragic sense of life of the Spaniard.

If we look ahead to Espina's other work of vanguard fiction, *Luna de copas*, published two years later by *Revista de Occidente*, we find more evidence for the view that Espina was perceived as more "human" (and hence a better novelist) than other vanguard writers. According to Luis Bello, *Luna de copas* contains all of the building blocks of traditional fiction—characters, a social milieu, intrigue, setting—but combined in a new, cinematic way.[25] For R. Ledesma Ramos what distinguishes Espina from Jarnés is that the latter cultivates the "poematic essay," while Espina cultivates the "pure novel."[26] Unlike the pure novel, which utilizes all of the traditional ingredients of fiction (even if it lets the reader combine them at will), the poematic essay tries to do without them altogether. For José Gorostiza also *Luna de copas* is "fundamentally a novel," with plot, characters, and an employment of detail reminiscent of Stendhal.[27] Salazar y Chapela again reviews Espina for *Revista de Occidente* upon the publication of *Luna de copas*, and though he now abandons his typology of flat and spatial literature, his evaluation of Espina remains unchanged. In language reminiscent of Gómez de Baquero's discussion of denaturalization, Salazar claims that Espina's achievement has been to return the novel to its nature—"a substitution or complete return to the essential nature of the genre."[28] This return had been anticipated by *Pájaro pinto* and is fully achieved in *Luna de copas*, which Salazar labels "the first authentic modern novel" (p. 388). And although he nowhere mentions Jarnés or Salinas by name, it seems clear that they are the ones alluded to when Salazar criticizes those who have led the novel astray by producing "superficialities, beauties of mere style" (p. 384). To judge by these reviews, Espina, though still clearly a member of the vanguard "team," was seen to represent a more legitimate novelistic alternative. His role in the criticism of this time was to create a nexus between vanguard fiction and the Spanish literary tradition. One could say that he provided a Spanish version of modernity, an autochthonous model for other authors who followed—or so it was thought—foreign fashion. Even if Espina's style, his mannerisms, his techniques had a modern stamp, the temperament that infused them was authentically Spanish, and reminded one of such canonic figures as Quevedo, Goya, Larra, and Valle-Inclán.[29]

The first moment includes one other work that did not form part of the "Nova novorum." Published in November of 1926 in Buenos Aires, Eduardo Mallea's *Cuentos para una inglesa desesperada* was immediately assimilated in Spain as a "repercussion" of the manner initiated by Salinas and Jarnés. Such an association had a sound historical basis, since Mallea was an early and enthusiastic admirer of *El profesor inútil*, as is evidenced by his glowing and extensive review in *Martín Fierro* (see note 23). This review is important because it demonstrates Mallea's familiarity with Jarnés and with the *Revista de Occidente* enterprise.[30] It begins, in fact, by evoking the periodic arrival of the magazine, in whose pages one would regularly find the "elegant toast" of Jarnés' notes and stories. In *El profesor inútil* Mallea recognizes "points of contact with Jarnés' way of gathering sensations and then displaying them like a deck of cards before a thousand astonished eyes." The book, a "marvelous spectacle," places its author "at the head of the modernist contingent." But if Mallea was aware of the good works of the Spanish vanguard, the Spanish vanguard also was aware of Mallea, and *Cuentos para una inglesa desesperada* was reviewed both in the *Revista de Occidente* and in *La Gaceta Literaria*. Writing in *La Gaceta*, Jarnés praised the book for its modernity, for constituting a first step toward "the novel of the future," a journey that in Jarnés' view began with Proust. Many of the qualities that Mallea had found in *El profesor inútil* Jarnés finds in *Cuentos para una inglesa desesperada*: bookishness, a precious style, a sportive, sunny disposition, lack of transcendence. And when he labels Mallea's collection "that pretty thing: a useless book," he echoes the title of his own novel.[31] It was left to Guillermo de Torre, however, to clearly stake out the common ground between Mallea and the Spanish contingent. In a joint review of *Cuentos* and of Pierre Girard's *Connaissez mieux le coeur des femmes*, he situates these works generically and lists the properties of the group.[32] His title, "Dos novelas poemáticas," already gives us an indication of where these novels are to be placed. According to Torre, Mallea has rescued the Argentine novel from the sterile emulation of the realistic and naturalistic novels of the previous century; he is thus a practitioner of the "poematic novel," a genre that originated in France with Giraudoux, and which has already had "traslaciones" in the Peninsula. Nevertheless, "in South America Eduardo Mallea is the first, the expert gardener who has succeeded in transplanting the delicate buds of the gardens of Giraudoux and Girard" (p. 118). But for Torre it is doubtful that this fictional manner can flourish in Spanish (or Argentine) soil. Echoing earlier criticisms of *Víspera del gozo* and *El profesor inútil*, he suggests that the "spirit" that informs the genre—gratuitousness, intranscendence, levity—is not compatible with the Spanish temperament. These novels are in some sense *feminine* (the reason for my emphasis will become clear later on), and their heroines live in a "paradise of pure poematism," in a "benign spiritual climate" nothing like the Hispanic milieu, which is "hard, abrupt, transcendent" (p. 119). These ethereal creatures feel right at home on the shores of Lake Leman, but probably could not survive in harsher climes: "Will a Spanish writer ever manage to move easily in that pure zone of gratuitous feelings and jovial emotive colorings, eliminating the violent contrast and dramatic chiaroscuro that gravitate around him? Or must a writer, in order to escalate those airy miradors and see from them the pleasing pirouettes of his characters, find himself in a more benign spiritual climate, in a sentimental atmosphere like that of the shores of Lake Leman?" (p. 119). In spite of these reservations, however, Torre's review is important for what it tells us about the developing status of the vanguard novel. Called upon to discuss Mallea's stories, Torre evinces a thorough awareness of a new narrative genre, with franchises in Spain as well as Spanish America. The genre is essentially foreign in origin, at odds with the traditional conception of the novel, and generally consistent with Ortegan aesthetics.

If Torre limits Mallea's anteriority to South America, it is probably because he was already aware of a parallel fictional flowering in Mexico stimulated by the writers who collaborated in the journal *Contemporáneos*, a kind of cisatlantic clone of the *Revista de Occidente*.[33] The first important work of vanguard fiction produced by this group was *Margarita de niebla* by Jaime Torres Bodet, published by the Editorial Cvltvra of Mexico City in the summer of 1927, about one year after the appearance of the "Nova novorum" collection. Widely reviewed in Spain and Spanish America, *Margarita de niebla* singled out its author as a leading exponent of the *prosa nueva*. The first thing we should notice about these reviews is the ease and uniformity with which they categorized the novel. The awareness of genre that we observed in Torre's review of *Cuentos* is equally or more evident in reviews of *Margarita*. According to Francisco Ayala, for example, Torres Bodet forms part of a "cycle," of a "renovating current," whose representatives are Giraudoux in France and Jarnés in Spain.[34] And he goes on: "When—less than a year ago—we had occasion to indicate the possibilities contained in the *manner* that Jarnés had incorporated into his *Profesor inútil*, no one could have foreseen such prompt transatlantic repercussions. But repercussions there have been, nonetheless. Especially perceptible in the *Cuentos para una inglesa desesperada* by the Argentinian Eduardo Mallea, and—better still—in the book that is the object of this commentary." Salazar y Chapela also has little problem classifying Torres Bodet's novel, although he takes issue with the invocation of foreign models. Torres Bodet, "in the last analysis," is a disciple of Jarnés: "Before this manner of constructing one speaks of France, of Giraudoux. Nonsense! Before Bodet's prose one speaks now of Benjamin, making unfair comparisons.—Pedantry? Before

Benjamín Jarnés' prose and before the prose of—in the last analysis: his disciple—Jaime Torres Bodet, one has no need to think about French literary influences."[35] Jarnés himself, in his review of *Margarita de niebla*, seems to take for granted Torres Bodet's discipleship. After pointing out the poematic character of the novel and its transitional status, he concludes with what amounts to a wink of complicity: "But this delicious period of transition cannot last too long. (Jaime, my friend, shall we call it quits?)"[36]

The claim that Jarnés was Torres Bodet's professor did not sit well, however, with those on the other side of the Atlantic. In a spirited reply to Salazar y Chapela published in the short-lived Mexican periodical *Ulises*, such a connection is disavowed.[37] There is no need, says the review, to resort to Jarnés or Giraudoux to account for *Margarita de niebla*, for the defining characteristics of these authors' works issue from a common source—a diffuse epochal mentality that molds the literary preferences of foreign and Hispanic writers alike. This review is noteworthy because of the way it situates generic questions. By insisting on their impersonality and their epochal dimension, it fixes with precision the mode of existence of generic concepts. A genre works through individual texts and authors, and yet it possesses a reality independent of them. Genres have, in fact, a causal role: "The tone of this kind of prose is required and provided by the spirit of the age" (p. 24). It is not the texts that produce the genre but the genre that produces the texts. One might say that, at the most general level, genres originate in a civilizational situation (to use David Jones' phrase), in a web of intersubjective (and intertextual) circumstances whose nodes or points of articulation will be individual critics and authors but whose overall coherence and organization transcend that of any individual's discourse. But let the appropriately anonymous *Ulises* reviewer speak for himself:

> In the book-review column of *El Sol*, in Madrid, E. Salazar y Chapela writes about *Margarita de niebla* by Jaime Torres Bodet. The note is intelligent and, almost always, just. We disagree openly only on one point. According to Salazar y Chapela, "Before Benjamín Jarnés' prose and before the prose of—in the last analysis: his disciple—Jaime Torres Bodet, one has no need to think about French literary influences." And we ask ourselves: Jaime Torres Bodet, a disciple of Jarnés? Not even in the last analysis. Benjamín Jarnés, a young writer of undeniable merit and author of *El profesor inútil*, is not yet, fortunately for him, anybody's teacher, not even his own.
>
> The tone of this kind of prose is required and provided by the spirit of the age. So as not to speak—as Salazar would have it—of the appearance

of Proust or Giraudoux in France, and of Joyce in England, let us remember the almost simultaneous, symptomatic publication of three books by new Spanish authors: Antonio Espina's *Pájaro pinto*, Pedro Salinas' *Víspera de gozo* [sic], and Benjamín Jarnés' own *El profesor inútil*, books that are irreconcilable because of their diverse personalities but nonetheless examples of the same approach to the writing of prose. Jarnés is not Salinas' teacher, nor is Salinas Espina's teacher, nor has Espina, in turn, taught Marichalar, who also cultivates a new prose that has not yet appeared in book form and that, like that of his contemporaries, rebels against the academic prose of the past.

Among us and as an imperious necessity, as a spiritual fashion, that new prose ('precious,' Jorge Cuesta would call it) has been cultivated. Examples: Villaurrutia, who has only published a fragment of his *Dama de corazones* (*Ulises* 3), written in 1925-1926; Salvador Novo's *Return ticket*, also an example of new prose (*Ulises* 2, 3, 4); Jaime Torres Bodet, who has already published his narration, and Gilberto Owen, who in 1925 published a novel entitled *La llama fría*. Does this mean that Owen, the first to publish a narration belonging to this prose genre, is the teacher of the Spaniards who published subsequently? By no means. Nor of the Mexicans who were writing earlier, or simultaneously, or afterwards. (pp. 24-25)

The exemplary class consciousness of the review makes its specific claims all the more persuasive. We have here one of the earliest and most encompassing acknowledgments of the vogue of a new kind of fiction, cultivated in Spain and Spanish America, which the reviewer characteristically labels "new prose." Some of the names and titles are already familiar: Salinas, Jarnés, Espina, Torres Bodet; others, like those of Villaurrutia and Owen, we will soon encounter again. Only Mallea is missing, but even so this notice represents an advance over Spanish reviews of *Margarita*, which installed the novel in the class but did not flesh out its profile so clearly.

One could say, then, that *Margarita de niebla* acted as a catalyst in the formation of the genre, for in addition to providing the occasion for diverse attestations of the existence of a new fictional class, it served to reveal more clearly the epochal significance of works that until then could not be definitively classified. A simple comparative exercise will corroborate this view. Let us briefly contrast the reception of Ramón Gómez de la Serna's *La Quinta de Palmyra* (1923) with that given Torres Bodet's novel. In a review published in *Revista de Occidente*, one of his earliest contributions to that journal, Benjamín Jarnés points out that *La Quinta* is an example of the to that employed by Jarnés apropos of *La Quinta*. *Margarita de niebla* also does without the typical fictional apparatus: "A novel without characters and without plot, lacking all anecdotal content"; "in *Margarita de niebla* nothing happens, nothing at all."[41] It too manifests complete artistic freedom—"its logic is completely illogical, gratuitous, purely artistic"—and erects an independent, autonomous world organized not mimetically but according to its own laws: "a lyrical reality, faithful only to itself, without external encumbrances. Without that formal discipline, good for lyceum exercises, that the poet—a creator—substitutes with the internal discipline demanded by his work."[42] In other words, to judge by these and similar pronouncements, we have here a work quite similar to Gómez de la Serna's, a work that would easily meet Jarnés' criteria for the new novel. The crucial difference is that Torres Bodet does not belong to a unipersonal generation. Like *La Quinta*, *Margarita de niebla* is an exemplary text, but one that exemplifies a class of works already in existence. According to one reviewer, for example, "it is such a clearly modern work that we dare catalog it among the very few novels that satisfy the strong aspirations of the American vanguard movements";[43] according to another, it is "a typical and genuine example of that poematic genre, so popular and prestigious nowadays, that is constructed, gratuitously, without setting and without plot, with a total lack of human materials."[44] And in the eyes of Francisco Ayala, the novel "joins to its individual characteristics, the most important and common features of the cycle to which it belongs."[45] Unlike *La Quinta* in 1925, *Margarita* does evoke a generic context constituted by other similar novels. In the few years that transpire between Jarnés' review and the appearance of Torres Bodet's novel, a new genre, defined roughly by the same criteria that Jarnés has set forth, comes into existence. The vanguard novel—a "cycle," a "manner," a "current," a "genre,"—joins Hispanic discourse about the novel in the interval between 1925 and 1927.

Among the novels that together with *Margarita* make up the second moment of vanguard fiction—its transatlantic or American moment—one should include: *Dama de corazones*, by Xavier Villaurrutia; *Novela como nube*, by Gilberto Owen; *La rueca de aire*, by José Martínez Sotomayor; *Extasis*, by Eduardo Villaseñor; and three other novels by Jaime Torres Bodet: *La educación sentimental*, *Proserpina rescatada* and *Estrella de día*.[46] As these works appeared, reviewers almost invariably made a point of grouping them. A few examples: in a review of *La educación sentimental*, Rubén Salazar Mallén furnishes the list of novels that form "the narrow shoreline of the modern

"new novel," a revolutionary form of fiction that differs sharply
nineteenth-century novel. Unlike the "old novel," the new novel
taneous, free and coherent."[38] It has severed its ties with reality a
doned the attempt to create "characters of iron" and "souls of steel'
While previous fiction derived its cohesiveness from that of the se
life it imitated, the cohesiveness of the new novel arises from the
constitution of the fictional organism itself. Reality intervenes o
initial provocation that is subsequently transmogrified. The new no
then be likened to "a protoplasm, a marvelous living worm," that as
and transforms surrounding matter according to its needs (p. 11:
over, because it is not bound by the conventions of traditional fic
new novel is "an art that is limpid and free of logic" (p. 116). By
the old novel is static, mechanical, subject to the constraints o
architecture; it is not a living and evolving substance but "a great
construction" (p. 113); it does not grow organically but "by juxta
by algorithmic increases" (p. 113).

Who are the exponents of the new novel? "By a strange fea
Spanish genius—they have the same name: Ramón Gómez de l
(pp. 113-14). Jarnés isolates a new genre, a new approach to the w
fiction, but one that lacks a suprapersonal dimension, existing by di
labors of one man. His analysis demonstrates, in fact, that a new g
the normal sense of the word, does not yet exist. His line of ar
which consists of using La Quinta to speculate on the differences
the old novel and the new, requires a generic horizon populated l
novels in which Ramón's work could be inserted. It requires, that i
a context, what the Ulises reviewer called "a spiritual fashion."
review mentions no one other than Ramón; in the absence of any
reference, he becomes a context unto himself, the member of a uni
generation. Jarnés' analysis of the differences between the old and
novel thus turns into a clever exercise in wishful thinking, more a
for future work—his own included—than a description of the prese
of affairs.[39] A year earlier, writing in Alfar, he had put the matter c
Ramón was not read and reviewed as he deserved, it was owin
anomaly of his work—"But these books by Ramón were barely
Without an epoch, without a school, without an obvious 'mover
which to refer, young critics remained silent. And perhaps they w
suspicious of such insulting abundance in this age of literary scarci

A few years later, when Margarita de niebla is published, that s
has changed. The language used to talk about this novel is strikingl

Mexican novel," and which includes *La educación sentimental, Margarita de niebla, Dama de corazones, Novela como nube,* and *La rueca de aire.*[47] The foreign models remain Giraudoux and Proust, "Adam and Eve in the Bible of current prose" (p. 187; he does not say who is who), and the distinguishing characteristic of these novels is their neglect of plot and character for the sake of style. Torres Bodet, writing in *Contemporáneos,* places *Novela como nube* in the "genealogical line of Giraudoux's style," to which Salinas, Jarnés, and Villaurrutia also belong, and identifies these writers' insistence on the theme of "incomplete idylls" as a unifying trait.[48] He also regards *La rueca de aire* as "within the refined school of the poetic novel, initiated in Europe by Giraudoux."[49] More explicit is José Gorostiza in his review of this novel: "*La rueca de aire,* written in that subtle prose that evaporates with each phrase into a metaphor, is a late flowering, though not an extemporaneous one, of the Giraudoux-Jarnés branch—the same one that brought forth *Margarita de niebla, Dama de corazones,* and *Novela como nube*—and thus offers us a material exhausted not so much in itself as Martínez Sotomayor in it."[50] It is striking that already in 1930, only two years after the appearance of Owen's and Villaurrutia's novels, and concurrently with the founding of the Colección Valores Actuales in Spain, vanguard fiction would be regarded as moribund or superannuated. *La rueca* is a belated addition, and yet the genre is no more than four or five years old. But as we will discover when we reach the fourth moment, another of the ironies in the history of vanguard fiction is that almost from birth the genre began to agonize. For vanguard fiction infancy and senescence coincide. I have already quoted an excerpt where Jarnés himself, "the aptly labeled captain of the poematic novel,"[51] calls for an end to this "transitional phase"—in 1927. And by the following year, if one is to believe his review of José Díaz Fernández's *El blocao,* his advice has been heeded, as the tendency to turn the novel into "a delicious sport for happy children" is receding before "the sharp imperative of deep life."[52]

Spanish commentators of the Mexican novels also noted their class standing. Jarnés, who regularly reviewed Spanish-American literature for *La Gaceta Literaria,* stated that *Dama de corazones* belonged to the "school" of Giraudoux, in which Jarnés also located his early work,[53] and that both Villaurrutia's novel and *Novela como nube* are examples of the modern novel's attempt to give expression to the sanguine spirit of the age.[54] In language reminiscent of his commentaries of Mallea and Torres Bodet, he remarks upon these works' levity, their sunny outlook on life, and their sense of humor. In the process he comes up with a couple of sentences memorable for their inaneness: "The great achievement of this art is to have forced sorrow into the farthest corner of the soul and to keep it tied up there, its barking stifled, its neck fastened to a collar adorned by elegant rattles: this is authentic humor. Today's art entertains itself by nourishing its melancholy with chocolate bonbons." In addition, he places *La rueca de aire* in the same genre: "The whole book unfolds with that carefree, light-hearted rhythm—at times to the point of childishness—that has become the patrimony of the best young prose writers of our time."[55] More probing is Salazar y Chapela's review of *Dama de corazones*. According to this critic, *Dama de corazones* is not a novel but a "narración," the latter a liminal genre akin to the lyric but quite unlike the novel or drama.[56] The narration, currently in vogue in France (Giraudoux) as well as in Spain (he gives no names, but none are necessary), is defined by the obtrusive presence of the author-narrator and the resulting disregard for the creation of a believable fictional world peopled by lifelike characters. Whereas the author of a novel or a play normally takes no part in the action, the author of a narration is constantly on stage detailing his thoughts, impressions, feelings. For this reason the work as a whole becomes a digest of "artistic occasions" unified only by a presiding sensibility. Salazar y Chapela concludes the review with an evaluation of the novel in a language that is by now familiar: "Very pretty prose, very jovial in style, enameled with 'Giraudouxian' imagery."

In Spain, between the initial impetus provided by "Nova novorum" and the subsequent stimulus of the Colección Valores Actuales, interest in vanguard fiction was sustained principally by Benjamín Jarnés, who in quick succession published several novels—*El convidado de papel* (1928), *Paula y Paulita* (1929), *Locura y muerte de Nadie* (1929), *Teoría del zumbel* (1930)— plus a number of shorter pieces in the *Revista de Occidente* and elsewhere. Indeed, of the Spanish practitioners of the genre, Jarnés is the only one who did so consistently enough to accumulate a substantial *oeuvre* in this mode. This posed a special problem for reviewers of his work, since they had to place his novels both in relation to those of other vanguard writers and in the context of Jarnés' entire output. The typical solution was to impose on Jarnés' trajectory a teleology that had him developing away from the ambiguous genre of the poematic novel or the narration and toward the novel proper. But since not everyone charted the trajectory in the same way, each new work of his was heralded by a different reviewer as enacting Jarnés' rite of passage into the novel. This process began as early as *El convidado de papel* and continued until the publication of *Lo rojo y lo azul* in

1932, the last important original novel he published before leaving Spain at the end of the Civil War.[57] A few examples will illustrate what I mean.

For Antonio Espina *El convidado de papel* was an authentic novel, unlike *El profesor inútil* and other similar works: "I say so because vanguard writers have the reputation of not knowing how to make novels but rather vague poems articulated by feeble plots. Well, it's not true. *El convidado de papel* is a biographical narration, with very human types and conflicts, developed in a marvelously limpid style (tone: ironic-lyrical) but without ever losing real control, in spite of the machinelike quality, of incidents and individuals."[58] According to Carlos Fernández Cuenca, nevertheless, only with *Paula y Paulita* does Jarnés become a novelist. In contrast to *El profesor inútil* and *El convidado de papel*, *Paula y Paulita* "is not a more or less fortunate novelistic sketch but an authentic novel that belongs to the eternal type of the novel as seen by the sensibility of a modern writer. . . . If in his previous novels one noticed an excessive intellectualism that diminished the emotional impact of many moments, giving them the coldness of pure cerebralism, in *Paula y Paulita* the author joins the phalanx of those true novelists who make a cult out of emotion."[59] Not so, would have argued Melchor Fernández Almagro, for whom *Locura y muerte de Nadie* is Jarnés' truest novel ("The most novelistic novel of all the novels produced by Benjamín Jarnés").[60] And José Díaz Fernández and Enrique Diez-Canedo defer the initiation even further, until 1932: not until *Lo rojo y lo azul* does Jarnés "abandon the ambiguous genre of the narration to install himself in the area of the novel proper [*la novela propiamente dicha*]."[61]

The lack of consensus among Jarnés' contemporaries makes it easy to find other critics who deny the novelistic status of each of the works mentioned above. Writing apropos of *El convidado de papel*, José Escofet claims that Jarnés should not be considered a novelist but a stylist, for as a novelist he is uninteresting. For José Gorostiza *Paula y Paulita* is not a novel but "a series of essays strung together by the slightest of plots." And where Fernández Cuenca praised this novel for its lifelike personages, R. Ledesma Ramos claims that the work lacks verisimilitude and that its characters are not human (though he does not regard this as a defect).[62] Even in the case of *Lo rojo y lo azul*, whose Stendhalian reminiscences would seem to guarantee its generic standing, there was little unanimity of opinion. In *Indice literario* it was called "a borderline narration, situated between the realistic determination of facts and objects and the vagueness of the lyric, written in a metaphorical, impressionistic style that offers up reality through recourse to figuration." And Miguel Pérez Ferrero thinks that even if this is where

Jarnés comes closest to writing a novel, his "indecisiveness" before the genre destroys the "unity" required by a novel.[63] Underpinning this controversy, of course, is that larger vexed question of the limits of the novel. The wide disparity of opinion about Jarnés' fiction is but another manifestation of the crisis reflected in "Reflexiones." If we leave aside the personalities and preferences of the critics involved, if we impersonalize our approach as the *Ulises* review recommends, Jarnés' divided reputation illustrates once again that, in the 1920s and 30s, criticism of the novel was constantly at odds with itself. The absence of a consensus does not merely stem from the quirks of individual critics. It should be explained instead as one of the constitutive properties of the critical discussion of this period, properties that are trans-individual or supra-personal, that speak to a level of description at which personal idiosyncrasies do not operate, or better, a level at which personal idiosyncrasies dissolve into formations of a higher order. But of this more later.

In spite of Jarnés' steady output and of the appearance of several other novels that attracted considerable attention,[64] after 1926-27 vanguard fiction did not again achieve much visibility in Spain until the establishment of the Colección Valores Actuales. This series provided an outlet for a group of "new" and not-so-new novelists whose production exhibited the "imagistic and pure" tendencies of the "generation of 1930."[65] The generational designation is interesting in this instance because it seems to be based on perceived literary affinities rather than on coetaneity—Jarnés, the patriarch if not the professor of the group, was already into his forties and had a substantial *oeuvre* behind him; Antonio de Obregón, one of the youngest, was scarcely into his twenties and publishing his first novel (a year earlier he had published a collection of poems, *El campo. La ciudad. El cielo*). What lent cohesion to the group was its program, advertised on the blurb accompanying the novels as follows: "In this collection Ediciones Ulises will group all the writers who are clear exponents of current literary values, that is, all those writers of the generation of 1930 who have an individual accent, who have detached, distanced themselves from the aesthetic creeds that constituted the previous literary vogue."

The following novels were published in the series: *Naufragio en la sombra* (1930), by Valentín Andrés Alvarez; *Cazador en el alba* (1930), by Francisco Ayala; *Pasión y muerte. Apocalipsis* (1930), by Corpus Barga; *Agor sin fin* (1930), by Juan Chabás; *Estación. Ida y vuelta* (1930), by Rosa Chacel; *Viviana y Merlín* (1930), more a fairy-tale than a novel, by Jarnés; *Tres mujeres más equis* (1930), by Felipe Ximénez de Sandoval; and *Efectos navales* (1931), by Antonio de Obregón.[66] Of these, Obregón's novel achieved the greatest notoriety. It was selected as "El libro del mes" for July 1931 and widely reviewed (between July and December, for example, three different notices appeared in *La Gaceta Literaria*). The language of these reviews is noteworthy for the way it echoes the idiolect of earlier criticism. The novel is praised (or condemned) for its lack of realism, its "scant humanity," its cult of metaphor, its lyricism. According to Jarnés, it exemplifies the age which produced it: "I don't know whether *Efectos navales* is predestined to figure in the future as an 'archeological marvel' or as a 'forgotten classic.' I tend to think that it will not be forgotten soon. It captures with such exactness this delicious, sportive, and youthful artistic moment that, at the least, it will be a precise, exact monument to the spirit of the age."[67] This accords with Obregón's own assessment in the preface to the novel: "My novel is unreal. One of its defects is that it is too entertaining, almost dizzying. Too many beaches go by in too short a time. The protagonists are constantly by the sea and moving to its rhythm. My novel is written freely. Nordic and sarcastic. It's worthless, but it's a document."[68] Clearly *Efectos navales* fits the same mold as the novels of the first two moments.

The other works in this collection, though less noticed, were perceived in much the same way. José Díaz Fernández calls *Estación. Ida y vuelta* "una narración tipo"—narration and not novel, he explains, echoing Salazar y Chapela's distinction, for *Estación* lacks plot and characters. Written according to the Ortegan recipe, it is morose, Proustian, "a subtle texture of images and insinuations," and a representative instance of the "novela minoritaria" (which is not really a novel at all).[69] For the same critic *Tres mujeres más equis* is a silly "game of images"; and for another it shows that "the writer has let his pen run madly after the new forms of the new literature."[70] Similar attestations could easily be found for the other works in this group. Although these novels differ in content and tone—the rain-washed melancholy of *Estación. Ida y vuelta* contrasting sharply with the frivolity of *Efectos navales*, for example—critics saw them as springing from the same innovative (and to some, wrongheaded and illegitimate) impulse that had produced the earlier flowerings of the genre. According to Ramón Feria, for example, the Spanish new novelists have discarded the "integral novel" for a new type of fiction that he characteristically labels the "poematic novel" or "essayistic novel" (the two terms are used interchangeably).[71] This kind of novel is defined by a reduced readership, a tilt toward the poetic, skimpy plot and characterization, and the creation of a self-regulating, self-centered, subjective world with tenuous moorings in reality. The works that embody these criteria—*Víspera del gozo, Luna de copas, Cazador en el alba, Efectos navales,* and Jarnés' novels—constitute a unit, "un conjunto de manifestación artística." The integral novel, in contrast, is represented by César Arconada's *La turbina* (1930) and Esteban Salazar y Chapela's *Pero sin hijos* (1931). This kind of fiction perpetuates nineteenth-century norms—objectivity, realism—and betrays the continuing influence of such writers as Balzac, Maupassant, and Zola.

Other critics furnish congruent or overlapping, if not identical, catalogues. For Guillermo de Torre in 1927 the "new novel" counts in its ranks: Salinas, Jarnés, Espina, Claudio de la Torre (*En la vida del señor Alegre*), Chabás (*Sin velas, desvelada*), and Valentín Andrés Alvarez (*Sentimental dancing*). A year later Salazar y Chapela gives his list of the practitioners of the poematic novel: Salinas, Jarnés, Espina, Chabás, Jaime Torres Bodet, and Dámaso Alonso, who had published a couple of stories in the *Revista de Occidente,* "Torcedor de crepúsculo y violín" (1926) and "Cédula de eternidad"(1928). Azorín groups Salinas, Jarnés, Ayala, and Chabás as young writers who have done away with the old rhetoric. And an anonymous omnibus review in the *Heraldo de Madrid* in 1931, after distinguishing between two forms of fiction, the "novela de evasión" and the "novela de regreso," includes in the former: Salinas' stories, Jarnés' novels, *Sentimental dancing,* and *Estación. Ida y vuelta.*[72]

The three works that comprehend the fourth moment in my account have one thing in common—all were regarded as belated reincarnations of an obsolescent or extinct fashion. As I have already stated, the critical fortunes of vanguard fiction do not follow the typical parabolic curve with its symmetrical ascending and descending slopes. Almost from the beginning vanguard fiction started going downhill, at least in the eyes of many of its commentators. Early death-notices are not rare: in Jarnés' review of *Margarita de niebla* and Gorostiza's review of *La rueca de aire* we have already come across two such reports. José Díaz Fernández, who regularly reviewed books for such newspapers as *El Sol, Crisol,* and *Luz,* made it a habit of greeting the publication of each new work of vanguard fiction with a declaration of the obsolescence of the form. *Tres mujeres más equis* is the kind of book "with which young writers amused themselves some years ago"; *Agor sin fin* prompts the statement that "the myth of a new literature" has vanished and that novels can no longer partake of "that light-hearted and almost cynical tone that more often than not served to dissemble the creative incapacity of young writers." And upon the publication of Samuel Ros' *El hombre de los medios abrazos,* he announces: "that sportive, superficial, cinematic world that enthused the writers of the last decade and created so many dehumanized topics in literature and in painting has already putrefied and only inspires repugnance, tedium, and fatigue."[73]

One of the strongest statements in this vein occurs in an article on Pío Baroja by Carlos and Pedro Caba:

A few spirited, carefree, and playful "idle youngsters," with bare calves, fillets, a jersey, and thick shoes, broke into the arena of art after stuffing all aesthetic ideas into the cubic zero of a soccer ball. Their first disrespectful gesture was even healthy, not only because it went along with the mood of the moment (our epoch belongs to the young, according to Ortega) but also because they prepared a new ground, a new sensibility, ejecting from the stadium hackneyed tropes, graceless, greasy prose, and baroque lyricism, swollen and grandiloquent. But the thing is that these young *équipiers*, with a stilted and cramped language, with the breeze of airplanes, jazz, and sportive allusions, began by declaring that they did not need a public, but only a select intelligent few capable of appreciating the aesthetic value of the show. And those intelligent few saw them indulge in innocent verbal games, in a picturesque dislocation of ideas, in the rebelliousness of spoiled brats, in a pursuit of metaphor. And the show ended with a pyrotechnic display; the new literary aesthetic flashed and pirouetted like a rocket and then disappeared, leaving behind a scattering of light and the faint smell of powder. All that remains of that sportive party are a few tattered books, characterized by the delicious coquetry of artifice and the divine intranscendence of toys.[74]

In light of testimonies like this one it comes as no surprise that when *Fin de semana, Hermes en la vía pública,* and *El profesor inútil* (2nd edition) appear, they are viewed as throwbacks to another age.[75] Gullón's novel prompts all of the familiar commonplaces. It is a novel "with the trajectory of a poem," a "Proustian narration," a member of the "poematic generation" which shares with its kin a "lyrical tone" and "a lively and humane cheerfulness."[76] By this time the distinguishing features of the genre are so well-known that several commentators, after placing the novel generically, excuse themselves from elaborating any further: "This kind of poetic observation has been applied to the novel with particular assiduousness. There is no need to cite names." Or, from a different source: "A modern literary fashion whose ascendancy and trajectory is known to all."[77] But such fame is largely posthumous, as is clearly indicated by the testamentary tone of J. López

Prudencio's review: "This kind of prose was much liked by the new generation. Its cultivation, difficult because of the dangers of absurd miscarriages,
produced monstrous conceptions, scarcely worthy of being taken seriously,
in the still recent and almost bygone times when this literature was popular.
The supreme master in the cultivation of this expressive orientation was
the admirable Jarnés, who knew how to exploit—in his *Profesor inútil* and
other subsequent works—all of its legitimate treasures, victoriously skirting
all of the surrounding dangers. The fashion, the fury, has fortunately
abated; and as always happens in such cases, what has survived has been
the rationally usable nucleus that this style contained."[78]

A similar reception awaits Obregón's second novel, *Hermes en la vía pública*.
Enrique Azcoaga, who considered the novel the "epilogue of a generation,"
thought that Obregón's dilemma was that he found himself between generations. Temperamentally unsuited to form ranks with his coevals (who have
"anchored" themselves in life), he nevertheless arrives too late to belong to
the vanguard; yet *Hermes en la vía pública*, with its levity, its lyrical bent, its
disregard for social concerns, is clearly a vanguard novel. Miguel Pérez
Ferrero, remarking also on the work's anachronism, compares it to a newspaper headline without an accompanying text. Guillermo de Torre makes
the same point by calling it "un libro-sismógrafo" that registers the tremors
of a bygone period. The most authoritative testimony, however, comes
from Jarnés, according to whom *Hermes* incorporates "the cleverest tech-
nical resources utilized by a sector of postwar novelists." It is thus "one of
the few Spanish novels that will be read in the future as a faithful testimony
of a light-hearted stage in the art of writing and describing." And yet it
belongs to another time; it constitutes, in a fitting phrase, "the last laugh in
a great literary feast that has already ended."[79]

The reappearance of *El profesor inútil* eight years after its original publication provides an even more apt denouement. Here we have one of the first
and most representative novels in the group surfacing again just at the
time when vanguard fiction was approaching its demise. The tone of the
reviews was appropriately elegiac. Antonio de Obregón used the occasion
to recall that this novel, in its original edition, had convinced him to become
a writer; *El profesor inútil* had been a "textbook of influences."[80] Juan José
Domenchina, about whom I shall have more to say in a few pages, was
equally alert to the significance of the professor's reincarnation, but was
less kind in his assessment: "This *Profesor inútil* comes before us now, in a
new incarnation, with its triad of 1926, as obstinate as before. This is very
much a 1926 book: a narrative attempt grafted onto an essay, of the type

Revista de Occidente, 1926. Its deterioration is evident. It's not just matter that wears down: the spirit also has perishable zones. Thus *El profesor inútil*, a creation of the spirit, succumbs today under the burden of numberless dead metaphors, just as Benjamín Jarnés, in the act of writing it, succumbed to the iconomanic vogue, to the fanaticism of images."[81] In 1934 the novel is consequently "a straggler," "a nostalgic melody of remote murmurings." But obviously this fact could not have escaped Jarnés, who for several years had been forecasting the end of the vanguard fashion. Accordingly the second edition contains a preface, "Discurso a Herminia," where he recognizes how dated his book must now seem. It begins: "It saddens me to think that you, faithful valkyrie, are my only listener, now that all of my companions regularly address their words—oozing doctrinal juice—to a whole nation at the least, if not to a continent, if not to all of humanity."[82] Vanguard fiction's always small readership is finally reduced to one imaginary interlocutor, Herminia. Times have changed and literature has changed along with them; in such circumstances a book like *El profesor inútil* cannot hope to elicit much interest. (Should Herminia be seen as a female Hermes and thus as the logical complement to Obregón's titular character? One thing is for sure: since valkyries look after the deceased—but wasn't this also one of Hermes' jobs?—Herminia makes an appropriate companion for the professor at this juncture in his career.)

The lifespan of vanguard fiction is thus bracketed by the two editions of Jarnés' novel: 1926 and 1934. Before 1926 there was no general awareness of the genre, nor was there a corpus of works that could have engendered it; by 1934—after the publication of perhaps three dozen works—the interest in this sort of fiction has all but dissipated.

iii. Class Struggles

My effort thus far has been to document the presence of a new fictional genre in the critical discussion of the eight-year interval between 1926 and 1934. To this end I have adduced what one can call constative and deictic information, that is, information that shows the existence of a class and catalogues its membership.[83] To conclude the demonstration at this point, however, would be to slight the disruptive impact of the emergence of the new class. Although I have identified the genre, listed its membership, and traced its fortunes, little has been said directly about the relations of the vanguard novel with other genres with which it might enter into contact, which it might overlap, complement, or displace. Little has been said, in other words, about the *consequences* of the inscription of a new class in the generic metalanguage of a given period. Such an event, nevertheless, is not as self-contained, not as inconsequential as it might first appear, for in order to accommodate the new class, older elements might have to be dislodged or redefined, and this will give rise to a struggle for dominance between the residual and the emergent genres, a struggle whose repercussions will be felt over a wide discursive field. In our particular case the many references to vanguard fiction's peculiar infringement on other genres—the novel, the poem, the essay—are already a symptom of this kind of unrest.

In this section, thus, I will be stepping back from the welter of names and titles to look again at the evidence, but from a different perspective. This perspective might—loosely—be labeled "archeological," since it privileges discourse over authorship and seeks to discern patterns that do not respect the integrity of any individual's opinions. For this reason, instead of focusing on what Jarnés or Díaz Fernández thought about vanguard fiction, I will be treating the pronouncements of individual critics as a medium for the expression of broader tendencies. In this way the narrative account of the preceding pages will acquire the necessary depth. If in the last section I traced the history of the reception of vanguard fiction, my aim now will be to identify the forces that shaped the contours of that history. Resorting to Salazar y Chapela's terminology, one might say that we will be passing from "flat" to "spatial" criticism, from a recounting of names, dates, and titles to a discussion of the configurations that underlie them.

This takes us directly to the interplay between the vanguard novel and other discursive categories: more concretely, to the problematic implicit in Torres Bodet's essay—the antagonism between the new and the traditional novel. For it is clear that from the moment of its appearance the vanguard novel presents itself as an alternative to the canonic genre. Its novelty is always gauged against the immediate fictional past. As in Jarnés' review of *La Quinta de Palmyra*, there is the "old novel," and then there is the "new." And the new novel emerges precisely from a systematic opposition to the conventions of the old. The vanguard novel is always defined negatively first: whatever else it may be like, it is foremost *not* like the traditional novel. If the old novel relied on plot and character, the new novel abolishes them; if the old novel was realistic, the new novel is surreal; if the old novel, simply by the accumulation of incidents and characters, was "renewable until the end of the world," the new novel "throws away the props and fires all the extras," thereby inventing "a new dimensional concept of the novel."[84] Even in those instances where a different generic conception is not yet available, this fundamental negativity still persists. Ramon Gómez de la Serna concludes his 1929 article, "Sobre la novela," with the following exhortation: "We have to react against the old-fashioned novel, even against the novel in the manner of Stendhal, that genre whose secret is possessed only by a few critics who could never write a novel and that has no definition other than that given by Mr. L. M. Forster [sic], 'any work of prose fiction of more than 50,000 words.' We must not write any of the novels that have already been written, nor any of those that were not written but could have been."[85]

The vanguard novel's hostility toward the canonic genre puts the two classes in head-to-head competition. It is not simply that the two genres are different, as an elegy is different from an ode; the point is that both aspire to occupy the same terrain, the same "discursive space," viz., that designated broadly by the term "novel." When in the article quoted above Ramón announces that "the novel, even if the old augurers deny it, is about to open its pages to lights that will cheer up its rooms,"[86] he is staking out the contested territory. Significantly, his forecast mixes metaphors, imaging the novel both as book ("pages") and building ("rooms"): as discourse to be written and space to be occupied. Spatial or geographical metaphors describe the situation best: at issue is the *domain* of the novel; that is to say, the specific content to be imputed to the label. Against what some of the critics of this time would lead us to believe, the inscription of the vanguard novel is not as much a matter of onomastics as of semantics, not as much a matter of finding new names for genres as of fitting the new genres to the inherited names—novel, poem, drama, essay, biography, etc. Until the appearance of vanguard fiction, *novel* meant essentially one thing—the nineteenth-century genre, what Antonio Espina liked to call "the biographico-analytical narration."[87] This form had exclusive claim on the territory; it owned the label. For a work to be considered a novel, it had to conform to the nineteenth-century model, and if a work conformed to the nineteenth-century model it was classified as a novel. With the onset of the "new" novel, however, the old novel's dominance is challenged, for a different set of criteria begins to encroach upon the label. Vanguard works lead a dual existence, they have a double life, as it were. Outwardly they look like novels, since they comprise fictional narratives in prose; but once one passes beneath the surface one notices how different these "new" novels really are. As critics are constantly reminding their readers, these works have little or no plot, little or no characterization, little or no humanity. They are lyrical, do not copy life, do not efface the personality of their authors. In short, they meet few of the criteria that had hitherto defined the novel. As a consequence a different definition of the label begins to take hold. The old novel finds itself under attack, its domain, its dominance (that is, its *dominio* in the two senses of the word in Spanish) threatened by the alternative generic option embodied in vanguard fiction and formulated in an accompanying body of criticism. The monopoly starts to quaver, and a class struggle results.

The complicated and tense connection between the new and the old novel can be seen clearly in an image which Azorín devised apropos of *Escenas junto a la muerte*. The piece in which it appears is titled "Jarnés, letal."[88] Why? Because the author of *Escenas* has dealt the traditional novel a fatal blow: "Lethal, deadly, because with this novelistic procedure he has mortally wounded the traditional novel." This is how Azorín explains Jarnés' deadly technique:

> Let's imagine a great circus of mirrors with us inside it. The glass walls are polyhedral: that is, the walls of the circus have been formed with an infinite number of mirror faces. In the center of this curious edifice there is a girating platform. We mount the platform then, and right away the artifact begins to go round. At first it girates slowly; later, vertiginously. We had closed our eyes instinctively, in spite of the assurances of the operator, and now we've opened them. What a marvelous spectacle! The platform turns and we see, as in a whirlwind, the reflection of the world's spectacle.

Reading *Escenas junto a la muerte*, then, is like climbing onto the whirligig and observing the "sobrerrealidad" of the myriad reflections. The aesthetic implications of the passage are suggestive and will be discussed in the following chapter; for now I want to stress the precarious continuity that the metaphor establishes between the traditional and the new novel. Azorín has retained the orthodox image of the novel as a mirror held up to life, but only after subjecting it to a radical restructuring. He keeps the mirror but shatters it to pieces. Like the reality it reflects, the exemplary icon of the old novel has been pulverized. And instead of having the novelist walking along a road (as in the famous Stendhalian version of the metaphor), he has the reader going around and around in circles. Equally important, by taking the novel to the circus, Azorín carnivalizes what was regarded as a serious and weighty enterprise. Ortega: "One shouldn't toy with the novel. It is perhaps the only serious thing left in the realm of poetry." And further, "But I doubt that [young writers] will find the track of such secret and deep veins [of novelistic matter] unless before writing their novels they feel, for a long time, fear. From those who have not perceived the gravity of the genre's condition, one can expect nothing."[89] We have here contrasting portraits of the artist: the novelist as coward vs. the novelist as clown. Azorín feels no compunction about playing with the novel. He takes the site of the Ortegan mine, with its deep and recessed deposits, and builds a circus on it.[90]

In this manner the new novel situates itself vis-à-vis the inherited fictional aesthetic. Even while rejecting the nineteenth-century genre, the new novel is still relatable to it in a way that sets the two classes in competition. Vanguard fiction, for all its innovativeness, still aspires to speak for the novel. It still aspires to that same general territory occupied by the nineteenth-century genre. Rather than making a fresh start, it seeks to recolonize familiar terrain, to tread the same old ground with fancy new steps. As in Azorín's image, it retains just enough of the old features to be recognized as a not-so-distant relative of the genre it wants to replace. This slight resemblance provides the backdrop against which the incompatibility between the old novel and the new rises in sharp relief, an incompatibility that Salinas will compare, as we will see in a later chapter, to the rivalry between siblings. Without this underlying likeness-in-difference the conflict would not take place, for the two genres would be different but not comparable. It would be impossible to speak about them as kinds of "novel."

This class struggle produces a number of interesting quirks in the criticism of this time. One finds, for example, that *novel* is no longer a sufficiently precise label to designate the nineteenth-century genre. In its place the term *novela novelesca* is sometimes used, a coinage that, even as it attests to the continuing influence of the canonic form, furnishes evidence that it is no longer the sole inhabitant of novel-territory.[91] Such a phrase supposes that *novel* has become inhabited by alternative meanings: although the true novel, the "novelistic" novel, remains the nineteenth-century one, the emergence of a diverse generic option, claiming the same rubric, makes necessary the apparently redundant qualifier. Were it not for vanguard fiction, "novela novelesca" would be a pleonasm; the intelligibility of the phrase hinges on the reader's awareness of competing claims on the same territory. The proliferation of names derived from "novel"—"noveloide," "pre-novela," "ultra-novela," "novela grande," "novela chica"—furnishes evidence of the same kind.[92] It too shows that the received conception is no longer powerful enough, entrenched enough in discourse, to control the range of meanings the rubric can have and the uses to which it can be put. "Novel" has in effect

become a chameleon word, constantly changing to fit its surroundings—
which suggests not that it has been emptied of meaning but that it is too
full with it.

The most striking and far-reaching effect of the class struggle is the
phenomenon of denaturalization. If the reception of vanguard fiction is
indeed the history of a struggle for dominance, one needs to inquire into
the tactics employed to achieve such dominance. How did vanguard fiction
attempt to unseat the dominant genre? How did the traditional novel parry
the threat? How in general is a genre disenfranchised? Since the two sides
are vying for the right to speak for the novel, the victor will be the genre
that can most legitimately lay claim to the contested territory. The argument, thus, will turn on the authenticity of the new and the old novel *qua*
novel, and the appropriate tactic will be to demonstrate that the opposing
genre has no right to the sobriquet. Hence the traditional novel will be
attacked for being impure, nonliterary, unartistic, while vanguard fiction
will be said to belong properly to a different genre, or to no genre at all. I
will name this tactic with the term *denaturalization*, employed in a similar
sense by Gómez de Baquero in his discussion of *Víspera del gozo*. *Denaturalization* describes the mechanism whereby the critical discourse of this period
sets up its own rules of inclusion and exclusion. As a kind of "principle of
rarefaction,"[93] it serves to police the organization and distribution of novel-
territory. Used against the vanguard novel, it removes the threat to the
continued hegemony of the nineteenth-century form; used against the
nineteenth-century novel, it clears the way for a recolonization. In both
instances denaturalization results in the disenfranchisement of one or the
other genre.

It is not difficult to find this tactic at work. The polemical stance of the
new novel evidently entails the denaturalization of the old. If the new
novel—the type of fiction that is wont to call itself "pure"—dispenses with
such things as plot and character, it can only be because, at least in the
conventional doses, they are not inherently novelistic.[94] Mimesis, the age-
old imperative of the novel, is now seen as the province of the chronicler or
historian.[95] To the extent that the nineteenth-century novel endeavored primarily to imitate life, it was impure, not especially literary. In fact, Torres
Bodet's central argument in "Reflexiones" is that the traditional novel is a
deviant form. He replies to Ortega's allegations of decadence by contending
that plot, character, and theme—the building blocks of nineteenth-century
fiction—are irrelevant to the "essence" of the genre.[96] The realistic novel in
the manner of Balzac is thus a "disfiguration" of the profile of the genre:

"When they said that Balzac was configuring the profile of the French novel, wouldn't it have been more accurate to say that he was disfiguring it?" And the new novelists, novelists like Giraudoux, Salinas, and Jarnés, are not only indifferent to plot, but actually incapable of telling a story.[97] Seen in this light, therefore, the traditional novel takes on the appearance of a bogus artifact, a heterogeneous admixture of nonliterary materials: "In order to construct the old novel, the metaphysician, the chronicler, the grammarian, the excavator, the decorator, the tailor collaborated. . . . At times the urgent help of special technicians was required: the final chapter of several romantic novels required the intervention of an obstetrician." The new novel, by contrast, is solely the product of the artist's sensibility: "The new novel prefers to begin and end alone with the artist."[98] Cleansed from impurities, it aspires to raise fiction to the aristocratic stature of the poem.[99]

The tactic of denaturalization is employed more openly—and with more effect—against the vanguard novel itself. Reviewers insistently undermine the generic standing of these novels by either lodging them in a contiguous category—the poem, the essay—or suggesting that they represent an uncertain cross of two or more genres. Rufino Blanco Fombona's equation: "Cinematógrafo + Poemita + Tontería − Talento = Novela," in which vanguard fiction is portrayed as a witless hybrid, could well serve as the emblem for this tendency.[100] There is hardly a vanguard novel that, at one time or another, was not denaturalized. A few examples:

And what is *Víspera del gozo*? The volume is an aggregate of novelistic visions of the world; one cannot say that these fragments are short stories or short novels; neither can one affirm that they are philosophical essays.

Is *El profesor inútil* a novel—or rather: is it a volume of novels? It is not a novel nor has its author meant it to be.

Margarita de niebla—the best book of poems by Jaime Torres Bodet.

[*Extasis*] a novel? In any event a novel without characters, without invention, without the pleasure of imagining possibilities and resolving them, of speculating in soliloquies. And why not a travel diary without a point of arrival or a point of departure?

The poet Antonio de Obregón, author of *El campo. La ciudad. El cielo*, gives us now *Efectos navales*; it too is a book of poems.

Jarnés has completed a book entitled *Escenas junto a la muerte*. It's something like a continuation of *Profesor inútil*, but with new preoccupations. A novelistic book, though not a novel.

The novelistic narration *Estación. Ida y vuelta* possesses all of the characteristics of a true poem. Rather than a novel, it is in reality a poem.

Proserpina rescatada, a book that is not a novel because in order to be one it needs both more and less than it has, is rather a very modern essay in dehumanization.[101]

This view was also expressed apropos of vanguard fiction as a whole:

A prose of poets or, at least, impregnated with a poetic quality by virtue of which these not very 'novelistic' novels become poematic.

That such books do not exactly deserve the rubric 'novel,' since their freedom, their fragmentariness, their plotlessness set them apart from the canonical form? Perhaps.

Benjamín Jarnés, Antonio Espina? . . . Well, but this group of pearly snails, drooling metaphors, remains outside the true novel.

That the writers who called themselves 'avant-garde' did not know how to make true novels but rather poems barely structured by feeble plots? In general the reproach is accurate.

Undoubtedly if nothing happens there is no novel. It seems to me futile to submit the novel to the canons of other arts. The novel has not had its Rimbaud or Mallarmé like poetry; it will not have them. There may be pure poetry, but there is no such thing as a pure, dehumanized novel, because the novel's raw material is human.[102]

As a result of this sustained indictment of its class standing, vanguard fiction became part of what Foucault has called "une teratologie du savoir."[103] Teratology is not too strong a word, for a denaturalized novel is indeed monstrous, so much so that it is sometimes described with the language of sexual pathology. In López Prudencio's reference to the "monstrous conceptions" of vanguard writers, quoted a few pages earlier, we already get an inkling of this. But consider the following remarkable declaration by Juan José Domenchina:

The novel subsists. It triumphs over all kinds of intrigues. It doesn't matter that in this or that novelist the genre degenerates. Neither does it matter that this one or that one band together. In the end, their mystification does not spread. Even if the mule props and nourishes its hybrid offspring, hybridism only highlights the deterioration of the creatures it produces. The pseudoart of the supergifted homunculus will not prosper. The craft of the novelist is a man's craft. Only a genuinely virile man can practice it. . . . The 'pure narration' is not a novel. The effeminate gestures of these narcissistic or androgynous stylists—who need no complement, since they are self-sufficient—produce an equivocal impression that only captivates others like them and has nothing to do with properly novelistic movements.[104]

By a trick of lexical legerdemain, a novel of indeterminate genre becomes one of indeterminate gender, and the consequence is a catalogue of terata hybrid in itself, where the human and the nonhuman combine. Degeneration is the biological equivalent of denaturalization. Vanguard fiction is degenerate literature, in both senses—without genre and thus without gender.[105] The extravagance of Domenchina's language suggests the importance attached to this debunking. As Foucault has shown, discourse does not merely reflect battles waged at other levels; it is also the medium and cause of such conflict: that for which and through which one fights, the seat of power to which one would gain access. Being contested here is the power to speak for the novel. Appropriately, Domenchina's opening sentences adopt the language of political conspiracy and insurrection. Before it becomes an erotic or even a literary problem, the presence of the vanguard novel is seen for what it is, a threat to the hegemony of the ruling class.

The tendency to translate literary inclinations into sexual preferences, illustrated so well by Domenchina, is fairly widespread. Exhibiting a peculiar kind of *machismo*, these testimonies generally call into question the virility of vanguard authors. A one-hundred page narration, with wide margins and lots of metaphors, and with a female protagonist, cannot be the work of a man. The true novelist fathers; he begets a world; his creations are his children. But vanguard novelists are sissies, fags, or simply impotent. Their puny and ambiguous offspring bear witness to their enfeeblement: "The vanguard writer, here as in Italy or Spain or France, is a poor kid who knows nothing of life. He does not know society, or women. . . . He writes very little: miniatures of a few lines, impressions. And after two or three years he publishes these little things in a volume of one hundred and twenty pages, with a lot of blank space. Of course, this writer, who is organically impotent, incapable of serious effort, will never be a novelist."

And again, "*Justo el evangélico* is a virile novel. Arderius' style is very far from that morose delight in form that is so popular with our young writers. Today's style, so composed, so polished and subtle, so mimetic, in most cases with a feminine soul and intention and attitude, shatters in the hands of this great ogre."[106] Even Jarnés, who was certainly the principal target of some of these attacks, indulged in a similar invective: "Above all, we must avoid the hermaphroditic book. The worst thing that can happen to men and women is to forget what we are: men and women. The worst thing that can happen to a book is also to forget its compass. In a not distant literary epoch amphibious books came to be preferred. Fortunately it's over. May it never return."[107]

Needless to say, the denaturalization of vanguard fiction was extraordinarily effective. In 1936, after the publication of well over two-dozen texts that were received as examples of the genre, it was still possible to state: "We're still waiting for the complete and authentic new novelist, a novelist with a clear-cut vocation who will represent this genre with originality and profundity."[108] In fact, during the early thirties the consensus was that for over ten years Spain had not produced novelists: "Today in Spain we do not have novelists other than those who remain from the generation of 98." "The fact is that during the advent of the so-called—for how long?—'new literature,' the novelist did not appear on the horizon. For that 'vanguard' team that approached throwing stones at puddles, the art of the novel was not important." Or, "Those in our country who are between thirty and forty years of age, those who tried their hand at the novel in these last years, what's become of them? . . . The group that we gleaned no longer exists; there are no novels; and hope has turned into despair."[109] Considering the richness and diversity of the production of such writers as Jarnés, Torres Bodet, Ayala, Obregón, and others, statements like these may strike us now as strange, if not incomprehensible. But more than a fit of critical blindness, what they evince is a simple discursive fact: by 1935 or 36 the vanguard novel has ceased to exist as a token of critical exchange; it has been effectively suppressed.[110] The assassination that Azorín had heralded did take place, but with the roles reversed. At the level of metalanguage, it was the old novel that did the new novel in—a murder so perfect that it succeeded in hardly leaving a trace.

We can measure the ground covered by juxtaposing the passages I have just quoted with "Reflexiones sobre la novela." Written in the thick of the struggle, Torres Bodet's essay splits its allegiance between the old and the new novel. The emergence of vanguard fiction creates a disposition to affirm the obsolescence of the traditional novel, a disposition counterbalanced by the opposite tendency to acknowledge the traditional novel's stability. "Reflexiones" balances, but does not quite manage to reconcile, these two forces. But several years later, once the crisis has passed, similar reflections exhibit no such ambivalence; manifesting a curious textual amnesia, they scarcely remember the new genre. The vanguard novel, with its present characteristics, has receded into a forgotten past.

2. A Pneumatic Aesthetics

In the last chapter we encountered different attempts to define the vanguard novel. They ranged from programmatic disavowals of the themes and procedures of the nineteenth-century novel to fairly extensive descriptions of the trademarks of the new genre. Most of this information, however, does not supply any real insight into the novels, nor does it adequately differentiate the class. Take, for example, the pervasive insistence on the lyrical or poematic quality of vanguard fiction. Even if one constructed a contextual glossary to track down the semantic nuances of terms like "poematic" or "lyrical," little would be accomplished. One would discover that "lyrical" frequently means nothing more than a first-person narration, a usage as ancient as the Aristotelian classification of poetry according to the manner of imitation. A novel presented in the voice of one of the characters, it is thought, shades into the poem, for the narrative perspective specific to fiction is third-person omniscience, "backbone of the narrative genre."[1] Other familiar criteria—internal coherence, lack of realism, metaphoricity—also suffer from insufficient specificity. Though generally useful, they do not delineate a sharp generic profile; there is more to vanguard fiction, one hopes, than what such broad concepts will allow one to discern.

I believe that this vagueness can be corrected by concentrating on the metaphorical tissue of vanguard-fiction criticism, rather than on its overt pronouncements. Thus in this chapter my examination of the metalanguage will aim to uncover recurring patterns of imagery, "obsessive metaphors" in Charles Mauron's phrase, that by conveying precisely how the genre was perceived, will supplement the criteria we have already seen. I do not propose, however, to embark upon a theoretical justification of this procedure, which will function here as a working postulate whose soundness can be gauged from the results obtained. I intend, further, to postulate from the outset the pertinence and centrality of a particular group of metaphors to which I allude in the "pneumatics" of my title. My contention is that a consideration of this imagery will take us directly to the central aesthetic issues raised by the reception of the vanguard novel. I hope to show that pneumatic metaphors are the means by which this criticism figures both its own aesthetics and its position vis-à-vis the dominant discourse about the novel. They constitute its "reflejo absoluto,"[2] understanding by *reflejo* both "image" and "reflex."

I have selected this approach, nevertheless, for a concrete reason. The accusation most frequently leveled at vanguard fiction by its contemporaries is that of iconomania. For Juan José Domenchina a vanguard sonnet and a vanguard novel differ only in the number of metaphors: fourteen for the sonnet versus three-thousand two-hundred and twenty-three for the novel.[3] By turning my attention to the critics' own metaphors, therefore, I will be searching for the synapses that connect narration and commentary in the area one would least expect them. I will be, in effect, redirecting the accusation back to its source in order to seek a similar iconomania in the criticism. But that such synapses exist is undeniable: look again, to give a preliminary example, at José Gorostiza's review of *La rueca de aire*: "*La rueca de aire*, written in that subtle prose that evaporates with each phrase into a metaphor, is a late flowering, though not an extemporaneous one, of the Giraudoux-Jarnés branch—the same one that brought forth *Margarita de niebla, Dama de corazones*, and *Novela como nube*—and thus offers us a material exhausted not so much in itself as Martínez Sotomayor in it."[4] At the very moment when Gorostiza is remarking on the metaphorical excesses of *La rueca*, his own prose evaporates into a metaphor—the metaphor of evaporation, which is soon followed by others. To judge from this sentence one would have to conclude that Gorostiza's essay represents still another offshoot of the Giraudoux-Jarnés branch. Of course, since commentary seems fated always to repeat, at some level, the commented text, this doubling is not unusual; but with vanguard fiction the repetition is uncommonly extensive, in part because many of the same people who wrote the novels wrote the reviews, in part because the newspaper article was regarded as a literary genre, and hence a suitable forum for the verbal fireworks otherwise reserved for poems and novels.[5] As a result novels and criticism mirror each other with exceptional clarity. The same quirks, the same excesses, appear in both.

My subject, then, is the iconography of vanguard-fiction criticism. In the last chapter one important element in this system, Azorín's circus of mirrors, was seen to mark a pronounced discontinuity between the old novel and the new. The metaphor I would now like to examine is not so easily grasped, nor so easily explicated, as this one. It is in fact not one metaphor but many, and cannot, as in the case of the circus, be reduced to one *comparant* and one *comparé*. Rather than as a metaphor, it is better regarded as an isotopy, a cluster of images that revolve around a shared semantic nucleus.[6] I will label this nucleus the "pneumatic effect." The term is purposively vague, for it spans a wide and variegated range of items. In the most general terms the pneumatic effect shows through in images which, in one way or another, convey a sense of dissolution or weightlessness. It represents an ascensional movement and a centrifugal force: up, and away. Pneumatics comprehends that branch of physics that studies the properties of air and other gases. The pneumatic effect, consequently, is the informing principle of imagery that embodies some of these properties. To say "informing principle," however, is already to betray the concept, since the pneumatic effect establishes a pattern of binary oppositions in which form figures prominently at one of the negative poles. More accurate would be to speak of an "unforming principle," or, if logic permitted, of an "informing unforming principle," where the second participle would designate the import of the concept, and the first its function. Pneumatic imagery will include metaphors of evaporation (as in the Gorostiza passage), of levitation, of various kinds of gaseous matter (mist, clouds, nebulae, etc.), of diverse inflatable organs and objects (lungs, soap bubbles, pneumatic tires). It will even include an air pump (to inflate the tire, of course). In addition, it will be predicated not simply of the novel as a whole, but also of its constituent parts—character, style, plot—as well as of the reading and writing processes. The brief conspectus that follows, though obviously not exhaustive, will help create a "feel" for this kind of imagery. The occasional glosses are furnished only to illustrate how some of these images might be naturalized, and not as an analysis of the isotopy. This task will be undertaken later in the chapter.

A. *Style*

1. The vision is expressed with the same arbitrariness, the dislocation, the incoherence of mental experiences, "in images joined together like rings of cigarette smoke."
2. Because of the fluidity of its subject matter and elaboration, because of the airy grace of its themes and their treatment—schematic essentiality, agility—Obregón's literature is made from water and crystal, snow, ice,

and steel, fluid like the most insubstantial thoughts, immense like the sea, whose images predominate in this book.

3. In our opinion, this novelist demonstrates his obsession with the ren-ascence of 'lightness' in 'Juno (Edad Antigua).' The whole first chapter of his 'scenes,' almost thirty pages of lightness, is designed to highlight the final nuance.
4. The characters move—sway—, come and go, meet, cross, like shadows, made of fog, while before them the words, exact, brilliant, rise, fall, dance like celluloid balls on a thread of water.[7]

B. *Character*

1. And who are all these imprecise women who don't begin or end any-where, like apparitions awakening from the footprints of a shadow?
2. *La rueca de aire* is a narration, a paper skiff that one should not cast upon the deep sea of the novel. Everything in it is fragile, brittle, weightless. Even the characters, formless creatures, seem able to filter through the walls. They have neither the dimensions nor the consistency of characters.
3. What happens here? Just the opposite of what usually happens in novels whose title is taken from the protagonist's name. On this occasion the novelist follows his protagonist, but not to sketch or characterize him; rather, to un-sketch [*desdibujar*] or de-characterize [*descaracterizar*] him.
4. Perhaps his heroes are, at times, phantasms, but they remain always deli-cious creatures. Women of flesh or devilings of smoke, what's the differ-ence? After all, the novelist can operate on an infinite number of planes.
5. The protagonist—a useless professor—hides from us his bodily bulk: he is an empty abstraction, an 'invisible man' with a weakness for beer and romantic adventures. And the women or spectres who act as accomplices in his hardly platonic pastimes also do not achieve the corporeality or human accent that would have freed them from being light, ephemeral love interests.[8]

The pneumatic effect has a dramatic impact on character. Traditionally a character's lifelikeness has been expressed in corporeal terms. The novelist's goal has been to create the illusion of mass and dimension: to elide the materiality of the word and install in its place the materiality of flesh and bone. A successful character, consequently, is one who cons the reader into overlooking his status as a verbal construct. A novel that accomplished this end would be praised as follows: "In *Las Galgas* there are no characters.

There are men and women. Pedro Caba's creations manage to be, with all of their positive or negative humanity, of flesh and bone."[9] The pneumatic effect precludes corporeality. It disembodies characters, stripping them of flesh and bone. They lose their bulk, becoming "devilings of smoke" instead of "women of flesh." Incorporeality, moreover, is accompanied by an obliteration of individuality. In physical terms what separates the self from the other is the finiteness of the body. A disembodied character, thus, imperceptibly merges with others around him. It becomes impossible, as one passage asserts, to tell where one character ends and the other begins. Instead of a cast of individuals, we find a fluid, undifferentiated matrix of character traits (the protoplasm with which Jarnés compared the new novel would be an apt image). There is characterization, one might say, but there are no characters. The paradigmatic title in this respect is *Margarita de niebla*, since it announces the narrator's inability to grasp his subject in her material distinctiveness. When Margarita enters the novel, in the first sentence, she is identified as "una cabellera de aire." As we will see in discussing this novel, subsequent events do nothing to correct this imprecision. The key words in these passages, then, are *desdibujar* and *descaracterizar*, techniques which rob fictional personages of their lifelikeness.

C. *Plot*

1. Was it Rémy de Gourmont who—in order to highlight the importance of style in art—asserted that every novel—from the time of the Greeks onward—could have been written, without any loss of variety, about the love of Daphnis and Chloe? The new authors in Spain, in Spanish America, in France, seem to be out to prove it, answering Ortega's complaint about the impoverishment of plot in the modern novel with the example of a brilliant series of subtle, agile narrations—some of which already possess an oblique and tendentious profundity. In these novels, if the plot has not disappeared altogether, it remains, like an amiable pretext, as a dew drop on whose surface one can see the reflection of a morning landscape with its slippery and tender colors.
2. Plot—the ballast of immediate reality.[10]

These two passages establish an important interlock: plot, one of the components of the traditional novel, is conceived of as a "heavy" substance, as the ballast that keeps a novel from floating away. Of Jarnés it was affirmed that "as a good connoisseur of the limits of art, he takes care not to ballast his works with foreign, extraneous elements; and in that sense, he fulfills the only possibility open to pure art."[11]

D. *Novels*

1. Agile, smiling, image-filled stories. In them a young imagination plays freely. Hardly touching the ground, just barely grazing reality.
2. At times a sharp desire to avoid the chronicle turns the book into a— refined, subtle—reflective breviary, two steps away from melancholy, always authentically lyrical. On the surface a fine, gray drizzle, but behind it the flights of the author's fancy.
3. As a result *Proserpina rescatada* ends up by disappearing herself. After so many experiments with diverse alchemical agents, she evaporates. The artificial lights with their agile and daring effects have shown her in a thousand guises. And when we want, finally, to see her as she is, to *rescue* her, she escapes us, like a subtle and vague essence.
4. His books are groupings of minute orbs—poetic milky ways—where the common microscope perceives little, where the clear lens of another good poet immediately begins to see—deliciously atomized—bright new worlds in the process of becoming.
5. *Dama de corazones* is a luxurious, cheerful art, a first-class ticket on an ideal ocean liner that does not take us too far from the planet, that rocks us between two undulating, fugitive surfaces: the sky and the sea. An art that does not touch, does not want to touch dry land, because it is repulsed by the rough sailors and shameless whores of the ports.[12]

E. *Vanguard fiction*

1. We wander through the fields of the essay, through the groves of the poematic idyll, in a word, through the literary nebula of the unfocused novel. But the reader feels cheated. Where's the novel? he asks upon finishing the book.
2. [The new novel] prefers first-person narrations that allow the author, without losing credibility, to alchemize each instant of consciousness, to atomize the I, the I's. If it sometimes suits this purpose to have 'central characters' it's only as sparring partners with which the writing I—or his alter ego—works out and shows off. There might also be—I've already mentioned it here apropos of Villaurrutia's novel—a deeper motive: a certain modern disposition against rotund, univocal integrations of per-

sonality (a phenomenon typical of the nineteenth century), and also, a certain repugnance toward the concentration of sexual affect, which is now subjected to cerebral dilutions.

3. The curious ambiguity of *Señorita 0-3* grows out of this duplicity of inclinations; before its pages some skeptics will ask: is it pure literature, that is, a literature suspended in the air that only uses the ground to push off? . . . Is it social literature, that is, a literature supported by a social theory and written to illustrate it?[13]

F. *Reading and Writing*

1. *Margarita de niebla* is a transitional book, a beautiful transitional book. It has one foot in the poem and the other in the novel. Hence—as is the case with other similar books—the oscillations, the vacillations that envelop in a fine mist Torres Bodet's shadowy prose.
2. When the book ends we leave, in effect, a warm shadow that had girded our spirit like a tunic made of fog.
3. If the poet is a violin where harmonious waves palpitate as they strike the marvelous box, the novelist is a lung that purifies the air around it, turning it into breathable artistic matter capable of being assimilated by the reader.
4. Jarnés' pen has theological flashes of dominance. Everything that it touches catches fire, burns, comes alive with living warmth, with sinfulness. The flattest tires—the most squalid themes—are raised, inflated with his marvelous pneumatic pump: renovating and inexhaustible.[14]

The last passage sketches an interesting picture: a portrait of the artist as automobile mechanic. This is not the only instance of the image, which is also used apropos of Giraudoux: "One day in the XXth century the novel fell in love with the poem and it seemed that it was inevitably going to derail, but Giraudoux had already invented a pneumatic tire that rendered the rails superfluous."[15] The metaphor is essentially a reworking of the ancient topos of the poetic afflatus, only here it has been "dehumanized," transformed from a spiritual into a mechanical operation. The third passage also revitalizes (and burlesques) a dead metaphor, this time that of the poet as Aeolian harp. The other end of the reader-writer continuum is represented by the first two entries; they portray the pneumatic effect as affect.

One could adduce supplementary examples for each of the contexts in which the isotopy appears. As it stands, however, the conspectus gives a fair idea of the variety of usage and formulation of the pneumatic effect, an idea that would not be substantially altered by a replication of instances. It shows that in the critical discourse of this time there exists a certain impetus, a certain (air) pressure, for which pneumatic imagery serves as an outlet. This impetus is as diffuse and expansive as many of the images it provokes. It is also of variable density. In some segments (B2 and E2, for example) it materializes as a determining presence that molds the visual and plastic content of very nearly every sentence. At other times (C1 and D2, for example) it incides unobtrusively, and its presence can be detected only in a word or an allusion. This is an important realization, for it shows that the pneumatic effect is both a discursive choice and a discursive reflex, that it evinces both the unintentional mannerisms of discourse and its deliberate phrasings. The pneumatic effect is a stutter as well as an utterance, and as such reveals or articulates preferences that cut across such distinctions as conscious vs. unconscious or explicit assertion vs. presupposition and implication. Since what we are striving to achieve is a historical definition of vanguard fiction, that is, a definition based on how the genre was inscribed in the critical discussion contemporary with it, it is imperative that the threshold created by such distinctions be crossed. One must be leery of taking commentary too readily at its word, for in so doing one might be overlooking levels of coherence inaccessible to an approach whose principal weapon is paraphrase. My assumption is that the way to avoid this pitfall is by giving precedence to the metaphorical tissue of commentary, by—in effect—submitting critical discourse to the same close reading to which one would subject a literary text. Explicit descriptions of norms will still figure in my analysis, but conditioned and controlled by interpretive guidelines derived from a consideration of pneumatic imagery. The pneumatic effect will be our text, and overt critical statements will act as scholia. The latter will help adumbrate the text, but will remain subordinate to it. These, broadly, are the hermeneutical principles that motivate and orient the following analysis. They will be applied, first, to an examination of the genesis of the pneumatic effect, and later to an exposition of its aesthetic implications.

> ¿Se puede perfilar en la niebla una arquitectura?
> ¿Se puede hacer una novela en la niebla?
> ... (Problema del arte nuevo—más en concreto:
> de la novela—planteado y aún no resuelto.)

[Is it possible to outline an architecture in the fog?
. . . (This is the problem of the new art—more
concretely: of the novel—formulated and not yet
resolved.)][16]

With respect to the new fictional genre, the "old novel" behaves much like
an institution. It acts as a coercive, constrictive force that curtails the
development of the emergent genre so as to prolong its own dominance. It
comes as no suprise, then, that when the traditional novel is visualized, the
image evoked is that of the edifice, the material symbol of institutions.
Thus, one of George Bernanos' novels is described as follows: "The writer
who conceives, feels, and writes a book like *Sous le soleil de Satan* is a total
architect. He has built an admirable literary edifice. It had been thought
that those ornate literary structures were no longer in use, that Proust had
atomized them, and that to retrieve them one had to go back to no less a
name than Flaubert. This man, G. Bernanos, has demonstrated that this is
not so, but by aspiring, of course, only to write—with talent—one more
novel, a novel in the grand French manner, and by remaining outside the
latest evolution of the genre. In this respect, the author of *Sous le soleil de
Satan* represents a reaction against today's poematic novels."[17]

The pilot metaphor in this quotation is far different from those we have
seen thus far. No question here of an ascensional movement and a centrifugal force. The pneumatic effect, present in the familiar reference to atom-
ization (cf. D4 and E2), surfaces only to be negated. *Sous le soleil de Satan*
strives toward form; like the great nineteenth-century masters, Bernanos
writes as an architect builds. This quotation puts in place the building blocks
for another isotopy, parallel to the first: the writer as architect; writing as
construction; the novel as edifice. Images like these occur repeatedly in connection with the traditional novel. A narration of this sort constitutes "the
most beautiful building in the world";[18] it requires "construction work."[19] If
the novel is going through a difficult period, the reason is the "lack of
architects to raise the new edifice."[20] Since the traditional novelist works in
the construction business, his raw material is "dense matter";[21] and his job
is that of "a luckless laborer for whom the concrete world exists."[22] Given
that biographies were considered near-relatives of the novel, they too par-
took of these images: "There is nothing more erect [*Nada más parado*] than a
geometrically constructed biography. Nothing more static and secure. I
think of Amiel's, of Shelley's, of the Duke of Osuna's. There are many. All
of them inert, restrained, shackled with the fetters of repose, silent and

clear, as if rejecting that mad dynamism, unrestrained and mindless, of modern life."[23] A few sentences from Ortega sum up well this way of conceiving the novel: "One has to accept things as they are. The novel is not a light, agile, winged genre. We should have been alerted to this by the fact that all of our favorite great novels are, from a different perspective, a little ponderous."[24]

One has only to contrast Ortega's opinion with the description of *Cuentos para una inglesa desesperada* as "agile, smiling, image-filled" (D1) to perceive the opposition between this imagery and the pneumatic aesthetics of vanguard fiction. The pneumatic effect figures a novel that is weightless, agile, incorporeal. The novel as nebula or phantasm. Its stock of tropes encompasses phrases like "nebulosa de novela," "novela gaseiforme," "novela amorfa, en estado de formación."[25] Gilberto Owen's narration provides the exemplary title—*Novela como nube*.[26] Other titles like Azorín's *Blanco en azul*, which also refers to cloud formations, and *La rueca de aire*, a description of the novel itself, echo the same idea. Architectural metaphors, on the contrary, figure a novel that is stable, even ponderous, fixed in space and endowed with an inflexible structure: not a nebula but a monolith (we will soon come across the phrase "cúbica mole"). We have, then, parallel but contrasting isotopies: first, the pneumatic effect, visual and plastic (dis)embodiment of the new novel; and in opposition to it, a contrary set of images embodying the traditional narration (to keep things tidy, I will call this second isotopy the "architectural impulse"). The competition between the two novel-forms thus finds a correlate in the clash between these two systems of imagery: the pneumatic effect against the architectural impulse. The latter tends toward form; the former toward shifting and evanescent contours. One feeds on the material world; the other, as in Martínez Sotomayor's title, processes air. One tends toward specification and concretion; the other toward dissolution. One sinks into the ground; the other levitates. One is iconolatric; the other is iconoclastic. In the most general terms, the architectural impulse reflects an ideology of fabrication, while the pneumatic effect reflects an ideology of deconstruction.[27]

The two isotopies have their corresponding mythological mentors. According to Jarnés, the tutelar spirit of the new novel is Hermes, god of surfaces, spirit of mobility, who skims "over mere circumstances, over the cheerful skin." The old novel's patron is Prometheus, avatar of "deep life" [*la vida profunda*] who cannot break the chains that attach him to the world.[28] These two figures appear repeatedly in the discussion of the old and the new novel. In the statement that biographies are "inert, restrained, shackled with the fetters of repose, silent and clear, as if rejecting that mad dynamism, unrestrained and mindless, of modern life," the personae behind the words are obviously chained Prometheus and winged Hermes. Hermes is also the protagonist of Obregón's second novel and serves as an explicit parallel in Torres Bodet's *Proserpina rescatada*. He is present in the alchemical references within the pneumatic network (cf. D3 and E2); in the allegations of generic "hermaphroditism"; and in the Ortegan notion of "hermetic" literature (of which more later). Some idea of his ubiquitousness may be garnered from the following: in the first chapter, while speaking of Jarnés' "Discurso a Herminia," I mentioned the possibility of seeing Herminia as a female Hermes, since, as a valkyrie, she also leads the dead to their last abode. The curious fact is, however, that the professor's discourse revolves around the homosexual leanings of Juan, one of his students (we are still moving in the realm of the hermaphroditic, the sexually ambiguous), who has been much taken with a young man who builds instruments, wind instruments, for a living. Juan has fallen for a maker of saxophones, trumpets, and flutes; he has fallen, in Jarnés' words, for a "splendid plebeian Hermes."[29] A certain textual logic, thus, dictated my identification of Hermes and Herminia. Hermes has left his footprints on the professor's discourse, as he has on many other vanguard texts.

The epigraph of this section confronts the hermetic and promethean conceptions of the novel: the novel as *niebla* and as *arquitectura*. The question is whether they can be reconciled, whether it is possible, as Ayala asserts, to sketch "en la niebla una arquitectura." The difficulty of the enterprise becomes fully apparent once we pause to consider the aesthetic implications of these isotopies. The architectural impulse supposes, first, that the novel is a discrete genre, clearly cordoned off from contiguous forms. Just like an edifice, the novel occupies a limited and well-defined space. This conception sanctions the traditional separation of genres, a division that was also rendered in architectonic terms: "Current literary thought lacks those corporeal and measurable excellences that until now have defined the novel, the drama, the essay. Literary edifices erected with their weight and volume in a moral space, just as architectonic constructions—like a cathedral or a windmill—are erected in physical space."[30] Architectural metaphors suggest, second, that the novel is firmly entrenched in reality. It rests on the material world, from which it is also constituted. Realism and mimesis are generic imperatives. Accordingly the novel has a prescribed form; Ortega believes, in fact, that it is the only extant genre with its own rules and conventions.[31]

Another architectural metaphor summarizes the genre's fixity: the novel is "a finished thing: well-made and prescribed."[32]

The pneumatic effect evidently entails a different set of norms. Unlike the edifice, the nebula does not allow for the drawing of clear boundaries. The vanguard novel is scandalously transgressive. It blurs distinctions by expropriating material from other genres; it does not hesitate to foray into the territory of the poem or the essay, or even of film. Like Hermes, it is expansive, mobile, never in place. And instead of anchoring itself in reality, it hovers "floating over things. Tied to them only by slight allusions"[33] (cf. also D1, E3, and E4 above). One can thus label it "surreal" in the literal sense of the word (the sense Azorín activates in *Superrealismo*). In addition, the novel as nebula will not stand prescription, for it lacks a structural paradigm to which individual novels must conform. Unlike the old novel, it is neither prefabricated nor prewritten. Again the analogue is Hermes, free spirit, and not Prometheus.

More generally, the pneumatic effect subverts the form-content dichotomy, while the architectural impulse endorses it. The image of the edifice readily doubles as a metaphor for the division of a work into form and content, a division that goes along with the view that the novel is a fixed genre. The frame of the building, its *armazón* (a word constantly used to subsume the categories of plot and character), serves as the "form" which the novelist imbues with a specific content. Although the content may vary with the times, the form remains unchanged: "The classical frame [*La armazón clásica*], filled out in a modern way, is what gives Moravia's novel its solidity, unheard of in these times."[34] This assertion, made apropos of *Los indiferentes*, "a good novel constructed from all the parts," can be contrasted with the following excerpt from a review of *Superrealismo*: "No question here of taking characters who are already complete, already created, already born, already alive with their I.D. cards in their pockets and their literary papers in order, so as to entangle them in situations that are also already created, preconceived, and worked out. In order to throw them into that traditional setting called a novel. No question here of ready-mades that one then places within the frame [*armazón*] of the well-studied genre."[35] Azorín's reviewer rejects both the architectural conception of the novel and the analytical categories to which this conception gives rise; he discards the view that there exists an inherited finite set of formal possibilities with which the novelist must shape his material. A gaseous novel dissolves this polarity. As form, how can a gas, itself of indeterminate shape, contain? As content, how can it be contained? how can it be enclosed in an *armazón*?

Instead of an artifact separable into form and content, the pneumatic effect figures a homogeneous (if unstable, surreal, and amorphous) novelistic vapor. And, we can add, vanguard fiction was criticized as frequently for its formlessness as for its insubstantiality.

The symmetrical opposition between the two isotopies serves as evidence of the postulated centrality of the pneumatic effect (a centrality at the margins, however, for we have seen that vanguard fiction never achieved dominance). This opposition corroborates the findings of the last chapter, which stressed the fundamental negativity of the genre. As pneumatic effect, the new novel remains, primarily, that which the old novel is not. Our examination of the isotopies must be carried further, however, for their relationship is more complex than simple contradiction. Because binary oppositions are easy to establish, they are somewhat arbitrary. A building is unlike a nebula, but it is also unlike a great many other things. To predicate the significance of the penumatic effect on this basis alone is clearly insufficient. One needs to show that the conjunction of these two clusters of images is motivated by something more than opposition. We can begin to do this by looking closely at the following excerpt from Antonio Espina's review of *Libro de Esther*:

> La magia, prodigio y hechicería de las fuerzas ocultas, cede sus más raros valores al estilo en la prosa de Jarnés, al estilo en la arquitectura de la prosa . . . (No. Si decimos sólo "arquitectura" no daremos la impresión verdadera de lo que queremos y debemos significar al referirnos a la fábrica especial de la prosa jarnesiana; felizmente cabe aditar al término una adjetivación bien moderna que trueca en ágil, veloz y siempre móvil la vieja idea pesada de la solemne arquitectura en reposo. La vieja arquitectura. La idea y la fábrica que también es idea en arquitectura. Precisemos, pues, con cuidado: "arquitectura aerodinámica." Porque, en efecto, el estilo de Jarnés puede compararse al que cuaja en la forma y movimiento del moderno navío, o en la volátil estructura de la cometa, o al del aire mismo—etéreo estilo—cuando cristaliza en efectos cromáticos y musicales en el espíritu, del idioma. Nunca nos recordará al duro croquis del castillo feudal con su cúbica mole asentada en la roca. Aunque la roca sea viva.)

>> [The magic, the marvel, the witchcraft of occult forces imparts its best qualities to the style of Jarnés' prose, to the style of his prose's architecture. . . . (No. If we say only "architecture" we will not give a true impression of what we want and mean to say in referring to the special fabrication of Jarnesian prose; happily it is possible to add to the word a very modern

adjective that will turn the old, solemn, ponderous idea of architecture into an agile, fast, and mobile thing. The old architecture. Fabrication and conception are also part of the architectural 'idea.' Let's be precise, then: "aerodynamic architecture." Because, in effect, Jarnés' style can be compared to that embodied in the lines and movement of a modern liner or in the volatile structure of the kite, or to air itself—an ethereal style—when it crystallizes as chromatic and musical effects in the spirit of a language. His style will never remind us of the hard outlines of the feudal castle with its cubic mass planted on a rock. Even if the rock is alive.)][36]

The two isotopies figure here explicitly and in detail. The phrase "la vieja idea pesada de la solemne arquitectura en reposo" could well function as a synopsis of the principal connotations of the iconography of the traditional novel—ponderousness, immobility, authority. Its concretization as a medieval castle perched on a rock connects not only with other building images but also with Prometheus, an association strengthened by the mention of a "roca viva." In contrast, the mobility and airiness ascribed to Jarnesian prose readily fall within the sphere of influence of the pneumatic effect. In addition, the reference to magic and occult learning in the opening sentence connects with the alchemical aspect of the isotopy, once again evoking the figure of Hermes. What is new is that the clash of isotopies actually generates the passage. The long parenthesis that spans the quotation is produced by the force I have called pneumatic, and whose distinctive characteristic is its incompatibility with the traditional novel. Significantly the parenthesis begins with *No*, a particle that embodies the typical gesture of vanguard fiction. Moreover, the setting in which the pneumatic effect appears is entirely in keeping with its nature. That it should surface within a parenthetical qualification underlines its role as a foreign substance, fundamentally noxious and subversive, embedded in discourse about the novel. Here the pneumatic effect disrupts the flow of ideas in order to offer a series of qualifications whose effect is simply to cancel out the meaning of the term being qualified (*arquitectura*). In this instance at least, the pneumatic effect overwhelms the architectural impulse. Moreover, it permeates the paragraph from which the quoted excerpt has been extracted, which concludes with a quotation from *Libro de Esther*: "She is all softness. She prefers to wear grey tones. She seems thus a patch of fog seeking definition. Even white, when she wears it, chooses to mute its brightness, to dissolve in a fine mist. And so with every color."

The process of qualification to which *arquitectura* is submitted will repay further scrutiny. The "solemne arquitectura en reposo," whose material counterpart is the feudal castle, is successively assimilated to a swaying ship, a kite, and finally, air. The setting moves from matter in its solid state (the rock), to matter in its liquid state (the ocean), to the realm of mist, clouds, and nebulae, into which the castle is finally dissolved. We witness, then, a gradual but complete *volatilization* of the feudal castle. It is detached from the rock, then set adrift, then cast in the air, then turned into air. What begins as a manifestation of the architectural impulse culminates as a manifestation of the pneumatic effect. Form is unformed and mass is vaporized. Adjectives like "volátil" and "etéreo" replace others like "duro" and "cúbica." The unforming power of our informing principle is clearly at work here. This process is important because it shows that the novel as nebula not only clashes with the novel as monolith—as "cúbica mole"—but *arises* from it. Indeed, the nebula is nothing other than a monolith volatilized, pulverized, atomized to the point that it levitates.

The rhetorical strategy of the passage—having the parenthesis develop as a qualification of *arquitectura*—thus emphasizes the interconnection between isotopies. It points to the relational complexity that binds old novel and new, a complexity that is dialectical in the true sense of the word, since each genre can only be defined by reference to its opposite. The monolith and the nebula are not only antitypes; more importantly, they represent opposite states of the *same* material. For this reason to name the old novel is implicitly also to name the new—and vice versa. The architectural impulse subsists in the pneumatic effect as a memory trace or phantasm: each of the nebular atoms was once a building block; each carries within the ruined memory of a wall or a cornice.

The transformation operated by Espina on the feudal castle is structurally identical to the one performed by Azorín on the topos of the novel as mirror. In both instances the fragmentation of an artifact is followed by the reconstitution, from the old material, of a different object. In one instance the new icon is a circus of mirrors; in the other, the constellation of images designated by the pneumatic effect. The "curiosa edificación"[37] of which Azorín speaks doubles—mirrors—Espina's "fábrica especial." The adjective in each phrase fulfills the same function: it acts to erode the semantic underpinnings of the noun it modifies. In this respect the relationship between the new novel and the old, and especially the mode of existence of the former, are neatly summarized in a nearly oxymoronic syntagm like "curiosa edificación" or "fábrica especial." Vanguard fiction possesses an adjectival, contingent existence. It depends on the old novel as the adjective depends on the noun, though when noun and adjective come together the result is a *contradictio in adjecta*. And we should recall that supplying the proper adjective was precisely Espina's aim in the quoted excerpt. Espina writes in order to add "a very modern adjective" to the noun "architecture." It is thus a peculiar kind of (in)subordination that attaches the new novel to the canonic genre—where the parenthesis around the prefix recovers the one in Espina's text. Indeed, to the extent that the passage concerns itself with onomastics, one can say that it names "(in)subordination": the diacritical dependence of text and parenthesis, monolith and nebula, noun and adjective, and now, of stem and prefix. And should there be any doubts about the place of adjectives in the pneumatic network, let me cite one sentence from *Libro de Esther*, the book that has prompted Espina's discussion: "Benjamin Constant, in whom the adjective—that window opened toward vagueness through which fog filters into the sentence—is one more way of circumscribing thought, could not join that dishevelled lot."[38] The adjective is to the noun as a window is to an edifice—a window through which the fog seeps in. Here again, within another parenthetical aside, the pneumatic effect unforms the architectural impulse.

But the resemblance between Azorín's and Espina's metaphors goes beyond homology. Can one not discover the circus of mirrors in the phrasing of the last step in the process of volatilization: "Jarnés' style can be compared . . . to air itself—an ethereal style—when it *crystallizes* as chromatic and musical effects"? Azorín's metaphor is thereby inscribed in the quotation, with the result that what had originally appeared as related but distinct texts might be better regarded as two different *loci* within the same text. The two-step destructive and constructive mechanism of these images was also described, with not dissimilar terms, in Torres Bodet's "Reflexiones sobre la novela": "Balzac, Flaubert, Dostoiewsky did not penetrate the spirit of their heroes with just one astute glance. They besieged them and then conquered them little by little. The modern novelist tires of this laborious process and prefers to work on a material that has already been defined. Comparing his effort with that of the sculptor, we could say that Balzac, Flaubert, and Dostoiewsky tore the original figure from the heart of the rock, while today's novelists are content to work on the figure they have received from reality or literature until it becomes transparent" [*tallar hasta la transparencia*].[39] Here also it is a question of fragmentation and crystallization—"tallar hasta la transparencia." It is also a question—why not?—of "reflections."

The iconography of the vanguard novel may then be said to have a double referent. Even as it embodies a new conception of the novel, it (literally) disembodies the iconography of the dominant novel-genre, which it aspires to supplant. The novel as nebula functions in one direction as a representation of the distinctive features of vanguard fiction, and in a different direction (perpendicular to the first, one might say), it functions as a representation of the connection between the new novel and the old. Thus, the pneumatic effect signifies both in reference to novels (which incorporate the characteristics represented by the imagery: diffuse characterization, lack of realism, etc.) and in reference to the state of the theory (the pneumatic effect as a product of the volatilization of the architectural impulse). It is at the same time a theory of the novel and a "theory" of the theory. This auto-referentiality poses some difficult interpretive problems, for the two functions may not always be easily reconciled. One referent could well interfere with or occlude the other. This, in effect, is what happens when one attempts to infer a poetics of the vanguard novel from the pneumatic effect. It is to this problem that I now turn.

Thus far I have identified several of the distinguishing features of the new novel and demonstrated how they organize themselves around the pneumatic effect. We have seen that this isotopy figures such qualities as diffuse characterization, lack of realism, and resistance to form-content dissection. Some of these qualities, nevertheless, because they arise from a negation of the attributes of the traditional novel, lack a specifiable content. Others seem only to skim the surface of the phenomenon; they do not, I believe, exhaust the interpretive possibilities of the isotopy. But since a pneumatic aesthetics by its nature precludes rigid definition, these shortcomings are inevitable. In order to overcome them one would have to arrest the deconstructive force of the isotopy, and this would mean, in effect, allying vanguard fiction with its nemesis, the old novel, whose trademark is precisely concreteness of definition. A process of specification such as that implied in the term "poetics" would transform the pneumatic effect into an architectural impulse. If the nebula solidifies it becomes a monolith; and it is the monolithic character of the old novel, "muy hecha y prescrita," that pneumatics sets out to explode.

One should not, therefore, impelled by a kind of meta-architectural impulse, reverse the process of volatilization from which the vanguard novel springs. A more fruitful procedure would be to study the deconstructive effort itself as it appears in the criticism of individual novels. The result would then not be a poetics of the genre, but a poetics of why a poetics is impossible, an antipoetics. One would focus on the dissolving power of the isotopy in order to reveal the features by virtue of which vanguard fictions are prevented from becoming like traditional novels. In this manner the difficulties of the double referentiality will have been averted, for one will no longer be utilizing a deconstructive metaphor for constructive purposes. By not suppressing the subversive force of the isotopy (when referred to the old novel) in drawing the (blurred) profile of the new, the two referents will have been reconciled. The question one wishes to answer is not, What are the distinctive features of the vanguard novel as a fictional form? but rather, What about the vanguard novel prevents it from becoming a "form" in the sense in which the nineteenth-century novel is a "form"? I should like to examine, thus, that aspect of the isotopy that relates to incompleteness: the ways (there are two) in which the pneumatic effect protects and sanctions the vanguard novel's imperfectibility as a literary form.

When Azorín labels *Superrealismo* a "nebulosa de novela," he employs the pneumatic metaphor to connote incompleteness. A nebulous novel is one which has not yet achieved its entelechy: an "amorphous novel, in a state of formation," whose constituent parts resemble so many "shreds of fog."[40] *Superrealismo* is, pointedly, not a novel but a "pre-novel." Since a nebula is constituted from matter that has not yet cooled into a solid mass, the novel as nebula is a fiction that has not yet developed sufficiently to qualify as a novel. In other words, it represents only a *beginning*. This is the positive sense that can be infused into the criteria mentioned already: the vanguard novel is generically indeterminate, unrealistic, formless, contentless, not populated by lifelike characters, in that it consists of a beginning only, of an intimation of what could (have) be(en) a novel. Its elements have not yet differentiated sufficiently for it to have a form and a content, belong to a genre, or furnish the illusion of reality. It remains "in gestation," that is, "not yet situated, not yet anchored in a precise zone of the universe."[41] Bulk and definition are postnebular developments. A nebular novel cannot be "anchored" in the universe or "situated" in a taxonomical space.

The frequency with which this trait is predicated of individual novels confirms the importance of the anticipatory, embryonic, or potential quality of vanguard fiction:

The book ends just when we were beginning to read it. When we knew for sure that something was going to happen.

As a novel without an ending, *Margarita de niebla* leaves in the reader's spirit an invitation to weave a refined denouement in accordance with the plot.

These novelists' inspiration does not lie, in effect, in the erotic story told in Longus' poem, but it is nevertheless an idyll: an incomplete idyll.

It seems as if we were fleeing from what begins to take shape, as if an internal contradiction animated the dialogue and, in the end, all possible adventures were erased.

If we insisted on determining the novelistic elements in *La rueca de aire*, we would find in it the environment for a novel or the background for a novel that was left unpainted, as in some unfinished pictures by Michaelangelo, but whose presence can be felt in the precise spot from which it is missing. Let the reader or I fill in the blank space with our own conflicts and the novel will instantly appear, as if produced by the chemical reaction of two substances.

Ruth is an introduction to another introduction: the discourse to Herminia. So many introductions confirm our idea of a *Profesor inútil* that will age along with its author. All of it is a prologue, a propitious theme, a part of a whole, an anticipation of things to come [*parte de un todo, porvenir*].[42]

The vanguard novel is thus all "porvenir": the fiction of the future. The paradigmatic title here is Salinas' *Víspera del gozo*, proclaiming the imminence of an event that never materializes. As one of the passages above suggests, this peculiarity involves "an internal contradiction," for the novel, even etymologically, should bring "news." The concept of a prenovel is, accordingly, profoundly antinovelistic, since it runs counter to the most basic expectations about fiction. But we know enough by now not to conclude from this that the prenovel simply opposes established practice. It too illustrates once more the contingency of vanguard fiction. A beginning is such only in regard to a certain end. In this instance the end, the *telos* toward which the prenovel strives but whose fulfillment would mean the obliteration of its distinctiveness, is the traditional novel. The prenovel can be grasped as such only by reference to that which it anticipates but never realizes. And that is simply the nineteenth-century novel form. One could say that for vanguard fiction the past lies ahead.

Because the prenovel ends at the beginning, it assigns to the reader a new role and importance. If the nebular novel is only a novel *in potentia*, it is up to the reader to bring to completion what the text leaves unfinished. The metaphor of the circus of mirrors already intimated as much, since

Azorín stations the reader on the whirligig in the middle of the circus. The reader thus occupies the center of the novel, and not only because of his vantage point, but also because undoubtedly the mirrors will show him the reflection of his own splintered self. In Azorín's circus the artist disappears, the world disappears, and the reader becomes both subject and spectator. Similar appeals to the reader's collaboration regularly accompany references to incompleteness. Thus, in one passage above, he is encouraged to fill in the "blank space," the pages that the novelist left unwritten, and in another, he is invited to "weave a refined denouement." The type of reading and reader required by the new novel is explained as follows:

> The pure novel needs readers to become an impure novel, a common novel. It only offers hints, profiles. Privileged profiles that tell the reader, without possible deviation, where the treasures are hidden [*Perfiles privilegiados que aseguran al lector sin posible desvío el punto donde se esconden las atracciones de los parques*]. For me *Luna de copas'* highest merit has been the frequency with which Espina leaves the readers to their own devices so that, all alone, they can exhaust the possibilities of a situation, resolve a conflict, even interpret a metaphor. What used to be curiosity has become tension.
>
> It's just the opposite of the old serial novels and the so-called psychological novels. In these everything is finished beforehand. The reader has nothing to do but skim the round surfaces without leaving his usual surroundings, since the novelists force him to experience common emotions, manipulate him, and make him take the worst part in the farce.[43]

Apparently the new novel's loss is the reader's gain. He is no longer a passive bystander whom the author can manipulate at will, no longer a victim of emotional blackmail. Vanguard fiction ends the tyranny of text and author, freeing the reader to actively participate in the making of the novel. Julio Cortázar has a name for this kind of reader: *un lector macho*. In this instance the name is all the more apt since the *lector macho* is exercising himself over a "feminine" or "hermaphroditic" text. The old novel presupposed masculine texts and feminine readers; the new novel presupposes masculine readers and feminine texts.

This conception, however, gets caught up in a troubling paradox. Were the reader to complete the novels in the manner indicated, the result inevitably would be a "common novel," the typical novel with a beginning, middle, and end. By resolving a conflict or exhausting the dramatic possibilities of a scene, one would be leading the prenovel in the direction it cannot go if it is to retain its identity. As Antonio Espina says of *Superrealismo*, "the *other* novel, the novel with bulk [*la de los bultos*], can of course begin where this one ends."[44] The vanguard novel, it seems, self-destructs in the act of reading. If it is carried to its anticipated conclusion (to any conclusion in fact), it vanishes before our eyes. The chemical metaphor in the passage about *La rueca de aire* should have alerted us to this subtlety: "Let the reader or I fill in the blank space with our own conflicts and the novel will instantly appear, as if produced by the chemical reaction of two substances." Although the interaction of the reader and the prenovel produces the novel, in the process the two substances that had provoked the reaction disappear, leaving a new element in their place. The reader, as well as the prenovel, are swallowed up in the "novela de bultos." But this is not inconsistent with the rest of my analysis, which has yielded an antipoetics and now logically yields as the object of that antipoetics not a novel but an antinovel, a novel predicated on the impossibility of its own fulfillment. To study the system of norms implicit in the reception of vanguard fiction, then, is to evolve the antipoetics of an antinovel.

One important feature of this antipoetics is that it seems to preempt the novels from naturalization by an interpretive act. According to the hermeneutics (or "hermepneutics") it postulates, the act of reading would dissolve the prenovel and install its reverse image in its place. The perversity of this maneuver cannot be overlooked. In order to distance itself from the traditional novel, vanguard fiction simply cajoles the reader into behaving as he usually does when he reads novels. It is a tactic devised for and against the *lector* (or *lectora*) *de novelas*, since the habits and expectations nurtured by conventional fiction are used to shield the vanguard novel from contamination by conventional fiction. In its own peculiar way, therefore, the new novel is no less manipulative than the old, as it also forces on the reader an attitude convenient to its own purposes. In fact, the explanation of the demands placed on the reader by the "pure novel" includes clearly coercive language. The pure novel presents "perfiles privilegiados que aseguran al lector sin posible desvío el punto donde se esconden las atracciones de los parques" ("privileged profiles that tell the reader, without possible deviation, where the treasures are hidden"). Significantly, a secondary sense of *asegurar* is to imprison or control. "Asegurar al lector," read in isolation, would mean to put him in handcuffs, which is not far from what is being attempted. Although the reader is cast in a more active role, he is not given freedom to exercise his creativity. The prenovel takes him, without possible deviation, where it wants him to go.

Vanguard fiction only begins. As we have seen, this involves a paradox, for it begins only with respect to the genre that has gone before it. Paraphrasing Torres Bodet, one could say that "la novela nueva, con sus características futuras, es un género de ayer." But one paradox does not an antipoetics make. It takes two: for if the vanguard novel depicts the beginning of a past, it depicts equally the past of its own future. That is to say, embedded in vanguard-fiction criticism we find another variation on the term "novel" whose purpose is not to stop the traditional novel from forming, as in the prenovel, but to make it disintegrate once it has been formed. The intent now is not to arrest the curve of development of the traditional novel in its ascending slope, but to propel it downward toward extinction. We are dealing, consequently, not with a novel or a prenovel, but with a postnovel or an "ultranovel," as it was once called. But prenovel and ultranovel accomplish the same end, since they both swerve away from conventional fiction. This was already perceived by Antonio Espina in coining the term; after pointing out the rationale for the sobriquet "pre-novela," he adds: "I could have also labeled it, strictly speaking, an 'ultra-novel.' Because where the other one ends *this* one, always advancing, can begin."[45] The prenovel ends where the novel begins; the ultranovel begins where the novel ends. They differ only in positioning: the prenovel is situated "before" the novel; it contains the novel of the future. The ultranovel is positioned "after" the novel; it contains the novel of the past. One is the novel that could have been, the other the novel that was. Put them both together and the result is a fiction that is both past and future, memory and anticipation; a fiction that is both—to reprise Torres Bodet once again—obsolete and "actual."

Now according to the criticism of this time, a text "degenerates" into an ultranovel when it becomes a vehicle for essayistic or critical speculation. Vanguard-fiction commentators regard "the critical sense" as a dissolving, centrifugal force, very much a part of the nebular network. The analytical faculty, which "shreds and annihilates," stands in opposition to the "novelistic sense," which "gathers, reconstructs, recasts, vivifies."[46] Once again pneumatics and architecture clash, the latter allied with the novel, the former allied with the faculty that takes apart whatever novelistic sense has constructed. If a novel indulges in essayistic digression, it collapses: touched by the intellect, "the novel volatilizes. It leaves our hands in search of rarefied air."[47] The ultranovel is thus nothing more than the old novel volatilized; and the catalyst of this reaction, the pneumatic agent, is the critical sense. Like their anticipatory character, the critical or reflexive orientation of vanguard novels is repeatedly stressed, often in conjunction with a reference to denaturalization:

It is very difficult nowadays to review a story without feeling the curiosity to study it as an aesthetic phenomenon. This dual character, this androgyny of the modern creator is prejudicial to the unity of execution indispensable to a work of art; it is a kind of strabismus that hampers the concentration of one's faculties. It has been said, and rightly so, that to write a novel today is to make a study of it.

Narration as a pretext for essayistic speculation may be profoundly characteristic of the novel of today and even perhaps—as a reaction against the 'all too human' manner of the past—what most vitally reflects the animating spirit of the age.

It could be said that today's novel is unlucky. When it is not born of a lyrical poet, it is born of an essentially cerebral writer who intellectualizes it. Treated with such rigor by the scrutinizing glance that observes it, and by the sharp instrument that extirpates all of its corruptible elements, a novel, thus mummified, is closer to the scientific essay, to the didactic composition, to the critical artifact.

Before, the novel used to follow the laws common to every living thing. The novelist carried the novel for a while inside his head, his heart, one of his vital organs, until the moment of birth. Now the opposite seems to happen: the novelist does not carry the novel; the novel carries the novelist. The novelist of today—less capable of falling in love, of romantic and fertile adventure—is not usually fecundated by a theme. Just the opposite: he goes out to find any old fragment and sticks himself inside it, there to lay his theoretical eggs.[48]

Subsequent chapters will bear out that observations like these accurately reflect the metafictionality of many a vanguard text. The paradigmatic title this time is Gilberto Owen's *Novela como nube*, since it presents, *in nuce*, an appraisal of the novel. By putting the novelist inside the work, this feature of the new novel, as Jarnés notes in the last citation above, inverts the traditional author-text relationship. This inversion parallels the collaborative role assigned to the reader of a prenovel, for if the prenovel privileges the public, the ultranovel does the same for the author. The difference, though, is that the two exchange places: the reader is brought in as author, whereas the novelist is brought in as commentator, as reader. But both mechanisms serve a similar purpose: they keep vanguard fiction from advancing, or retreating, toward the canonic genre.

Because the prenovel and the postnovel share the same dissolving, pneumatic force, they represent the ways in which vanguard-fiction criticism conceptualizes its rejection of the received fictional aesthetic. They are the objects at once described and constituted by the antipoetics of the genre. It remains to be seen, however, how well these notions account for the novels themselves. Since my reliance on the "primary" texts has been limited to the occasional mention of a title or an incident, we (I mean, you) have no guarantee that the critical prescriptions will match the fictional realities. Do the prenovel and the postnovel adequately portray the genre? Or are they utopian constructs, critical fictions, that far exceed any given work? What, in brief, is the usefulness of these concepts for "practical" criticism? In the second part of this book we will have the opportunity to consider these and related questions, for there I will be trying to *test* the interpretive power of the metalinguistic image of vanguard fiction. We will then discover whether these concepts "apply," whether they can support a close reading of the primary texts. But so as to end this section on a less tentative note, I will conclude with a quotation (from a *novel*) that furnishes a first clue:

> Impetu de ascención. Las cosas se abren paso entre los ángeles fieros que custodian la escala de Jacob. Anita se ha puesto nerviosamente en pie. Lo reconoce: ella también es fuerza de ascención. La recóndita voluntad que la impulsa tiene ya dirección: la hélice. ¿A dónde? ¡Qué importa! Subir, elevarse, desarraigar. Agotar el impulso, realizar la fuerza. ¿Hacia dónde? ¡Desarraigar!
>
> > [An ascending impetus. Things make their way among the fierce angels that guard Jacob's ladder. Nervous, Anita has stood up. She knows it: she is also an ascending force. The recondite will that impels her has found its direction: the spiral. Where? It doesn't matter! To ascend, to rise, to fly away. Exhausting the impulse, exploiting the force. Where? Away!][49]

Pneumatic effects, still.

Part Two: Novels

3. Closed World

There is a certain pertinence to inaugurating a series of readings of vanguard fiction with a consideration of Salinas' "Mundo cerrado," one of the stories in *Víspera del gozo*. As we have already seen, the fashion of vanguard fiction began with the collection "Nova novorum" of the *Revista de Occidente*. The first title in the collection is *Víspera del gozo*; the first story in *Víspera del gozo* is "Mundo cerrado"; the first sentence in the story is, "He spent two hours reading."[1] It might be said, then, that vanguard fiction begins with a meditation on reading. My own discussion, in turn, will begin with a reading of this meditation: the circularity of the process is part of what the title, "Mundo cerrado," wants to convey. To read the story, thus, is to find ourselves at or near the chronological point of departure of my subject, at or near a beginning whose importance is enhanced by the theme it develops. For "Mundo cerrado"'s concern with reading is symptomatic of one of the dominant strains in vanguard fiction. In the preceding chapters we saw that on the metalinguistic level the "new novel" constitutes itself as a revisionary outgrowth of the old. We will now find that the same might be said of the novels themselves. They too need to be understood by reference to the canonical fictional forms which they reassess and displace. They need to be understood, that is, as a subversive reformulation of traditional novelistic concerns. The significance of Salinas' story lies precisely in this: it demonstrates that, conceptually as well as chronologically, vanguard fiction begins with reading. What will then follow, the "new" novel, will be, like the story, an account and evaluation of the matter read.

The story is brief, no more than a dozen pages in a recent edition,[2] and tells of a trip by train to a city named Icosia. The central character, Andrés, has been invited by a newly married friend, Alicia Chesterfield, now Lady Gurney, to spend a few days with her and her husband. Upon his arrival, a letter from Lord Gurney informs him that Alicia has just died. The account ends as Andrés is driven away from the train station, past a cemetery, toward Lord Gurney's house in the country. On one level, then, the theme of this story, as of others in the collection, is the frustration of desire. The longed-for reunion with Alicia, formerly his lover, never materializes. Her death forecloses what he had envisioned as a new world of adventure and romantic possibilities. All but the last paragraph of the story seems to have been written under the auspices of the title of the book: as Andrés rides on the train he indeed feels himself on the eve of pleasure, remembering his liaison with Alicia and anticipating its renewal. The last paragraph effaces the title of the collection and writes over it the title of the story. The expectancy nurtured by the former dissipates in the hermeticism of the latter. His hopes and illusions crumble when they enter into contact with the "world." In the train Icosia had seemed a ripe and savory fruit that Alicia was making accessible; but when he finally tastes it, when he arrives and learns of her death, it turns bitter and unpleasant (pp. 26-27). Thus construed, the story appears as a simple parable of innocence and experience. By tasting the fruit Andrés leaves behind the garden of illusion and enters a world troubled by human mortality. As he is leaving the station, his car passes by a cemetery—a sight markedly different from the attractive countryside he had observed from the train window, and one that reminds the reader of the change Andrés has undergone.

A more abstract way of recasting the plot of the story is to say that it is built on, or revolves around, a nonevent. The opening sentences already make this clear: "He spent two hours reading. Next to him, on the seat, the book remained closed." The closed book, echoing the closed world of the title, signals at once that in this book-world unrealized possibilities will prevail. Andrés does not read the book, and neither will he get to know Icosia or see Alicia again. In this as well, "Mundo cerrado" anticipates later pieces of vanguard fiction, many of which also evince a predilection for the abortive, the unrealized, or the unrealizable. It is often said that in vanguard novels "nothing happens." This is true only if one reads a certain affirmative impetus into these words: nothing *does* happen, it *happens* all the time. In vanguard fiction the nonevent is as obtrusive a presence, as powerful a force, as actual occurrences. My discussion of *Locura y muerte de Nadie* will make this clear enough, since in this novel the life of the protagonist, Juan Sánchez, consists of a succession of increasingly strident nonevents. It too does not advance past the eve of its own fulfillment.

But "Mundo cerrado" does depict events, though of an entirely different order. Andrés' trip to Icosia is presented primarily as an excursion through a sequence of texts. The story begins with him reading, and as it unfolds, his attention will be successively drawn to other texts. His adventure is eminently a textual one. Even the culminating revelation of Alicia's death is mediated textually by Lord Gurney's letter. It is as if he were being told: the world is closed, here is a letter instead. This is how the narrator describes Andrés' handling of the document: "On leaving the train station he saw nothing, not even the short and voluptuous avenue full of acacias, reminiscent of that look with which a woman or a city invites us to follow her, to go too far. He felt his soul settle in his hand, from where it weighed, calibrated the closed letter, stiff, unbearable, undoubtedly with something big inside" (p. 26). Not only does the letter completely blot out the outside world; it hangs from his arm just as Icosia, likened to a fruit, had dangled from the branch that Alicia was lowering to his reach (p. 23). The letter performs as a denial and replacement of the world, and it does so in two ways: both by its physical presence and by the information it conveys. This substitution of verbal for real experience, of a letter communicating the inaccessibility of Alicia for Alicia herself, characterizes the entire story. It is intimated in the closed world = closed book formula of the opening passage and will be sustained throughout. To complete the equation, however, we must add one more term: *mundo cerrado, libro cerrado,* and now, as in the passage just quoted, *carta cerrada.*

The account of Andrés' trip begins with a riddle: Andrés is reading but the book is closed. The riddle is drawn out through several more sentences which explain in some detail why the book remains unread. They also offer a first illustration of the discourse-producing power of the nonevent. Like Don Cayetano Polentino's *Historia de los linajes de Orbajosa,* whose subject is another kind of closed world, the relation of Andrés' expedition to Icosia concentrates on what did not happen rather than on what did. The riddle is finally solved when one realizes that Andrés' reading-matter is rather unorthodox: he is reading the landscape, refracted through an extended scriptural comparison. A pastoral scene is "a moving, tender page, as classical in its simplicity as a Homeric leave-taking, written in a crystalline phrase by the river's course, adorned by trees and greenery—fit epithets—and with two or three superb images, pure and colorful clouds, crowning the period" (p. 11). On the other hand, the sights at a dilapidated train station compose "an astonishingly realistic 'excerpt,'" so unlike the pastoral setting "that one, not understanding how they could have been created by the same author, suspected an apocryphal interpolation" (p. 12). The "book" even has blank or illegible pages that appear sporadically when smoke clouds the window or the train passes through a tunnel (p. 14). Thus, and this is the sentence that unravels the riddle, "he spent two hours reading without a book, his gaze fixed on a sheet of glass—that of the train window" (p. 10).

As the last quotation explains, this striking conceit rests on a simple analogy. The page is to its contents as the window pane is to the sights it discloses. One frames the text just as the other frames the landscape. This transposition produces something very much like a palimpsest: beneath the characters on the page one can discern the phenomena of nature, the subtext as it were, which they have almost but not quite effaced. A "crystalline phrase," thus, names both a group of words and a river. The palimpsest effect becomes more pronounced once we realize that these metaphors are distinctly reminiscent of a well-known passage in Ortega:

> Let the reader imagine that we are looking at a garden through a window pane. Our eyes will adjust so that they will look through the glass without hindrance and settle on the flowers and fronds. Since we are focusing on the garden, we will not see the glass; our gaze will pass through and not perceive it. But later, making an effort, we can disengage from the garden and, refocusing, set our sight on the glass. Then the garden disappears and we see only shadowy masses that seem stuck to the pane. Thus, seeing the garden and seeing the window are two incompatible operations: they exclude each other and require different ocular adjustments.[3]

It turns out that Salinas' transposition of words and objects is itself a transposition into a fictional key of a metaphor from *La deshumanización del arte*. The principal difference between the two passages is that whereas Ortega keeps the two poles of the comparison distinct, Salinas confounds them, thereby arriving at such locutions as "crystalline phrase" or "page from a third-rate station" (p. 11). Salinas has also reversed the direction of the metaphor. In Ortega a landscape seen through a window stood for, among other things, a literary text; in "Mundo cerrado" the literary text (Homeric poem or realistic slice of life) stands for the landscape. But that "Mundo cerrado," arguably the first example of Hispanic vanguard fiction, should begin with a paraphrase of *La deshumanización del arte*, precisely that work that is usually regarded as the breviary of the whole movement, is a revealing coincidence.

It is pertinent too that Ortega employs this comparison to illustrate the difference between aesthetic and nonaesthetic pleasure, and hence between "pure" and "impure" art, between the kind of art that is sui-refential (or, in Ortegan terminology, intranscendent) and the kind that opens out into the world by embodying human problems. Ortega is in effect distinguishing between a work like "Mundo cerrado" in which, as he puts it, art plays with art, and traditional fictional forms where, instead of texts meeting texts, people meet people. The latter type of fiction, we can note, also figures in Salinas' story. But significantly, it is the book that goes unread, lying at Andrés' side "like a disdained virgin" (p. 10). By all accounts this book is a conventionally plotted novel: it has "an intricate and attractive plot" and is designed to be read at night by a fireplace or while one is traveling (p. 9). It is, we can speculate, exactly the kind of story that would have resulted had Andrés' adventure gone according to plan, since the ensuing romantic triangle would certainly have had the makings of an intricate intrigue. This suggestion is reinforced by the pleasure promised by the unopened novel— "un placer totalmente exprimido y sabroso" ("a totally expressed and delicious pleasure") (p. 9)—a phrasing which takes us back to the description of Icosia as a fruit offering "un sabor deliciosamente nuevo" ("a deliciously new taste") (p. 23). On one level the unopened book represents and anticipates Alicia's death; on another, complementary level it represents vanguard fiction's attempt to do away with the "old" novel. The problematic of displacement and substitution that I discussed in earlier chapters is fully at work here. "Mundo cerrado" denies the world and the kind of fiction whose generic imperative has always been to represent it. Both denials are couched in similar terms and have familiar sexual overtones: not reading a book is likened to disdaining a virgin; when Andrés, weighted down by the letter, ignores Icosia, it is as if he were spurning the seductive glance of a woman. And in place of the world and of books about the world we have a story that begins by invoking in *La deshumanización del arte* its own theoretical defense: a closed, hermetic world indeed.

But my discussion thus far has missed the most obtrusive Ortegan echo in the story—the title, which recalls Ortega's definition of the novel as a "recinto hermético," an "ámbito cerrado," or a "mundo completo."[4] Indeed, as we will see shortly, this story is not the only piece of vanguard fiction in which the phrase "closed world" is used to paraphrase Ortega. The interesting thing about Salinas' title, however, is that it evokes a different, and not necessarily compatible, frame of reference, for the alluded work here is not *La deshumanización del arte* but *Ideas sobre la novela*, where Ortega employs this image to represent the novel's ability to envelop the reader, monopolize his attention, and thus make him forget that he is reading a work of fiction.[5] Closed world is thus the Ortegan figure for the anesthetizing power of fiction. Vanguard art, however, strives after a different effect, for it is constantly making us aware of its status as a constructed object. The traditional novel has the power to blur the boundary between art and life; the dehumanized art-work counts as its highest achievement its careful delineation. The difference can be seen clearly in Ortega's metaphors for the novel's enveloping power: not just anesthesia, but also imprisonment, somnambulism, trance, amnesia.[6] The contrast with the self-consciousness—on the part of both text and reader—of vanguard art could not be sharper. Traditional fiction puts us to sleep, confounding the categories of art and life; but dehumanized art wakes us up to the fact of their divorcement.

"Mundo cerrado" thus has an ambiguous referent. The title also contains a kind of riddle, since it refers both to the closed world of vanguard art, closed to involvement with life, with human concerns, and to the nineteenth-century novel. But clearly Salinas privileges the first referent. The story begins, in fact, by debunking the idea of the anesthetic power of fiction. The novel that lies unopened by Andrés' side holds no interest for him; it cannot put him to sleep; it cannot even goad him into reading. The closed world of traditional fiction is itself shut and replaced by the very different hermeticism of the window text.

For Andrés the outstanding feature of the window text is that he cannot govern its reading. Since each new sight is a page in the book, the pace of his reading will be determined by the speed of the train. And aesthetically the train engineer just doesn't measure up. He will tarry on a realistic passage, even though it is "poor and insignificant" (p. 12), but rushes past a Homeric poem. Eventually tiring of his passive role, Andrés interrupts his reading. All he does, however, is exchange one text for another: "Finally he grew tired; he was no longer a rich and idle devotee who reads at his leisure. And without heeding the whistle with which the train, at the end of the tunnel, invited him to renew his arbitrary reading, he grabbed his briefcase and took out two thick address books" (p. 14). Unlike the window text, the notebooks allow more scope to his imagination and initiative. In one Andrés has written down the names and addresses of all of his acquaintances; the other contains a list of cities. By matching names and places he forms a "geographico-sentimental" map of the world (p. 16). The active hermeneutics that the notebooks require works in two ways. First, Andrés has to fit together, collate, the two texts. Secondly, since each of the entries in the notebooks offers only minimal information, he has to mentally reconstruct its significance (as he does with Alicia's name). Andrés states that with each new city that enters his notebooks "a concrete point of the world unveiled itself, lost its mystery and its threat" (p. 18). Textualization is his

way of domesticating the world and its horrors, and his goal is total domina-
tion—a web of names and places "complete and without holes, with no
undiscovered territories" (p. 16).

His last text is the letter. One can observe a certain progression from
window to notebooks to letter. It is, in one sense, a progression toward
"normal" textuality. The metaphorized landscape gives way to a literal text,
but one which is all names and numbers. The notebooks in turn give way
to a text of sentences. It is also, complementarily, a movement away from
reality and into the closed world of discourse. As in the expression "crystalline phrase," in the window pane text and world intertwine. Words have
been placed over nature but have not managed to efface it altogether.
Indeed, it is difficult to determine where one ends and the other commences:
"crystalline" refers as much to the water of the stream as to clearness of
expression; "phrase" refers both to the linear course of the river and to a
string of words. In the notebooks the disengagement from reality is more
clear-cut. Here the world appears encoded and subordinated to Andrés'
interlocking system. In the letter the disengagement is complete, as Alicia's
death effectively truncates Andrés from the world (or from the part of it in
which she lived). If one had thus to summarize in one word the subject of
"Mundo cerrado," the word would be *imposition*. Imposition of word upon
world, of word upon word, of title upon title, of genre upon genre, of text
upon reader and of reader upon text. The procedure is inscribed in the
story: when Alicia marries, Andrés erases her maiden name from his notebooks and writes over it her new name: "Next to Icosia something had been
written and erased, like an abandoned hope, and then, in a very recent
handwriting: Lady Gurney" (p. 19). This writing over (in the sense both of
writing again and of writing on top of) is, I think, "Mundo cerrado"'s
definitive gesture. The kind of text that results from this operation can be
described with a phrase that occurs in another of the stories in the collection. The phrase, "incomplete palimpsest," which appears in "Aurora de
verdad" (p. 88), suggests to me two complementary types of incompleteness. The first, embedded in the adjective, works horizontally on the text,
interrupting its syntagmatic flow. "Palimpsest," on the contrary, suggests
an incompleteness that can be called vertical, since it results not from
truncation but from superposition and effacement. Both kinds, we have
seen, surface several times in "Mundo cerrado." The first appears when the
reading of the window text and of the notebooks is interrupted, when the
story ends abruptly, when Andrés' reunion with Alicia fails to take place.
The second materializes in the window text and again in the notebooks.

My discussion of other novels will demonstrate that these two types of incompleteness are the concrete forms that the prenovel assumes in individual works. A prenovel will be either a narrative whose linear development is aborted, or one the integrity of whose events is constantly being undermined by the transparency of other textual layers. In this way too "Mundo cerrado" constitutes an apt beginning, since its incompleteness anticipates, brings us up to the eve of that which we will subsequently encounter. And this means that, with only a little metaphorical stretching, to read Andrés reading is to read ourselves reading vanguard fiction.

"Mundo cerrado" can be read on two different levels. On one level the subject is Andrés' foiled expectations, his disillusionment and frustration upon being told of Alicia's death. On the other level the focus shifts from Andrés to certain details in the composition of the narration. The fundamental difference between these two levels of analysis is that, in the first instance, the story appears to deal with questions of human concern, whereas, in the second, its subject is nothing other than the work's status as a fictional construct and its relationship to other such objects. Returning to Ortega's categories, one can say that the first reading presupposes a "transcendent" text, one that appropriates to art some of the qualities of life (in this instance the problematic of desire and its frustration). The second reading strips the text of its lifelikeness by revealing that the story deals not with "human" but with "artistic" questions; this reading turns "Mundo cerrado" into an example of "intranscendent" art.[7]

Now inasmuch as the opposition between transcendence and intranscendence describes the difference between traditional fiction and dehumanized art,[8] and inasmuch as that opposition is already implicit in the title of the story, these two readings do nothing more than retrace, on the plane of interpretation, the movement of the text. By passing from the transcendent to the intranscendent level, we are reproducing the transition, at the beginning of the story, from the unopened novel to the window text. We are, in effect, occupying Andrés' place and mimicking his own preferences, and by so doing abandoning the Ortega of *Ideas sobre la novela* in favor of the Ortega of *La deshumanización del arte*. These two options result, moreover, from the operation of the optical mechanism described in *La deshumanización*. In passing from the transcendent to the intranscendent reading all we are doing is shifting our focus from the garden to the window pane. From the transcendent perspective the garden moves to the foreground and the medium through which we are viewing it becomes invisible. But once our ocular apparatus is readjusted, the garden fades and the medium itself comes into view.

This possibility of a double focus is a feature not only of "Mundo cerrado" but of many other works in the genre, and it tells us a great deal both about this type of novel and about the hermeneutic avenues open to its interpreter. Perhaps the distinguishing mark of vanguard fiction is its recalcitrance to generic description. The central problem of the genre is, precisely, generic. As *novels*, these works do seem difficult to read—so much so that for many critics they are not novels at all. As reviewers repeatedly insist, what distinguishes them are features that speak to a different level of description (syntax, imagery, vocabulary, tone), features that do not address the formal or generic specificity of the texts. In order to isolate the indicia of the genre it seems necessary to leave the level of description on which the properly novelistic elements of the novels would be engaged. And the reason is not simply that these novels lack plot and character, though this is true often enough; equally significant is the fact that many of them, when read in the manner novels traditionally have been read—for the human interest of their stories, to find out what happens next—seem only *too* conventional. To a considerable extent this was already true of "Mundo cerrado," even if here the incipient novel never gets off the ground. But the ingredients for a novel, one with "an intricate and attractive plot," "of those that we buy a winter day to read by the fire," are all present. This means that for "Mundo cerrado" to be read *as* vanguard fiction a different approach has to be adopted, one that shifts the focus of the analysis from the conventional elements in the work to a whole stock of devices that lend themselves to construction as indices of intranscendence. My reading was geared to the elucidation of just such devices.

Jaime Torres Bodet's *La educación sentimental*, a work similar to "Mundo cerrado" and like it susceptible to a dual reading, will provide a second illustration of the double focus. The plot centers on the friendship of two adolescents, the unnamed narrator and Alejandro. Being more mature, more precocious and better read, Alejandro is the dominant force in the relationship, though he is also shrouded in mystery. The narrator knows nothing of his origins, of his social station, and Alejandro never speaks about himself. The climactic episode arrives when the narrator decides to visit his friend's home, for it turns out that, besides hailing from the wrong side of the tracks, Alejandro is the illegitimate son of a prostitute, upon whom the narrator intrudes during business hours. Given this summary of its contents, *La educación sentimental* would have to be regarded as a slight and conventional *Bildungsroman*. The final and none too surprising revelation introduces the protagonist to life's seamier side, undeceives him about Alejandro, and thus ushers him past the threshold of adolescence and into adulthood. After the narrator has left Alejandro's mother, we see him approaching another prostitute, about to have his first sexual encounter. This punctuates his rite of passage, underscoring that he has become fully a man. Although the ending contrasts sharply with that of "Mundo cerrado," which concludes with an episode of sexual denial, not gratification, the point is the same: in both works the protagonists exit a world of illusion and enter the "real" world.

By reading the novel in this way, however, one does nothing to account for its "vanguard" standing. One could, it is true, speak of Torres Bodet's striking imagery, or of his use of language, but this would again involve slighting *La educación's* specificity as a work of fiction. Fortunately, there are clues in the novel that alert one to the availability of a different reading. At one point the narrator describes his friendship with Alejandro in the following manner: "We lived then in a closed world [*un mundo cerrado*], like the perfect poem that contains nothing but poetry, or like the perfect canvas completely saturated by painting. The same impersonal atmosphere in which we met gave each of our meetings an abstract, almost eternal, character."[9] These similes open the way for an allegorical reading not unlike that enabled by the window-text passage in Salinas' story. *La educación* changes from a novel of formation to a covert commentary on Ortegan aesthetic theory, since here also one seems to be dealing with a fictional transposition of the notions of transcendent and intranscendent art. As the passage encourages us to do, the plot of the novel—the course and evolution of the friendship between the two adolescents—should be treated in an "abstract" and "impersonal" way. The self-sustaining friendship of the protagonists should be read as an emblem of the intranscendence of "pure" poetry or painting—a closed world into which the fresh air of life does not carry.

Or does it? Paradoxically, if this Ortegan allegory is carried through to the last scenes in the novel, one has to conclude that such closed worlds cannot remain shut forever. Should we not now interpret the open door that discloses the sight of Alejandro's mother on the lap of a man as a repudiation of Ortegan hermetism? "He was going to knock again when the door, gently giving way to the light pressure of his knuckles, swung open" (p. 137). One might say that the pressure on the door leaf is that of transcendence, a figuration of the inevitability of "life" impinging on "art." Once the "impersonal environment" of the boys' meetings is replaced by the real-life circumstances of Alejandro's existence, the perfect poem collapses. Just as their friendship cannot resist the disruptive effect of Alejandro's sordid biography, the perfect poem cannot shield itself from the impure substance of life. Specifying further, one can add that the crack in the closed world of art is caused by a revelation of origins. Since art results from human agency, since—like Alejandro—a poem or painting has a human author, the attempt to detach art from life is doomed from the start.

Interestingly enough this is precisely the criticism that Torres Bodet levels at Ortegan aesthetics in one of the essays included in *Contemporáneos*. Art, he there asserts, cannot help but be human; even dehumanization presupposes a core of humanity that one then subjects to stylization. "We might accept the death of art, its disappearance. We will never accept the existence of an inverted art, without roots, without branches—only flower and scent."[10] This statement could well serve as a gloss of *La educación sentimental*. Roots and ramifications are precisely the issue in the concluding scenes, which expose Alejandro's "roots" and detail the ramifications of this revelation on the narrator's awakening sexual curiosity. The novel raises aesthetic rather than psychological or emotional issues, although the moral is that the psychological and the emotional—that is, the human—will always impinge on the closed world of the aesthetic. This interpretation thus winds up rehabilitating the position it set out to surpass (or *transcend*), for if the moral says that human intervention in art cannot be avoided, then there is no reason not to read the novel as a *Bildungsroman*. Curiously, the allegorical reading validates the nonallegorical one: the text is a "perfect poem" that tells us that perfect poems do not exist. Once one reads the novel as aesthetic allegory, the next step would be to read it again—literally.

Even so, this backhanded rehabilitation of literalism rests on unsteady foundations. The problem is not that the allegorizing attempt is misconceived or unjustified but that it hasn't been carried far enough. Although I have argued that the novel's conclusion leads away from literature and into life, these last few episodes possess a distinctly literary cast. The spirit that animates them is the breath of art, not life, as the following examples show. When the narrator enters Alejandro's neighborhood, the rain that begins to fall seems to him to belong to the "domesticated storms" of *The Barber of Seville* (p. 124); the door-keeper at Alejandro's home has been lifted from a naturalistic novel: "a door-keeper from a naturalistic novel, obese, lame, aggressively senile" (p. 130); the sight of Alejandro's mother making love is presented as if it were being read, not experienced first hand: the open door discloses to him "the *fragment* of an unexpected intimacy" (p. 138; my italics). And even the narrator's astonishment and disillusionment, the crucial, initiatory moment in his transition to adulthood, is couched in literary and artistic terms: "My surprise lasted only a few moments. Only as long as it took me to compare that murky, almost grotesque scene with the elegant old print in which, while trying to imagine Alejandro's private life, I had gotten used to placing Alicia's name and person, now suddenly reunited" (pp. 139-40). As in Andrés' inspection of the landscape in "Mundo cerrado," the narrator's perception of reality is always mediated by literature. He does not witness events but "scenes." And his coming to terms with his discovery means simply finding the proper literary correlate for the information that the world offers him. The passage just quoted continues: "Consequently, my disillusionment was not more pronounced than that I had already experienced before poor illustrations of illustrious books: Gustave Doré's ridiculous Don Quixote, which I found—as if turning the wings of its windmills—among the pages of that deluxe edition" (p. 140).

Of course, the presence of these references can be explained without abandoning the "transcendent" perspective. One could argue that Torres Bodet, in conveying his character's innocence by invoking his bookishness, is simply resorting to a venerable literary device. The reference to *Don Quijote*, the canonical instance of such a procedure, would only underscore his intentions. But this explanation falls short on two counts. The first is that the narrator never does confront life first hand, since even *after* his "disillusionment" he still persists in seeing events through the prism of illustrations from *Don Quijote*. He never does manage to disentangle himself from the arms of this windmill. The revelation has forced him to readjust his lens, but not to discard it for the naked eye. Second, even the way in which this explanation is set up announces its insufficiency. The allusion to Cervantes only highlights the fact that Torres Bodet's appeal to literature in such circumstances is nothing if not stalely literary. Using literary references to signify a character's naiveté cannot help but smack of literature. In the manner of Gustave Doré, *La educación* merely furnishes another "poor illustration" of the Cervantine procedure. The reader is not lead into life. He is led back to previous literature. But how can one expect anything but pallid imitation from a novel published in 1929 with a title like "La educación sentimental"?

La educación sentimental presumes to be the authentic memoirs of the unnamed narrator. In the prologue a fictitious editor informs the readers that the author has insisted on this title because his account was written under the "protection" (*amparo*) of Flaubert. This same imitative impulse also presides over the behavior of the narrator, who on several occasions remarks that his identity has been borrowed from various models—his parents, his teachers, and Alejandro himself. Constantly "besieged by [his] imitations" (p. 79), the narrator speaks with "borrowed voices" (p. 78) and lacks all "inner consistency" (p. 78). Even when he falls victim to a typhoid epidemic he is simply succumbing to the "imitative frenzy" that grips the city (p. 78). And in the presence of Alejandro he always remains in the "aureola of his imitation" (p. 104). The pervasiveness of the motif of imitation provides another indication of the literary hermeticism of the novel. Like the narrator, the text possesses only a derivative identity; it basks in the aureola of previous literature and makes no effort to conceal it. Indeed, *La educación* is a story about "roots," and roots that are buried not in human soil but in the not less fertile humus of literary tradition. And it shows that the "perfect poem" achieves its intranscendence by excavating—Ortega would say playing with—its origins.

The puncturing of art's closed world is therefore bracketed and negated by the literary context in which it is inserted. As the intrusion of the "naturalistic" doorkeeper demonstrates, the retrieval of Alejandro's past does not take the narrator beyond literature—just the opposite. Although the text focuses on the question of origins, it does so from an "intranscendent" perspective. Rather than on the garden, our attention is fixed on the window pane. From the title on, thus, *La educación sentimental* bears witness to the diacritical dependence of vanguard fiction on the "old" novel (old like the doorkeeper, who is also called an "anachronism"). Like the narrator himself, the novel speaks with borrowed voices, and nowhere is this more apparent than in the conclusion, which does indeed seem cribbed from a naturalistic novel. In Salinas' description of Icosia, the city at the end of Andrés' journey, "Mundo cerrado" contains an appropriate emblem for this text and for the kind of literature it typifies: "A minor European capital, with an elegant, timid, and quiet charm, like that of a famous beauty's little sister, who is less handsome, less intelligent, but yet possesses an always happy and smiling countenance, a distinctive secondary expression [*una expresión secundaria y muy suya*]" (p. 19). Vanguard fiction is also derivative, like a younger sibling, its family likeness undeniable. And yet, like Icosia, it possesses a charm and identity all its own. The paradox of "una expresión secundaria y muy suya," which in the context of my analogy refers to literary and not facial expression, captures accurately the ambivalence of the genre, which is original *and* secondary, unique *and* derivative. The characters, the plots, the themes are very often familiar. But their reappearance is marked by a degree of self-consciousness that transforms them. Like the narrator of Torres Bodet's novel, vanguard fiction is fully cognizant of its secondariness, and this awareness distances it from its models. This phenomenon, which I described in a previous chapter with the word "(in)-subordination" and which surfaces again in "Mundo cerrado" as "imposition," makes possible the double focus. One focus reveals the stock of resemblances that joins vanguard fiction to its ancestry; it shows us, for instance, that both "Mundo cerrado" and *La educación sentimental* descend from the novel of formation. The other focus lets us see how these works manipulate their ancestors, disinterring them, profaning them perhaps, constantly alerting the reader to their existence.

This means that vanguard fiction is a closed world, but a closed world in orbit. The body around which it revolves and whose gravitational pull it cannot elude is the nineteenth-century novel. The genre is poised in an even balance between centripetal and centrifugal forces, between the pull of tradition and the desire to proceed its own way. In my discussion of Salinas and Torres Bodet, I have tried to trace the dynamics of this orbit in broad terms; carrying the metaphor one step further, I might say that my attempt has been to locate and identify the twin foci that generate the orbit's elliptical route. In the chapters that follow the principle of the double focus will again be employed to study several of the important elements of a work of fiction—characterization (chap. 4), authorial control (chap. 5), and novelistic structure (chap. 6). This will allow us to chart with more precision the coordinates of the genre's path.

4. Decharacterization

The gramophone prevails—like cinema, like sports, like dance. Where they reach, it reaches; their domain is the same. But its true comrade is the cinema, and those who aspire to give a voice to the silent bodies on the movie screen have heard the anguished cry of two phantasms who ask to be united, even if their union will not result in a genuine, physical life, but will instead create a bigger phantasm, stranger and more unbalanced.

Fernando Vela, "Literatura
fonográfica" (1929)

How much we've heard about "character"! Fifty years of disease, the death notice signed many times over by the most serious essayists, yet nothing has yet managed to knock it off the pedestal on which the nineteenth century had placed it. It is a mummy now, but one still enthroned with the same—phony—majesty, among the values revered by traditional criticism. In fact, this is how this criticism recognizes the "true" novelist: "he creates characters."

Robbe-Grillet, *For a New Novel*

If Torres Bodet were a "true" novelist, *Margarita de niebla* would have two principal characters: Carlos Borja, the narrator, a young professor of Spanish and "writer without a will," and Margarita Millers, a young woman of German parents whom Borja meets while conducting an examination. The book would then narrate the story of two young people who meet, fall in love, and after some difficulties and hesitation, marry. In the course of the courtship Borja's attention would be temporarily diverted to another woman, Paloma, Margarita's best friend. Likewise, Margarita's affection would waver with the appearance of her cousin, Otto Schmiltzer, who comes to spend a vacation with the Millers. Mr. Millers' decision to leave Mexico, however, would put an end to the flirting; Borja and Margarita would marry; and with her parents at their side, depart for a new life in Europe.

If I have just summarized hypothetically the actual plot of Torres Bodet's novel, it is because *Margarita de niebla* resists being read as a conventional love story. Anchored in the categories of plot and character, such a reading runs into omissions and ambiguities as soon as it attempts to pass beyond mere paraphrase. One is hard-pressed, for instance, to account for the behavior of the characters. The motives behind the actions of Margarita, Paloma, and Otto remain obscure. Even Borja, whose position as narrator would normally afford good insight into his motives, is something of an enigma. Although he states early on that he never errs in assessing his love affairs,[1] his feelings toward Margarita are puzzling. Apparently in love with Paloma, he marries Margarita; once married, he declines to consummate their union. And it is not simply that his behavior—as well as that of the other characters—is inconsistent, or that it oscillates between alternative courses of action. The difficulty is rather that this inconsistency or indecisiveness is not grounded in or attributable to a clearly etched psychological profile. If one of the requisites for a believable literary characterization is a well-rounded personality, then the shadowy figures that populate *Margarita de niebla* are not characters in the full sense of the word. Torres Bodet admits as much when he states in his memoirs that his purpose was not to depict psychological states, but to describe landscapes, moods, thoughts: "I was less interested in the personalities of the characters I meant to sketch than in the landscape where I was going to put them, the atmosphere of the drawing rooms where they would meet and perhaps live, the car and boat rides, the thoughts that adorned their letters or their conversations. . . . I was convinced that a story like the one I was preparing to write would be closer to the prose poem than to the novel."[2] Other commentators, taking a similar stance, have argued that the characters "are not convincing as real people," and have thus attributed the merits of the book to its "poetic style."[3]

Nevertheless, while it is true that the work does not offer consistent and well-rounded characters, the filiation of *Margarita de niebla* with the novel should not be so easily dismissed, for the problematic of the work, as novel, is intimately tied in to this lack. That is to say, though *Margarita de niebla* cannot be read fruitfully as a novel of character, it can be regarded as a novel *about* character, as an inquiry into the question of characterization in fiction. In this respect it is not a prose poem, as Torres Bodet would have it, but belongs firmly within a long novelistic tradition whose central concern has been the delineation of a thorough and lifelike portrait of an eponymous character. *Margarita de niebla*'s contribution is a critique of that tradition. In its failure to come to grips with Margarita it provides a prenovelistic rendition of the classical novel's concern with "particular character."[4] This critique can be embodied in the concept of *descaracterización*, used by Esteban Salazar y Chapela apropos of Gómez de la Serna's *Chao* but equally applicable to Torres Bodet's novel: "What happens here? Just the opposite of what usually happens in novels whose title is taken from the protagonist's name. On this occasion the novelist follows his protagonist, but not to sketch or characterize him; rather, to un-sketch or de-characterize him."[5] *Margarita de niebla* places itself in a similar polemical position with regard to previous novels. The biographical narrative mode heralded by the title is not realized in the text itself. Since Borja never manages to grasp what he terms Margarita's "life," since the closer he gets the more elusive she becomes, it can be said that the novel's accomplishment, if not its intent, is decharacterization.

By suggesting that *Margarita de niebla* is a novel about character, and that the character it is about is Margarita, I am thereby also suggesting that the connection between Borja and her is more epistemological than romantic. To the reader Borja is essentially a voice trying to grasp and render its vision of an Other. From the beginning their relationship is oddly impersonal. The fact that they first meet in a classroom, with Borja as the examiner and Margarita as the examinee, can be taken as emblematic of the general tenor of their intercourse. She is there to be inspected, quizzed, evaluated. I have already said that Borja's behavior cannot be adequately explained as stemming from a romantic interest in Margarita. Less incompatible with the novel is the proposition that his interest is "academic." Already in the scene where he introduces himself, as he is helping her into an automobile, he reflects: "Beneath the whiteness of her skin I visualize a coral skeleton created by the confluence of many perfect veins, where her life, stirring without disorder, comes and goes: a life that is not mine and can thus become my *object*" (pp. 20-21; emphasis in the original). His attitude is strangely detached, especially when one considers that this is his first opportunity to come into close physical contact with her. The biological precision of his description makes one think more of a vivisectionist than of a suitor, for Borja is not interested in Margarita's immediate physical presence, which he scants in favor of radiographic penetration. A few sentences earlier, when he had first taken her hand, his reaction had been the same: "A straight hand in which I can count the intelligent bones and phalanxes, not because of excessive thinness—that would be a defect—but because of the artistic simplicity of its architecture or, perhaps, because of the generous gesture with which it reaches out" (p. 20). Borja's detachment involves at the same time a distancing and an approximation. Although he withdraws emotionally, his withdrawal entails a redirecting of attention toward Margarita through less intimate channels. He replaces the sense of touch, which can only function in direct contact with its object, with the sense of sight, which not only works at a distance but is capable—as here—of penetrating beyond the epidermis. On neither of these two occasions does Borja relay any impressions gathered other than through the sense of sight. He looks; he counts; he makes connections. Tactile appropriation immediately gives way to contemplation, to a studied consideration of her features. What holds his attention is the perfection of the veins, the pattern they weave, the artistic simplicity of her fingers. He behaves like a painter or sculptor inspecting and evaluating a possible subject. They are now outside the classroom but Borja still scans her with an examining eye.

Borja intends, thus, to apprehend Margarita as an "object," to pass beneath appearances and capture the distinctive "life" that palpitates within. Now I do not wish to claim that he does not become romantically involved with Margarita or that, outwardly, the book is not a love story. What I would argue is that the love interest, like his holding of her hand, acts as an enabling pretext. It serves to link incident to incident and gives the novel a context from which to undertake the critique of characterization. For this superficial resemblance to a love story allows *Margarita de niebla* to invoke, and thus react against, a certain fictional tradition. As we have already verified in our discussion of *La educación sentimental*, the incorporation of features of the traditional novel in order to establish a frame of reference within (but also against) which to maneuver is one of the distinguishing marks of vanguard fiction. In Torres Bodet's narrative that frame of reference empowers the critique that goes on within it. Just as Borja reduces the flesh-and-blood complexity of Margarita to a "life" that animates the whole being, *Margarita de niebla* may be said to reduce the complicated mechanisms of a certain type of novel to their enabling principle: the accurate and detailed portrayal of character. This preoccupation underlies the love interest in the novel and lends coherence and purpose to Borja's actions.

The full significance of Borja's intention to objectify Margarita does not emerge until it is joined to a consideration of the epigraph of the novel. Lifted from the first part of Goethe's *Faust*, where these words refer to another Margarita, the epigraph reads: "¡Si me muevo de este sitio, si me aventuro a acercarme, no puedo verla sino envuelta en niebla!" ("If I move from this spot, if I get closer, I can only see her enveloped in fog!").[6] By showing that the purpose of the narration is to apprehend Margarita, to see her clearly and continuously, the epigraph announces Borja's intention. It also shows it to be unrealizable. In two ways: first, because it stipulates that attempts to delve into Margarita's inner being, into her "life," are doomed to fail. The "acercarme" of the quotation is the equivalent of the X-ray vision of the later passages, and indicates that the deeper one probes, the more inaccessible she becomes. This motif will be sounded repeatedly in the book. Secondly, the epigraph implicitly posits a privileged post of observation, at which the speaker is stationed, from where Margarita's outlines can be clearly discerned. If he moves, if he draws closer, she appears enveloped by fog; but, one can infer from his words, if he remains stationary, he will be able to see her. For the speaker of the sentence, however, this position is untenable. He feels compelled to move, to approach her. And, in fact, this point of view, much like the quotation itself, remains just outside the novel. As the title makes clear, Borja, as narrator, will occupy no such vantage point. The only image available to him is a blurred and nebulous one. As we will see in a moment, the Margarita contemplated from the threshold will never materialize inside the text.

The quotation from *Faust* raises the issue of finding an appropriate post of observation for the perception of Margarita. The question it implicitly asks is: from where does one look at one's subject? It thus posits, as a principle of organization for the novel, a changing and varied setting. In the narration proper this principle is put into practice. *Margarita de niebla* consists of twelve unnumbered chapters, each of which narrates a separate episode. Most of them place Margarita in a different environment: in school (first), on the street (second), at her house (third, sixth, tenth), at the movies (fourth), in the countryside (fifth), in a car (seventh), at her uncle's estate (eighth), on the phone (ninth), on the train (eleventh), at the dock (twelfth). The only milieu that occurs more than once, at the beginning, middle and end, is the Millers' home. By and large, the book is constructed like an album of photographs: the same subject in a succession of poses and circumstances. It is as if Borja were searching for the appropriate backdrop against which Margarita's figure would emerge in relief. The apparent fragmentarism of the novel is thus part and parcel of Borja's project.[7] Each of the chapters constitutes a separate experiment in contextualization, a separate act of knowledge, as it were, which, from a broader perspective, appears as but one moment in an ongoing epistemological enterprise.

The design of the book also bears out the validity of the epigraph, for only as a result of his viewing Margarita in different surroundings does Borja discover that his enterprise will not succeed. He discovers, that is, that she lacks an intercontextual identity. His experiments in contextualization tell him that Margarita is nothing but the aspect that her surroundings temporarily imprint on her. The unchanging core of "life" that he had postulated as the objectifiable essence of her being turns out to be a mirage. In this instance Borja's radiographic vision has misled him; there is no apprehensible substratum of identity beneath appearances. This realization dawns upon him forcefully when he observes the change that comes over her at the movie theatre: "For a month and a half I have been seeing Margarita twice a week. Once, at her house, on Thursdays. A second time, on Saturday afternoons, at the movies. Is Margarita two different women perhaps? Hasn't one of them prevailed yet? Is the personality that I like to stimulate during our conversations the result of her own vehemence or the sum total of the coincidences, of the picturesque circumstances that affect her?" (p. 35). Later in the same chapter he will reiterate this insight: "I understand the dangers of the ease with which she acquires the consistency of others, even the fluid weightlessness of movie characters. And I recall Paul Morand's title, *Temperature Sheets*. Because that's what she is, above all: an unmarked temperature sheet in whose blank spaces [*claros*], wisely apportioned by the lines of custom and tradition, anyone can jot down the fever of the moment" (pp. 40-41). Since she does nothing more than mirror her environs, Margarita possesses no fixed identity. Early in the novel Borja calls her a "continuity of absences" (p. 9)—as precise a description as he will ever achieve. Margarita possesses a personality only in the sense that she remains herself in changing settings—she is thus "continuous." But there are no concrete character traits to flesh out that continuity. The comparison with the blank sheet of paper also reminds one that what is at issue in the novel is Margarita's enclosure in a verbal work of art, what one might call her "scriptiveness." Since in the realm of fiction to "objectify" (to turn into an object, as Borja puts it) can only mean to transpose into verbal terms, to find, as in the case of the temperature sheet, a scriptural equivalent of a nonscriptural fact, Borja's endeavor is primarily to find the means to *write* Margarita. And part of the difficulty lies in that, being akin to a blank sheet (itself a continuity of absences), she passively receives impressions from the outside but is not herself of any substance. Each of the chapters in the novel thus resembles the *claros*, the blank spaces on the temperature sheet on which one records the temperature of a given moment and place, and whose script coheres only because it is inscribed on the same page.

This brings us back to the questions raised by the epigraph, for now we can speculate that the privileged post of observation which the epigraph acknowledges but the novel excludes can only be a nonverbal one. Since the motion referred to in the epigraph is, as we have just seen, coincident with the organization of the book, it can be identified with the act of composition. We can thus say that the fixed and untenable perspective from which the epigraph is uttered is absent from the text precisely because it is nonverbal. It is untenable also for this reason: about to launch into the text, a voice that the reader must attribute to Borja expresses a desire to move, to draw closer to its subject: what is this if not the setting-in-motion of the narration itself? But as he begins Borja loses his subject, which could only be apprehended so long as he remained in place, so long as he refrained from embarking upon the act of composition. The Margarita of the epigraph is not Margarita-the-character but the postulated "real" Margarita, not Margarita "de niebla" but Margarita "de verdad," who relates to her fictional counterpart as a body to its shadow. Borja's task consists in establishing a nexus between the real and the textual Margarita, between the one he sees and the one he writes. The epigraph, situated on the threshold of the text, just outside the novel, marks the distance that separates them. At one point Borja asks Paloma: "Hasn't it ever occurred to you to compare this house to a radio box? Mr. Millers would be the antenna. His wife, the speakers. But what to do with Margarita? Being too real, she would disappear in the transposition into metaphor" (p. 62). The impulse toward metaphor that Borja here evinces produces the novel. As the metaphor embedded in the title indicates, this is the intent: to find the suitable metaphor for Margarita, to transpose her nonscriptural reality into a scriptural fact. "What to do with Margarita?" is the question that Borja attempts unsuccessfully to answer. In the translation into discourse the Margarita "de verdad" vanishes and her nebulous counterpart is installed in her place.

When a moment ago I compared *Margarita de niebla* to an album of photographs, I could just as well have likened it to a newsreel.[8] Cinematic images are everpresent in Borja's reflections on Margarita. From her entrance into the classroom, which he likens to "the appearance of a winter landscape in the artificial warmth of a movie theater" (p. 7), Margarita is repeatedly projected onto a movie screen. The most significant instance of this occurs, not unexpectedly, when Borja describes their going to the movies, for during this episode he concludes that she lacks a stable or uniform identity. This lack, he says, gives her "the fluid weightlessness of a movie character." To understand why Margarita's mutability lends itself to construction in cinematic terms, it is first necessary to realize that Borja's approach supposes a departure from the way in which novelistic characters have traditionally been conceived. In the classical novel the portrayal of character is undertaken by analogy with painting or sculpture. One thus speaks of fictional personages as being round or flat, well-rounded, well-drawn, consistent, and of the process itself as delineation, sketching, or portrayal (as I have just done). When the analogical model changes from the painterly to the cinematic, however, an entirely different conception obtains. As Walter Benjamin has pointed out, the techniques of mechanical reproduction inherent to film (and photography) set these art forms apart from others (like painting or sculpture) which not only do not involve mechanical reproduction, but would be in fact denatured by it.[9] Whereas a painting derives much of its significance from the fact that it is a unique individual, photography (still or speeded up) renders obsolete the notion of the uniqueness or authenticity of the art work. As Benjamin remarks, it makes no sense to speak of the "authentic" print of a photographic or film negative. Each is as authentic as the next; there are no originals, only copies. A photograph thus is not nested in a tradition in the same way as a painting or a piece of sculpture. To belong to a tradition means to have a *place* in it, but the category of location no longer applies when one speaks of reproducible media. A film belongs in as many places as have prints of it, and consequently belongs nowhere in particular. Another way of putting this is to say that such art works lack a biography. Because a painting exists truly only in the original, one is able to reconstruct something very much like its life-history. One can trace its passage from hand to hand, identify its successive owners or keepers, locate the sites where it has been housed. All of this becomes impossible in the case of film. One might say that film, like Margarita, lacks an intercontextual identity. Although every print presumably contains the same pictures, the material uniqueness of the images disintegrates in the proliferation of copies.

We can now begin to understand the justification for Margarita's filmic semblance. From the recognition of the lack of individuality of the art work there is but a short step to the recognition of the lack of individuality of the artistic subject. The reproducibility inherent in the medium impinges on the uniqueness of the images it presents. Because we identify the image with the person, the multiplication of images seems to suggest a concomitant fragmentation of the person photographed. In the case of the film the fragmentation is twofold, for the proliferation of prints finds a correlate in the montage of shots that constitutes what we perceive as one continuous image. The integrity of a filmic character is shattered twice, first by the number of different copies of its performance, and then, more fundamentally, by the astronomical number of photographs into which the performance breaks down. That Torres Bodet was aware of the implications of photography is shown by the following: "What did he think of Piedad? Our way of seeing others, even those closest to us, is often so hurried! For our gallery of images we require only a brusque memory, a psychological snapshot, a daguerreotype of an inner life. This summary procedure is incompatible with our own covert desire to leave a pleasing image of ourselves in the souls of our friends. Like the prison archivist, we are satisfied with a dirty fingerprint [huella], with a spectral passport picture. And yet we want others to retain a full-body portrait of us, painted in oils by a great artist. How can we achieve this? How do we make the portrait reach our friends? Its individual quality, the fact that it is an important, uncopied painting, makes it worthy of affection."[10] This excerpt from Estrella de día clearly distinguishes between the painterly and photographic modes of representation in a way congruent with my discussion. Photography is a residual medium, capturing (or imprisoning, as is suggested by the reference to the record keeper in the prison) only a spectral image, a trace (the other sense of huella) of the flesh-and-blood individual. Painting does not imprison, it "conserves," and what is conserved is a full-bodied and irreproducible likeness of the person. Appropriately the object of this meditation, Piedad, is herself a movie star, and thus more susceptible to photographic representation.

Margarita de niebla oscillates between these two competing models of characterization, the painterly and the photographic. Because his ambition is to describe Margarita's distinctiveness, her "life," Borja's project lends itself to articulation in painterly terms, the dominant idiom of the fictional tradition to which Margarita de niebla belongs. And yet Borja's approach reveals a preference for the camera's instead of the painter's eye. When I earlier discussed Borja's detachment upon first meeting Margarita, I omitted from my analysis one important connection: the similarity between Borja's perspective and that of a camera. Borja's paradoxical detachment when holding Margarita's hand can best be seen as reproducing the equally paradoxical detachment or impersonality of the camera—paradoxical because it originates in its ability to establish an unprecedented visual intimacy with reality. A camera can see deeply, but the more intensive its focus, the more pronounced the close-up, the more it leaves out. Like Borja, who achieves such a detailed perception of Margarita's hand only at the expense of scanting the rest of her, the camera can only perceive detail by blurring the larger view. The analytical appreciation of detail makes impossible a broader, more encompassing perspective. During this scene Borja evidences the same perceptual habits that Torres Bodet bemoans in the passage from *Estrella de día*. Even though Borja wants to create a "full-body portrait" of Margarita, one that would retain her "individual quality," his photographic vision will only produce a shadowy figure, precise in its attention to detail but with little more than a spectral or residual resemblance to the original.

The detachment of the camera explains the coupling, at the beginning of the novel, of cinematic metaphors and a classroom setting. It also reveals the underlying logic of Borja's choice of profession. The camera is an examining tool, a form of testing. Interested only in what Benjamin labels "segmental performances of the individual,"[11] cameraman and examiner share a similar myopia that blurs everything but isolated features or performances. It is already symptomatic that Borja's initial attempt to portray Margarita, in the opening sentence of the novel, yields: "dentro de una cabellera de aire, una mirada de zafiro" ("locks of air and a sapphire gaze"). Two details, two fractions of a whole that, here as elsewhere, does not materialize. That Borja's job is to go from school to school administering exams is thus not an irrelevant detail, for this too contributes to an understanding of the peculiarities of his enterprise. Unifying the diverse settings in which he places Margarita is the uniform analytical perspective from which she is seen. Margarita never does leave the classroom, least of all when she goes to the movies.

On the most general level *Margarita de niebla* is a novel about representation. More narrowly, since Borja's representation of Margarita must involve the substitution of one thing for another, of the verbal for the real Margarita, it is also a novel about metaphor, its uses and limitations. This is one reason why this text is among the more interesting pieces of vanguard fiction. The abundance of metaphor in Borja's account does not merely reflect the iconomania usually attributed to this kind of writing, and neither is it simply the necessary accompaniment of a "poetic style." Even if not every metaphor in the text is motivated thematically, the presence of metaphor generally evokes and underscores the theme of representation. This is especially so if one pauses to consider Borja's choice of metaphors. His comparisons will frequently incorporate at one of their poles a reference to literature or art, and particularly to the visual (that is, the *representational*) arts. Thus a person or a thing is not likened to another person or thing, but to a painting, engraving, photograph, illustration, sculpture of another person or thing. A landscape seen from an automobile is likened to "the fake scenery with which the cinematographer simulates motion" (p. 71); the light that bathes it resembles "the halo that surrounds the angels' foreheads in some canvases by Echave" (p. 77); a broadening panorama is an enlarged photograph (p. 72); a room in disarray is out of focus (p. 74). Mrs. Millers' face looks like "a lively illustration of the book of Genesis" (p. 59). When she and her husband run into Borja on the eve of the departure for Europe, "they greet him with the same warm gestures with which the father in the parable welcomes back the prodigal son" (p. 111). Otto not only recalls Baudelaire's albatross (p. 65), but seems to have been sculpted— "designed in a hurry on the surface of a porcelain mug" (p. 59). And when, after their marriage, Borja contemplates Margarita sleeping, he describes her thus: "The small forehead gives her face the serenity of a pagan statue, while her mouth recalls the gracefulness of different smiles, those I have lovingly studied in the canvases of some precursors of the Renaissance. Not the academic, unmistakeable grimace of the Gioconda. Rather, the beatitude of a German Madonna of the XVIth century. Perhaps the smile of that virgin by Stephen Lochner, discovered centuries ago by Dürer" (p. 102).

Borja's bookishness undoubtedly accounts for much of this. He is, after all, in profession as well as demeanor, a near relative of Jarnés' useless professor. But this language fulfills a specific thematic function as well, for it makes the theme of representation reverberate throughout the entire novel. Comparisons like these give Borja an outlet for the representational urge thwarted by Margarita's recalcitrance. In the last passage quoted we can sense his frustration as he flits from one image to another in pursuit of the right metaphor. Expressions like "rather" and "perhaps," as well as the oscillation between painting and sculpture, and between painting of various styles and periods, communicate his uncertainty before his subject. In other passages we witness the familiar hesitancy between the painterly or sculptural and the cinematic. Because Borja cannot make up his mind about which model to employ, the novel can be regarded as an exploration of the different senses that, in the arts, accrue to the verb *to see*. The nuclear word in the epigraph is the infinitive *verla*, cordoned off by an efflorescence of qualifiers: "¡Si me muevo de este sitio, si me aventuro a acercarme, no puedo verla sino envuelta en niebla!" ("If I move from this spot, if I get closer, I can only see her enveloped in fog!") In the course of the narrative Borja will test the different ways of naturalizing that infinitive, the different ways of "seeing" Margarita—as a statue, as a figure in a painting, as a movie character. But the model that prevails is the cinematic (hence, in the context of my discussion the *acercarse* and *moverse* of the epigraph allude also to the movement of the camera). And this choice implies that Margarita will not really be seen at all, that—as in the epigraph—she will remain enveloped by fog. In this instance metaphor is not a sign of equivalence, of identity, but of distance. Margarita, "being too real," disappears in "the transposition into metaphor."

Because *Margarita de niebla* is a novel about transposed seeing, about representation, it is also a novel about memory. In Borja's intercourse with the world this faculty plays a crucial role. On several occasions he indicates a preference for experience at one remove, not as it is immediately available to the senses, but as it is re-presented by memory, an attitude that recalls his scanting of Margarita's physical presence. "I don't know how to enjoy any pleasure that is not apprehended through the exercise of memory. The reality of what I can directly smell, touch, feel displeases me as if it were a compromise" (p. 54). Here he manifests that same aversion toward the material, toward what can be felt or touched, that characterized his first meeting with Margarita. Significantly, his list of exclusions seems to pre-empt every sense but one, vision. Sight, like memory, keeps reality at a distance. The "carrying over" that lies at the etymological root of metaphor applies equally well to memory, which also transposes and defers the material object. To the extent that any mental image substitutes for the real thing, it is metaphorical. To the extent that metaphor distances the thing itself, it is mnemonic. And for Borja one flows into the other. Memory and metaphor, the psychological and aesthetic correlates of the theme of representation, combine as two interacting mechanisms in one continuous operation: "Like the crumpled portrait of a woman, Margarita's image, barely contained by the window where I place her, becomes filled with gaps and silences" (p. 84). His recollection of Margarita naturally takes the form of an artistic comparison; his mind's eye places her at a window, and the window then becomes the frame of a painting.

But the convergence of these two mechanisms results, as in this passage, in a double distancing of the object: distanced once because it is not being experienced first-hand and distanced again because the recollection is then framed (as in the instance just cited) as metaphor. Although Torres Bodet has sometimes been compared to Proust, the operation of memory in *Margarita de niebla* is unproustian both in that it is not involuntary and in that it acts not to recapture but to alienate the past.[12] The alienating power of Borja's reliance on recall can be seen most clearly in a description of Margarita that occurs early in the novel:

> I remember her on several planes, as if her image were reflected in a row of parallel mirrors. The first image I see is large, precise, a bit hard because of its reality, barely detached [*despegada*] from the reflection that imprisons it. Then I see a smaller, more abstract one, flooded by my presence, and then another and another, each springing from a deeper layer of intimacy, until I reach the final image, small and completely my own, drowned in memory's mirror, which has just, like the Red Sea in a schoolbook illustration, covered over the minute submerged caravan. (p. 12)

One of the striking things about this excerpt is that it occurs after Borja has seen Margarita only once, briefly, during the examination. At this point he has not even had a chance to meet her. And yet his long corridor of mirrors suggests something quite different—a prolonged acquaintance whose stages would correspond to the succession of "planes." Each succeeding mnemonic image would then lead us ever closer to the "real" Margarita, to her "life." But this is not what happens: on the contrary, the deeper we travel in Borja's memory the farther away she moves. Borja describes, in effect, Margarita's staged effacement, the process that I have been discussing under the rubric of *descaracterización*. Of the sequence of images, only the first bears the imprint of the real. Successive images, increasingly smaller and more abstract, are no longer "glued" to reality. By the time we reach the last plane memory's flood has all but effaced her. The question: where is Margarita in this rather tortuous passage? She materializes, at the very end, as the minute submerged caravan from the Biblical illustration, as a represented object whose presence can only be inferred, since it has been swallowed up by the water. Margarita escapes the bondage of reality, but only to be vanquished by the flood of memory: "drowned in memory's mirror." (The reference to the Jews' escape from Egypt would seem to follow from the language used earlier in the passage, where the hold of reality is portrayed as an imprisonment—"barely detached from the reflection that imprisons it.")

Margarita's fragmentation into a succession of mirror images results from the same radiographic perception that Borja employs in his daily commerce with the world. Here as elsewhere he insists on penetrating beneath or beyond surfaces. In his search for Margarita's essential image he accedes to increasingly more fundamental, more intimate layers of consciousness. Paradoxically, however, this procedure fails to produce the "in-depth" perception of the object that one would expect, for Borja does not so much see into Margarita as through her. The very idea of depth, in fact, is called into question. This procedure seems to demonstrate that depth is nothing more than an illusion created by the multiplication of surfaces. In probing deeper and deeper Borja replicates images, but he never abandons the realm of the superficial or epidermic, since beneath the surface there lie only other surfaces. Depth thus appears as an *effect* of rigorously superficial superpositions. Another way of putting this is to say that Borja perceives Margarita as a palimpsest, an object which furnishes us with an exact textual correlate of Borja's corridor of receding mirrors. A passage from another of Torres Bodet's novels clearly reveals this correspondence: "Speaking with him was like conversing with a palimpsest. A multitude of super-imposed versions, many of them inaccurate, had erased the true meaning of the original text."[13] *Margarita de niebla* presents also a superposition of different versions of Margarita, each projecting a different image of her without however being able to recover or reproduce the original. The effaced script, the swallowed caravan, and the figure shrouded by fog are equivalent images of the same inaccessibility.

The alienating action of memory thus operates in two ways: it not only distances the object of recollection, it fragments it. Memory multiplies images. In this its action cannot be distinguished from that of the camera. It too tells us that identity is always plural, especially if, as in the case of Margarita, the bottom layer of the palimpsest has been effaced, for then there is no original. Just as the proliferation of prints of a photograph replaces the irreproducible, authentic copy of the painting, the accumulation of textual layers takes the place of "the true meaning of the original text." As a result characters thus portrayed will always be "flat." Consisting only of a superposition of surfaces, they will lack psychological depth. Borja's results are in this respect exemplary: every time he probes into

Margarita, instead of discovering the motivation for certain actions, instead, that is, of passing from effects to causes, he encounters only a series of images that lack explanatory value, that have themselves to be explained. Xavier Villaurrutia's *Dama de corazones* contains a paragraph that in its imaginative combination of superposition and flatness could well serve as an emblem of this process: "Of course I am mistaken. Susana is not so different from Aurora. Just as in Susana's head there are crests of darker-colored hair, in Aurora's there are headbands of a deeper hue. Thus Susana in Aurora, Aurora in Susana. . . . Now they superimpose in my memory, like two negatives destined to form one photograph. Though not the same, they seem united by one body, like the queen of hearts."[14] First superposition and then, as a natural consequence, a flattening out. This is one specific illustration of the often-repeated remark that vanguard fiction is superficial. It is superficial inasmuch as the personages it depicts lack roundness, depth, psychological density.[15] As the quotation from *Dama de corazones* suggests, these novels are peopled by figures as flat as playing cards. And underlying these depthless portraits is the principle of plural identity, which finds expression in such images as the gallery of mirrors, the cinematic montage, or the palimpsest.

If one considers in sequence the titles of Torres Bodet's first three novels, *Margarita de niebla, La educación sentimental* and *Proserpina rescatada*, one gets the sense of an increasing assurance in their grasp of their subjects. Having gone through the learning process of *La educación*, the narrative voice of *Margarita* reemerges in the third novel now able to command its material in a way that would have seemed unthinkable in the earlier work. The impotence inscribed in the title of *Margarita* would seem to have been replaced, in *Proserpina rescatada*, by a reference to the successful completion of the novel's project, which in this case consists also of the portrayal of an eponymous character. Although Margarita may have been lost in fictional fog, Proserpina is "rescued."

By thus comparing the two novels I am not arbitrarily playing with words, for if we pass from the titles to the texts, we find affinities that warrant such comparisons. The photographic vocabulary I have been using will serve us well here, for these two novels resemble nothing so much as prints of the same negative. In both novels the disposition of character relationships is the same. Like *Margarita de niebla, Proserpina rescatada* is a narration given in the first person, this time by Delfino Castro-Valdés, a physician who recounts his involvement with the titular character, Proserpina Jiménez, his school mate, patient, and sometime lover. One can notice already that here also the connection between the protagonists has both a personal and a professional dimension. Although Delfino is not Proserpina's teacher, he is her doctor, and if this novel does not open in a classroom, it begins in an equally analytical setting—the doctor's office. In this respect there is no distinction between Borja's examining and Delfino's surgical eye, for both presuppose the same detachment from the object of contemplation. In fact, within each novel the roles of teacher and physician converge. In *Proserpina rescatada* Delfino gives Proserpina what he calls "lecciones de cosas," during which he teaches her the names of things; and in *Margarita de niebla* Borja X-rays Margarita's bone structure. This overlapping stems from the fact that both physician and teacher occupy a privileged point of observation from which to size up and describe other human beings. Because conventionally doctors and teachers are pictured as possessing a surplus of information and insight, these occupations provide Torres Bodet with an ideal framework for his enterprise. It has often been remarked that some of the most striking achievements of modern fiction have resulted from the placing of the responsibility for the narration in the hands of a character whose ability to grasp and transmit information is severely limited, in the hands, say, of a child or, more radically, of an idiot. In Torres Bodet's novels (and this applies to vanguard fiction in general), one encounters the opposite tendency. The narrative voice is given every advantage. It is impersonated in characters who, by nature as well as profession, should prove able and articulate relayers of information. As we will see in our discussion of *Escenas junto a la muerte*, however, the cards (queens of hearts) are stacked in the narrators' favor only to make the failure more striking and the diagnosis of its causes easier. In *Proserpina rescatada* as in *Margarita de niebla*, the narratorial perspective seems to provide optimum conditions for intelligibility. But the novels themselves bear out that, even in the most propitious circumstances, the storyteller's enterprise is fraught with uncertainties.

For in *Proserpina rescatada* also the narrator's attempt to represent the titular character does not succeed. Indeed, and notwithstanding the title, his failure is a great deal more visible than Borja's. But "visible" is not the right word to use for this novel, since here the sense of sight is not privileged as it is in *Margarita*. Sound has replaced vision; unlike Margarita, Proserpina projects a phonic, and not a visual, image of herself. Suffice it to say that, instead of pictures, she distributes to her friends recordings of her voice, a custom she has inherited from her parents and grandparents, of whom she preserves, not portraits or photographs, but recordings.[16] The point is not simply, nevertheless, that Proserpina should be heard and not seen. Were this the case, the novel would self-destruct. As a purveyor of words, of text, Delfino must endeavor to transform his acoustic perceptions into verbal images. Just as *Margarita de niebla* turned on the different senses of *to see*, *Proserpina rescatada* turns on the dual meaning of *to record*—aural and scriptive. Even if Proserpina comes across primarily as a voice, he needs to convert her into an icon. We must be allowed to *see* her. There is thus in the novel a general effort to pass from the acoustic to the visual, to transpose sounds into sights. Appropriately, the reader's first "glimpse" of Proserpina is phonic: in the opening scene of the novel Delfino receives a phone call from Proserpina, with whom he has not had any contact for several years. But this is how he records the incident: "Suddenly, on the table, the dark flame of the telephone begins to burn. On the other end of the line, silence stretches, crackles, breaks until it yields up, like a drum beating, the serene, invisible, unforgettable face of Proserpina, who says hello" (pp. 20-21). The passage conveys a sense of effort, of expended energy, of barriers pierced or overcome. This sense arises from Delfino's attempt to transubstantiate Proserpina's voice. Sound stretches, breaks, until it finally yields up the visual image. Her voice becomes her features. In the process, though, the hierarchy of perceptual fact and inference has been inverted: the realm of the acoustic intervenes ("like a drum beating"), but only as a metaphor subordinated to the *fact* of vision. Her voice becomes her face, which then recovers its original acoustic grounding by being compared to the clangor of a drum. Although the operation is circular, by the time sound returns it has been denatured and rendered contingent. Even the ringing of the telephone, imaged as a dark flame, is endowed with visual shape.

Delfino's task is thus rather more complicated than Borja's, since he has to do more than inscribe his subject. He needs to transfer his impressions through two different media: sounds into pictures and pictures into words. But if his difficulties only stemmed from this staged conversion of Proserpina, his enterprise would not be nearly as precarious as it actually is. His principal difficulty, in fact, involves the initial phonic stimulus, for it turns out that Proserpina is a medium. She makes a living letting others speak through her, grafting onto her voice others' voices. As a result her speech ceases to signify as a token of individual identity. Consider then Delfino's dilemma: Proserpina is preeminently her voice—but her voice is not hers, since it does not originate in the person who emits it. As he puts it: "Why must there always be that disparity between a medium's voice and her soul, between the sound and the images in a speaking picture?" (p. 134). Another way of phrasing the question might be: How does one obtain a voice print from a ventriloquist? Who speaks in a *recording* of a seance? At the same time, Delfino's recourse to a cinematic vocabulary brings out the similarity between this novel and *Margarita de niebla*. What in the latter was called "life," Delfino here labels "soul," though we know enough by now not to identify someone's "soul" with his/her photograph. The asymmetry of sound and image compounds that of image and soul, but the underlying dilemma remains the same. As Fernando Vela points out in one of the epigraphs to this chapter, cinematic characters and recorded voices share the same ghostly immateriality.

Proserpina, a happy medium, oscillates between a disembodied voice (on the recording) and a voiceless body (in her capacity as medium). Or rather, between a disembodied voice and a multivocal or polyphonic body, since the problem is not lack but abundance. This novel, in a more striking way even than *Margarita de niebla*, demonstrates the thesis of plural identity. When Borja wonders whether Margarita might be several people, he has to give an ambiguous answer. Insofar as she lacks an intercontextual identity, she contains several people; but insofar as she remains continuous, she is only one individual. With Proserpina one can be more emphatic in answering this question affirmatively. Proserpina contains not only several versions of herself (during one of the seances she retrieves her childhood self) but several other people as well. As a medium she lives multiple lives. She explains to Delfino: "Like infusorians, I have lived segmenting myself" (p. 170). Just like the recording of her voice, of which she had made a hundred and fifty copies, Proserpina herself proliferates—in segments. This takes us back again to the earlier novel, to Borja's *segmental* perception of Margarita. More narrowly, it sends us to the image of Margarita as a "minute submerged caravan." In this image one can read an anticipation of Proserpina, one can read the Proserpina in Margarita, for Proserpina's life-long segmentation does transform her, in effect, into a caravan of people. And if Margarita disappears in the flood of memory, Proserpina drowns in a chorus of voices.[17]

Margarita and Proserpina illustrate successive stages in the process of *descaracterización*, a process that we first observed in the scene where Borja scrutinizes Margarita's hand. This, by way of contrast, is Delfino's description of Proserpina on her deathbed: "All of the redness in her blood, in her lips, in her makeup has flowed into her nails. As in the arms of an Egyptian mummy, the tips of her fingers are agate-colored. The rest of her skin,

completely white, can no longer be distinguished—not even by its outlines—
from the snowy sheets" (p. 177). We find here the same attention to hands,
to fingers. Delfino seems to share Borja's belief that an individual's identity
asserts itself most palpably in the body's extremities, as if one's "life" or
"soul" concentrated in those places where the body reaches out to meet the
world. But the vestigial liquid that deposits in Proserpina's fingertips hardly
resembles the intricate network of veins and arteries of Margarita's hand.
Delfino's enterprise ends by dissolving his subject into a background of
whiteness that cannot but remind one of the blank page. In the end he
draws a blank—and yet, this had also been the inferred result of Borja's
endeavors: a blankness of fog that might also be assimilated to the script-
less page. In both instances *descaracterización* culminates in the effacement of
the titular characters.

But let us return for one last moment to Proserpina's bedside. Upon
seeing that she is about to lapse into a diabetic coma, Delfino administers a
fatal dose of morphine. Thus, in spite of Ortega's "ideas," *Proserpina rescatada*
propitiates the narcosis of its *protagonist*, not of its readers; it seems that in
vanguard fiction it is the characters, and not the readers, who are put to
sleep. Proserpina's sweet demise signals the extinction, in this kind of
narrative, of the age-old novelistic concern with lifelike characters. In their
places one finds volatile and pneumatic figures, "devilings of smoke" in
Jarnés' phrase, figures as rigorously superficial as playing cards, and hence
incapable of impersonation. Like the queen of hearts, they are so slight, so
slender, that as soon as one begins to probe, as soon as one turns them
sideways, they disappear.

5. From Palimpsest to Pastiche

Let us approach Benjamín Jarnés' sixth novel, *Escenas junto a la muerte*, by way of two of the early reviews of the work. Writing in the *Revista de Occidente* in 1931, Agustín Miranda Junco considers the novel "un libro agónico," a kind of literary correlative of Velázquez's drawing of the dying Christ, and as such profoundly typical of the Spanish people's obsession with death.[1] For Miranda the novel is essentially serious and philosophical. The following extract gives a fair idea of his views:

> Jarnés' book is an anthology of agonies. The transcendent theme, the preoccupation with life at its moment of highest tension are not new in Jarnés' work. In this book they reach full development. In these scenes where a man drags his angina through all the streets of an indifferent city, stumbling at every corner, livid under the neon lights. In these scenes where the protagonist pales under the pressure of a murderer's gun while cabaret lights dance in his pupils. In these scenes where, on a woman's body, a man discovers the footprints of his fleeing passion. Death scenes. Always unfolding in the tormented red light of dawn, for the dawn is the agony of the night.[2]

This impression, however, was not shared by other reviewers, and I am thinking particularly of Azorín, whose remarks on the novel have been discussed in earlier chapters. Azorín's reading is festive or carnivalesque, and not agonic. In the place of an "anthology of agonies" he erects a circus of mirrors. What is memorialized, says Azorín, is not any human death but the demise of traditional narrative. Even his title, "Jarnés, letal," with its figurative use of the adjective and its playful inversion of vowels (a-e, e-a), presumes a certain emotional distance that Miranda does not achieve.

Considered together these contrasting readings offer a striking illustration of the principle of the double focus. Miranda takes the novel at its word. Caught in the simulacrum, anesthetized, he does not stop to ponder its fictiveness. A man is shot; he agonizes; his pain is real. The distinction between art and life does not figure in his interpretation, which monolithically insists on the novel's agonic content. By means of a dubious interpretive leap, even the temporal setting is made to echo the principal theme: dawn is "the agony of the night." It is thus not surprising that Miranda's phrasing recalls the Ortegan notion of transcendence: "the transcendent theme, the preoccupation with life at its moment of highest tension." Such a preoccupation with life is missing in Azorín, from whose intranscendent perspective life and death hardly matter. He begins in fact by undermining any possible appeal to such considerations: "About death, Epicurus already said everything there was to say."[3] If death there is, it consists in the obsolescence of old ways of representing reality. Unlike Miranda, who has his eyes intently focused on the garden beyond the window pane, Azorín sees only the glossy surface of the glass.

The wide divergence between the two reviews leads one to ask how it is possible for the same work to elicit such incompatible responses, especially from contemporary reviewers. Even if one disallowed one of the reviews as eccentric, one could still ask what in the text triggered such eccentricity. And the point at issue is not simply the merits of the book, about which one would normally expect disagreement. Both reviewers give it a glowing appraisal. Their disagreement stems from a basic difference of opinion as to what the novel is about. Its very contents seem to be in dispute. Indeed, were it not for mentions of names and titles, one might be hard put to ascertain that Miranda and Azorín are glossing the same novel. How can the same sentences suggest agony to one man and carnival to another? Is there not in the text an immovable core of meaning that would prevent such disparate impressions from arising? At least in this instance these questions should not be shrugged off with an appeal to pluralism, or to literature's richness, or to other examples of similarly clashing readings of the same work. I want to argue, first, that something peculiar to Jarnés' novel permits, indeed fosters, such contradictory responses; and second, that the pertinence of the novel to vanguard fiction emerges from an examination of precisely those features in the text that lend themselves to ambiguity or equivocation. It will become apparent, however, that I too am more amused than unsettled by these scenes.

The feasibility of both an agonic and a carnivalesque reading arises from a serious erosion, within the novel, of the narrator's claim to authority.[4] Because he cannot effectively situate himself at the point of origin of his own discourse, the events in the novel spin away from him and, in the manner of Azorín's circus, give off myriad reflections. Like other novels we have considered, *Escenas* revolves about the problem of personal identity. In this it differs little from *Proserpina rescatada* or *Margarita de niebla*. But *Escenas* does break new ground by making the narrator the victim of the identity crisis. In moving from *Proserpina rescatada* to this novel one finds that the polyphonic voice has migrated from the periphery to the center of the text. No longer does a stable narrator pursue a fleeing and fleeting voice. The narrator himself has been set adrift. *Escenas* therefore poses for the reader the same conundrum that Proserpina posed for Delfino—that of apprehending the personal quality, the timbre, of a ventriloquist's voice. As we shall see, Jarnés' narrator is in his own way a medium, a Proserpina-figure, and thus only partially responsible for these scenes. His mediative performance, however, will affect them profoundly.

The novel consists of a string of episodes narrated in the first person by the same "useless professor" who had been the protagonist of Jarnés' first novel, published five years earlier. As in *El profesor inútil*, most of the action centers on the professor's flirtations with several of his students, principally two young women named Susana and Isabel. Unlike Jarnés' first novel, though, where each of the vignettes is joined to the others solely by the presence of the protagonist, *Escenas* exhibits a more sustained narrative line. Isabel, on whom the professor (identified in the novel only as *el opositor número 7*) bestows most of his attention, is introduced in the first chapter and figures in all of the subsequent ones. Susana, a character who has been carried over from *El profesor inútil*, appears at the beginning and is not heard from again. Most of the book, then, deals in a rather conventional manner (I am referring to the behavior of the characters, not to how it is rendered) with the progress of the professor's romance with Isabel. In the second and third chapters they meet again, and it is already rumored that they are lovers. In the fourth chapter the professor undertakes the education of Isabel and they fall in love. The seventh and last chapter recounts their meeting in a museum after a separation of five years. The novel also contains a preface and an interpolated "film," "Charlot en Zalamea" (chap. 5), which finds Charlie embroiled in the abduction of Isabel Crespo, the character of the Calderonian play.

Although the preface is not related to the rest of the novel (Jarnés calls it a "prelude"), it is perhaps the place to begin our search for authority. Paradoxically, we first meet the professor as he is about to jump off the roof of a building. Tired of life, in the grip of a profound despair, he wants to end it all; only the fortuitous intervention of the *opositor número 43*, who pulls him back from the ledge, prevents the suicide. The reader is thus given to understand that the chapters following the preface contain the professor's recollections as he contemplates suicide, the proverbial life-in-a-nutshell newsreel that flashes before one's eyes moments before extinction. This preliminary scene is important, I think, because it represents an attempt on the part of the professor to occupy the terrain of absolute narrative authority. Because the narration unfolds in the shadow of death, the professor's account acquires a credibility it would not otherwise possess. As Benjamin has remarked, the death-trance constitutes the privileged narrative occasion.[5] Nothing can sanction a tale as death can; last will *is* narrative will—a story that we are bound to believe and act out. In this respect every tale is told implicitly in collaboration, in partnership with death, *junto a la muerte* in this sense. The storyteller always speaks perithanatically, as if with one foot in the grave. That *Escenas* begins by reenacting and literalizing the primal narrative scene is already an indication of the novel's vexed preoccupation with authority. This stratagem is essentially like that of making Borja a teacher and Delfino a physician, except that here the advantages are compounded, for we are given a teacher on the brink of death. In this way every possible advantage is squeezed into the narrative setting. Lucidity *in extremis*—this is how one might characterize the narrative voice in the novel. And yet this positioning is not enough to unencumber the professor's voice. As if the dying man were not allowed to speak his piece, as if his account were constantly interrupted and amended, the professor will be gradually dislodged from the vantage point in which the preface places him. Candidate #43's action is prophetic: just as he yanks the professor away from the ledge, others will pull him away from the terrain from which he might authoritatively speak. He will not succeed in securing a place *junto a la muerte*.

Inside a novel one can generally locate a central controlling consciousness —be it that of an omniscient narrator, that of a character narrator, or that of a simple character—which orders and places in perspective the events that constitute the narration. Though this consciousness does not limit the possibilities of interpretation altogether, it does establish a certain tone, a certain attitude and distance toward the narrated material. It supplies the text with a "reality principle" that channels the reader's range of response. It functions thus to exercise control over events, to police them, and by so doing convey to the reader a certain general impression of the work's contents. Henry James' term for a character who performs this function is *ficelle*, which he aptly defines as "an aid to lucidity."[6] Despite the professor's precautions to the contrary, *Escenas junto a la muerte* lacks such a controlling presence. The professor fails to provide the reader with an authoritative and, in the novel's terms, final characterization of events. The events that make up the plot escape his surveillance and acquire a life of their own, one incompatible with the designs and desires of their author and protagonist. The ambiguity of the novel stems directly from the problematic relationship that thus obtains between the first-person narrator and the fictional world he is in the process of begetting. A small example is offered by the excerpt from Miranda's review that I quoted above. Miranda states that at some point in the novel the narrator "pales under the pressure of a murderer's gun." But the incident alluded to is actually an attack of angina that, in the narrator's hallucinatory state during that episode, is taken for the pressure of the barrel of a gun upon his chest. This type of equivocation, unimaginable in the classical novel, springs from candidate #7's inability to get a firm grip on his text.

Events, I have just said, acquire a life of their own. Let me now illustrate what I mean. Part of the first chapter deals with the scuffle that ensues when Susana is discovered flirting with the professor. Her enraged boyfriend enters the cafe where he has found them, whacks Susana in the face, and when he is about to attack the professor, stumbles on a chair, wreaking havoc with dishes, glasses, and window. This is the event, the "fact": only a stroke of luck has saved the professor from a beating. But immediately after the incident a strange thing happens: a many-faceted process of emendation and amplification begins to transform the event. The *vox populi* turns a barroom scuffle into an epic battle. The amount of damages and the number of participants are systematically incremented. The waiters, labeled by the professor "the first singers of the deed" (p. 46), testify in court that no less than thirty blows had been exchanged, and assign to the professor the heroic role of defending the maiden from a bully. The judge, not thinking a man as frail as the professor capable of such a titanic struggle, reduces the number of blows to seven, and subsequently to three. This becomes the official, the definitive version of the event, recorded for posterity in the deposition that all parties to the incident (presumably even the professor) sign. In addition, a body of oral legend ("provisional truths"), according to which the professor is a "paladin," "a legendary type" (p. 47), supplements the court's account ("the juridical truth that is already a lie, because it contains two extra punches" [p. 47]). The historical record of the incident thus hardly resembles the actual event. Resigned to the fabrications, the professor states: "Well, sir: the punch was so powerful that it even shattered the truth. I'll have to accept my splendid role. From now on I'll be a terrible man. My presence will suffice to destroy iniquity and correct injustice. My case has been rigorously examined. Everyone agrees that I am a hero" (p. 48).

In the second chapter something similar transpires. The narrator's attack of angina is taken either for a stab wound or for drunkenness. Try as he may he cannot set the record straight. As he returns home in a taxi he reflects upon his impotence: "This horrible skirmish with my frenzied heart —can it be capriciously transformed into an embarrassing incident in a cabaret? My heroic march through the city next to my own murderous shadow—will it become a pedestrian bacchic episode? Solemn death scenes: a chauffeur has taken you for a young man's stupid carousing!" (p. 79). By the next morning what had been a night of anguish has become, in the eyes of the world, a drunken revelry. The taxi driver's assessment is now common knowledge; a friend meets the professor the next day with the salutation: "Greetings, future professor. We have all heard about your priceless nocturnal adventure" (p. 80). In *Escenas*, one might say, events happen twice: once as fact and a second time as fiction. And the version that is perpetuated, that lives on by word of mouth or in documents, is the fictional one. The novel evinces an ineluctable movement toward historicization, an archival impulse, in which the integrity of the actual event is lost. In the angina episode, as in the barroom brawl, when one passes from the incident itself to its record one enters the realm of the apocryphal. The narrator's truth gives way to another truth (the "juridical truth" or the "provisional truths") utterly at odds with his own.

This proliferation of "truths" suggests that in *Escenas* the fictional category of the event acquires a new and distinctive sense. It can no longer be defined, say, as "something that takes place," since it is never entirely clear what that "something" is. Recalling Miranda's vocabulary, one should say instead that the novel elaborates an "agonic" conception of the event. Events here are best seen as contests between explanations, as agons of conflicting reports. An incident like the barroom scuffle is primarily the locus of a struggle for interpretive priority. The emphasis falls not so much on what happens or on whom it happens to as on the process of emendation and amplification that begins as soon as the first (and last?) punch is thrown. As a result the factual (fictionally factual, of course) basis of the narration collapses. Being only one of the exegetes in the novel, the professor cannot impose his own version as the factual one. When in the passage quoted above he mentions the title of the novel ("Solemn death scenes: a chauffeur has taken you for a young man's stupid carousing! [*cierta imbécil juerga de señorito*]") he is at once acknowledging the relative autonomy of the text and removing himself from its center. The scenes can be interpreted as one wishes, and there is nothing that their author (demoted now to a *señorito*) can do about it. The waiters, Susana, her boyfriend, the judge—all usurp the author's territory. It may be said, then, that *Escenas* dramatizes the crisis of novelistic authority present in so many twentieth-century novels. The author (or in this instance, since the story is narrated in the first person, the narrator), once master and lord of *his* fiction, now finds it difficult to sustain and dominate the novel. One can sense how completely out of character with the narratorial stance of the typical nineteenth-century novel such a statement as the following would have been. Reflecting on the turn of events of the first chapter, the professor asks: "Why should my program of studies have been interrupted by a fact, a fact that no one will relate accurately until the gods let that chair speak? Do I even know what happened? What is a fact? Where does it begin and end?" (p. 49). The rippling effect of the agonic event prevents the professor, whose puzzlement contrasts sharply with the godlike powers of the narrators of earlier fiction, from keeping abreast of everything that happens in his tale. And if the narrator himself cannot ascertain the facts of his fiction, it is no surprise that different readers would emerge from the novel with contradictory impressions.

Since distortion of this kind impinges on the professor from the outside, one can call it extrinsic. One can also concede that it damages but does not quite shatter his authority. Though other characters in the novel will not know the truth, and though the reader, like Miranda, might be misled, it is still possible, if one is careful, to keep fact and fiction apart. It does, however, demonstrate the tentative and problematic stance of the narrator. But there is another type of distortion, which I will call intrinsic, whose impact is graver. Unlike the first it is not imposed on the narrator from without, does not grow out of the incompatibility between his opinion and that of the other characters; rather, it inheres in his own voice. For this reason it will do irreparable damage. The barroom incident can again serve as a first illustration.

In the course of narrating the scuffle and the ensuing court hearing, the professor profusely interlards his account with mythological, biblical, and literary allusions. The girl is alternately Juno and Andromeda; he is, by turns, Perseus, Hercules, David, and Don Quixote; his run-in with her boyfriend (now a nameless giant, now a monster) reenacts the battle between Perseus and the dragon, or between David and Goliath, or between Don Quixote and the windmills. So just as the number of slaps is multiplied manifold, the one event is refracted through several parallel incidents. This multilevel parallelism, which will hold throughout the novel, is advertised in the subtitles of each of the chapters: "Edad antigua," "Edad media," "Delirio decimonónico," "Edad contemporánea," "Edad futura." It is typical of Jarnés' use of parallelism, however, that the pattern of inscribing each chapter in a different allusive matrix is not consistently followed through. We have just seen that the first chapter, whose correlative is supposedly classical literature, contains also references to more recent sources. Similarly, the other chapters also interweave parallels from different temporal frames. Isabel, for example, is identified as Chloe both in "Edad media" and in "Delirio decimonónico," and as Andromeda in "Edad contemporánea." Azorín's circus, in which the same object is splintered into a large number of reflections, would seem an appropriate image for this aspect of the novel. Here also one witnesses a struggle for interpretive dominance between the different allusive matrices, each of which tries to overwhelm the others.

Jarnés' use of mythology is thus casual in the sense that no one parallel undergirds the entire novel or even one complete chapter. No sooner is one allusive matrix invoked than it is discarded for a different one. In addition, the characters who accept the new identity never quite measure up to their models. Susana's boyfriend is certainly no dragon; Susana herself is hardly an Andromeda; and least of all is the professor another Perseus. As Azorín's image indicates, there is something carnivalesque, even campy, in this mythological method. The art-deco poster which I have used as a frontispiece, where the myth of Hermes and Proserpine is adapted to an advertising campaign for the London underground, could well serve as the exemplary instance of vanguard kitsch. The caption of the poster—"the underground brings all good things nearer"—relies on the kind of far-fetched and slightly ridiculous parallel in which the professor excells. One might even say that the caption "thematizes" the procedure, which consists in bringing all good things nearer, but so near, so close to the commonplace circumstances of modern life, that they are denatured in the process. Something is lost (but also gained) in this translation from the acropolis to the metropolis. The underworld becomes the underground. Proserpina becomes a daffy medium. And in Obregón's *Hermes en la vía pública*, whose title echoes the subject of the poster, Hermes reappears as a record-company executive. A detail in Torres Bodet's novel will help us find a name for these transmutations: Mr. Lehar, a devotee of Proserpina and himself a latter-day version of his homonymous predecessor, nicknames her Pop.[7] Her nickname captures the essence of the procedure—one takes mythology and turns it into a Pop-art. Pop-art, like pop-art, involves a surprising recontextualization of cultural items that alters our perception of them: Hermes in the subway, the can of soup in the museum, Charlot in Zalamea.[8] Vanguard fiction not only uses mythology; it "pops," explodes, exploits it. As in Obregón's novel, sometimes the clash between the classical and the modern contexts is such that the original story is barely visible. Everything has been changed but the names.

In *Escenas* this exploitative employment of mythology has two important consequences. First of all, the thick allusive web in which the novel's events are caught does not, as in other modern novels, supply the reader with a handy frame of reference for purposes of contrast, intelligibility, or prefiguration. Jarnés' mythological method, unlike Joyce's, fails to impose a narrative order on a chaotic existence—just the opposite. It acts to obscure the "real" event, which gets lost in the allusive shuffle. The third chapter, for instance, which deals mostly with a romantic triangle in which the professor, for once, is only a spectator, never does identify the parties involved. The girl is identified only as Elvira de Pastrana, the character from Espronceda's *El estudiante de Salamanca*; other women who appear are also given literary names (Jarifa, Teresa, Mimí). Even the professor at one point assumes the persona of Félix de Montemar. Barely visible behind this elaborate literary facade is a rather trivial story of marital infidelity. The second consequence is that, because of the abundance of parallels for every incident, one forms the impression that the events in the novel are essentially repetitive. In the first chapter the professor asks: "But isn't this an old legend incrusted in the origins of candidate #7's life? A mythological episode, the trivial episode of a woman angry at not having gotten the apple?" (p. 50). Later in the novel he will pose the same question: "Why, why ask anything, if the answer is always an old, lethargic line of poetry?" (p. 101). These questions reflect the corrosive effect of Jarnés' (or the professor's) mythological method. One gets the feeling that *Escenas* is basically an "old story," a novel without novelty. Just as the professor has been carried over from an earlier work, his tales have been grafted from earlier sources.

This is not, moreover, the only instance of repetition in the work. One can note how insistently, in how many different ways, the figure of repetition is itself repeated.

1. The novel both begins and ends with repetition. In the dedication Jarnés states that *Escenas* constitutes a "continuation" of *El profesor inútil*.

When one begins reading the first chapter, one discovers how literally this is meant, since the opening scene, with some minor additions, repeats almost word for word the closing section of the earlier work. The beginning of the novel is not an authentic beginning, but only the transcription of old discourse. The first sentence, with its self-conscious emphasis on continuance rather than on inauguration, makes the point: "*Sigue*—aturdida—deslizándose la pluma" ("The giddy pen *continues* writing") (p. 23; my italics). In the last chapter a similar situation obtains. The professor and Isabel meet after five years in a museum where he used to take her for art lessons. Nothing in the museum has changed. Their behavior, dictated by a "logic of reedited sensations" (p. 225), reproduces exactly that of five years ago. They perform like actors rehearsing well-memorized parts; as the professor states: "Our faces, our hands know the scene so well that they can repeat it word for word, without adding a comma" (p. 219). *Escenas* thus concludes by repeating for one last time what has been the principal component of the plot—the professor's on-and-off affair with Isabel.

2. Repetition intrudes also in the body of the novel. Calderón's *El Alcalde de Zalamea* (Calderón's play itself apparently a rewriting of Lope's, which in turn is based on folklore) appears in three different forms. Its plot is narrated first to Charlie when he visits Zalamea (in the fifth chapter, the "film"). Then Charlie's elopement with Isabel is given as a duplication of her abduction by Alvaro de Ataide (pp. 173-74). And the seduction of Isabel (the character in the novel, who doubles, or is doubled by, the *dramatis persona*) is also projected onto the play (pp. 147-48). El *Alcalde de Zalamea* is thus staged three different times by actors from three different media—the *dramatis personae* of Calderón, the cinematic characters of the "film," and Jarnés' fictional creatures. Even the underlying plot idea, the seduction of Isabel Crespo, is considered a repetition of an age-old drama. When Isabel Crespo relates her story to Charlie (in the process mixing in Zorrilla's *Don Juan*, another derivative creation), he remarks, underscoring the triteness of it all: "Always the same walls! . . . Always the same couch!" (p. 173)

3. Jarnés' blurring of temporal barriers, exemplified by Charlie's retroactive reincarnation in seventeenth-century Spain, also works in with the motif of repetition by transforming the novel into a uniformly anachronistic artifact. The chapter subtitles, which proceed in an orderly sequence from Antiquity to the Middle Ages to the Modern Era and on to the future, create the illusion of a rigorous diachrony. But one soon realizes that this is a misconception foisted on the reader by the text, for the novel's commingling of modern, medieval, and ancient sources, its blend of past and present

events, produces a timeless, synchronic texture. In the preface the professor states that these scenes took place "some centuries ago, in an unspecified time" (p. 13) and he is right. An incident in the novel captures well this anachronism. The professor enters a church where he observes side by side statues of men who lived in different periods. The scene produces the impression of time negated, for as one walks inside the church seems "a small world where all historical boundaries have been erased and the men of the past and the present meet" (p. 207). Reading the novel we also gain access to a similarly timeless world, where past, present, and future shake hands.

These varieties of repetition complete the erosion of the begetting, initiatory authority of the novelist started by his inability to establish or control the facts of his fiction. In the first instance he finds himself in competition with other voices in the novel. His authority is challenged by popular opinion, by written records, in general by sort of a para-novel not of his own contrivance. In the second instance he finds himself, unwittingly, being collaborated with. What happens in *Escenas* is that the narrator's discourse is constantly being penetrated by *other* discourse, be it that embodied in the para-novel or in the mythological, Biblical, or literary references. As a result he cannot enforce upon the novel that provisional closure necessary to its integrity: *Escenas* never does erect itself as an alternate world in whose rarefied atmosphere the reader can lose himself. There are too many distractions. The assaults on the professor's authority undermine the novel's integrity, and the final blow is the text's repetitiveness, which on the one hand does not allow him to begin, and on the other dispossesses him of his discourse, of which he can no longer be said to be the origin. It is then fitting that as the first chapter opens we see the professor jotting down some notes on one Pero Guillén de Segovia, for he is less an author than a copyist, medium, or scribe. His function is less to engender discourse than to relay it, in this resembling the man he is studying, himself a translator. In the preface to the second edition of *El profesor inútil*, the professor puts this clearly and exactly: "Reminiscences of foreign timbres, of strange modulations filtered into my voice. Because from then on I would not be the only one to speak; my voice would be a commissioned voice, representative of all of my illustrious ancestors, from Seneca to Menéndez Pidal. Thus, a symphonic and borrowed voice that I was going to oppose to the incipient personal melody of my students."[9] Like Proserpina, like the narrator of *La educación sentimental*, the professor speaks with a borrowed voice, as a ventriloquist would speak. This quotation, I think, pinpoints a crucial moment in vanguard fiction. The clash between the professor's borrowed voice and his students' personal melodies marks the distance that separates the two foci of the genre's elliptical orbit, the distance that separates the prenovel from the novel, and thus, Azorín's carnivalesque reading from Miranda's agonic one. Even if the preface of *Escenas* is called a "prelude," a personal melody is exactly what the detached, highly self-conscious discourse of vanguard fiction cannot orchestrate.

Although in *El profesor inútil* Jarnés' protagonist is the examiner and not the examinee, he persists in seeing his task as *oponer* ("a voice that I was going to oppose," etc.). The reason is that *opositor* and teacher share essentially the same function: to reproduce discourse. During his lessons with Isabel the professor explains that words fall into three classes: those that are mute, those that talk, and those that sing. Unlike the last two, mute words only supply connectives; they are "bridge-words [*palabras-puentes*], the passageways of the sentence, the black iron chains that join together radiant express wagons" (p. 153). As a verbal figure, candidate #7 could only be imaged as one of the *palabras-puentes*. Unable to intone a personal melody, he neither sings nor talks; he simply transmits information.[10] The *papeletas* he redacts unceasingly, and which at times cannot be distinguished from the novel, represent the textual equivalent of the cathedral where past, present and future shake hands. And, to top it off, he moonlights as a mailman—another text-relaying profession. (Though in a way different from Delfino's, the professor too walks in the shadow of Hermes, god of messages, spirit of the letter.) Thus, the novel as mausoleum, *fichero*, or mailbag—which is to say also, the novel as pastiche.

Let me backtrack for a moment and quote more fully the opening sentences of the first chapter.

> The giddy pen continues writing: "Pero Guillén de Sevilla, born in Segovia, in Segovia, in Segovia. . . ." No! "Pero Guillén de Sevilla, born in Sevilla, in Sevilla, in 141341313333. . . ."
>
> It caracoles around a sentence, stops on the verge of an abyss from which periods fall like pebbles. Confused, without fluid with which to form new syllables, with the caravan lost in the lime desert, with the pulse weakening, with the last nerve about to snap. But the senseless pen keeps scribbling numbers, letters, numbers, letters.

This is the beginning of a first person account in which the first person does not figure, or figures only marginally, encased in the emphatic but ineffectual *No*—an empty gesture that fails to produce the intended restraining effect on the runaway pen. Even before anything has transpired in the novel, the professor already finds himself in a stuggle for the facts: what is Pedro de Segovia's real name? where was he born? in what year? These few lines stage the first agonic event in the text. Coming on the heels of the Prelude they immediately neutralize whatever narrative advantage the professor had there tried to secure. In the place of a narration under control they offer grafted discourse, pastiche, ventriloquy—and a ventriloquy gone haywire, that repeats and repeats itself with the automatism of repeating integers. The professor's pen, meandering across the page like a caravan lost in the desert, is nothing if not dizzy and dizzying— "giddy," "confused," "senseless," and a bit further down, "unrestrained." Undoubtedly something of this dizzying motion carried over into Azorín's whirling circus, whose central platform "turns vertiginously." Undoubtedly also another image underlies both this passage and Azorín's review—that of a broken record, which also repeats itself without stopping. But isn't the professor's garbled account a "broken record" in the scriptive sense? And if so, doesn't this remand us to *Proserpina rescatada*, which also activated both senses of "record," and to *Hermes en la vía pública*, with its gramophone magnate? And in case the connection seems tenuous let us think only of that "caravan lost in the lime desert." Where else have we encountered caravans in the desert? *UnJaimeliche* Torres Bodet—sometimes vanguard fiction itself reads like a broken record, sounding the same notes over and over and over.

Escenas junto a la muerte opens with candidate #7 taking notes for his examinations. A number of different texts are mentioned as he tries to pursue his studies while at the same time keeping an eye on the attractive young woman sitting nearby: there are his notes on Pero Guillén de Segovia (or is it Sevilla?), fragments of which are interspersed throughout the chapter; there is Segovia's translation of the *Salmos penitenciales*, also reproduced fragmentarily; there is a letter that the young woman is writing to her boyfriend and whose contents the professor guesses at and transcribes; there is a sonnet by Lope, introduced as a gloss to the letter; there is the pathology textbook that the girl is intermittently reading; there is a manuscript that an old scholar is deciphering; there is a book about revolution that a young revolutionary is avidly reading; there is a newspaper story being composed by a journalist; there is. . . . The enumeration in fact could go on indefinitely, since the scene takes place in a library. From the outset, thus, we enter something very much like Salinas' closed world, only more so. Jarnés' novel, like Salinas' story, like the library, is a storehouse of texts; Miranda's observation that the novel constitutes an "anthology of agonies" is not far off the mark, for *Escenas* is indeed anthological. What has to be added is that the professor's accomplishments as an anthologist diminish his effectiveness as an author. For anthologist and author are contrary callings. One gathers; the other begets. One extracts; the other infuses. The professor's dilemma consists in that he wants to author, to beget, but seems capable only of gathering. That inaugural *No* with which he asserts his rights intones the first, abortive note of an incipient personal melody that he lacks the vigor to sustain.

The erosion of narrative authority that *Escenas* illustrates applies generally to all of vanguard fiction. Even if it is not possible to subject every novel to an equally detailed analysis, the problematic of authority remains diffusely there, a hovering presence over the genre. Take, for instance, Azorín's *Superrealismo*, a work that figured largely in my discussion of pneumatic metaphors. This work is usually considered a deliberate inquiry, in fictional form, into the gestation of a novel: Azorín, or the authorial voice in the novel, is willfully experimenting with fictional form and matter.[11] As Antonio Espina put it: "Azorín is putting into practice the most audacious theories of vanguard art. Because he has not limited himself to studying contentedly these or those formulas so as to incorporate their easiest and most accessible elements into his novelistic technique. Azorín has gone in for experimentation. Having acquired a thorough cultural and theoretical knowledge about the avant-garde, he has set up his laboratory and begun to experiment."[12] Azorín's laboratory, however, takes on a new significance when it is placed in the world of *Escenas*, for then the same effects have alternative causes. It does not then appear that *Superrealismo's* experimentation stems from a youthful, innovative spirit (Azorín called the sequence of which *Superrealismo* is a part "Nuevas Obras"). Whatever the connection between this work and Azorín's own career, in the history of the novel *Superrealismo* is as much an instance of belatedness as of innovation. Viewed in the light of other vanguard novels, Azorín's machinations become the futile exertions of a novelist whose authoring fiat no longer works. Behind the sunny Levantine landscape and the apparently deliberate experimentation one can perceive as vexed and problematic a narrative stance as that of *Escenas*.

The applicability of Azorín's sobriquet to Jarnés' novel, which also displays the amorphousness that Azorín identifies as a prenovelistic indicium, affords a first confirmation of this view. In the preface the professor talks about *Escenas* in a language strongly reminiscent of Azorín's nebular imagery:

> All of that—these scenes—took place some centuries ago, in an unspecified time, a time without measure. I'm not sure. I barely remember anything.
>
> I only remember that then I had no contours, that I vainly and uncertainly strolled among the soft, slippery, crumbling walls of something I—like a monk—thought was a dungeon. I only know that between the world and my dazed eyes, between the world and my fingertips, there were cobwebs, patches of fog, mist from some lost river, from concepts no philosopher has ever expressed: smoke from some machine that dragged my fugitive nebula to unknown stations.
>
> How should I lose myself if I had never found myself!
>
> I rolled across the earth like a germinating star. I was a chaos, not a form. (p. 13)

"I was a chaos" reprises Azorín's description of a prenovel as a "chaotic novel";[13] the reference to nebulae echoes "the nebula of the prenovel" (*Superrealismo*, p. 79); "germinating star" recalls "the germ of the future novel" and the labeling of the protagonist "an imperceptible, microscopic germ" (ibid., pp. 12, 30); just as a prenovel consists of "shreds of fog,"[14] the professor is made up of "patches of fog." And notice that the pneumatic effects of this passage are aimed against an architectural entity—the jail or monk's cell, whose walls have been volatilized; this structure, with its "soft, slippery, crumbling walls," belongs with the medieval castle as another of the targets of the dissolving power of vanguard fiction's pneumatic machinery. The preface to Jarnés' novel clearly places the reader in that same rarefied atmosphere where pneumatic phenomena subsist.

But the contagion also spreads in the opposite direction, for if the concepts derived from *Superrealismo* apply just as well to *Escenas*, the vocabulary I have developed in discussing Jarnés' novel is equally pertinent to Azorín's. *Superrealismo* opens, in fact, with events as "agonic" as any in *Escenas*. Its opening chapters stage the indecisions, the changes of direction, the false starts of what Azorín terms "el pensamiento gestor" ("superintending thought") (p. 18). In them the novelist successively incubates and rejects different plot ideas. First captivated by the contrast between two locales—the monastery cell of an anchorite (a reminiscence of the monk's cell in the passage from *Escenas*) and a luxurious salon in a casino, his attention soon shifts to the mental image of a beautiful woman, then to a mysterious traveller from the East, and finally, beginning with the third chapter and continuing for several more, to an angel who will convey to the protagonist-to-be unmentioned secrets. Such flitting about from character to character and from one narrative situation to another is a symptom of powerlessness. In spite of the generally optimistic tone of the narrator, something of this powerlessness filters through into his language: "A struggle between two images" (p. 12); "Not knowing where to begin the novel" (p. 13); "Not able to withdraw from the moment in which one writes, from the books one is reading, from the enthusiasm and despair that one is experiencing" (p. 14); "Entanglement of other images" (p. 14). These phrases alert the reader to the author's uncertainty in the face of his material: he struggles; he despairs; he cannot decide—indications all that the authorial voice of *Superrealismo* confronts some of the same dilemmas as the professor. If these embryonic scenes had been developed more fully, the resulting conflagrations would no doubt have resembled those of *Escenas*.

A telling corroboration of this view comes in the fact that the prenovelistic musings of the initial chapters never develop into a shaped narrative. One of the striking features of *Superrealismo* is the extent to which the narrative itself, or a large part of it, remains extraneous to the theoretical concerns of the opening chapters. The reader who launches into the novel expecting a sustained exploration of fictional begetting is quickly undeceived, since of the nearly fifty chapters no more than a dozen fulfill the promise of the subtitle. The others are given over to a detailed description of the Alicantine region—its landscape, foods, customs, people, towns. This so overshadows the initial experimentation that Azorín, goaded by his editor, later changed the book's title to *El libro de Levante* and suppressed the subtitle.[15] As a result *Superrealismo* contains a great deal of information but very few stories. Excepting the opening chapters it is less a prenovel than an un-novel, for one cannot see how the travel-brochure sections on Alicante could be utilized as the building blocks of a narration. Of the three ingredients for a story—plot, character, and setting—*El libro de Levante* supplies only the last. For this reason the transition from the initial chapters to the later ones, and from one title to the other, bears witness to what can only be called an atrophy of narrative will. Overcome by the difficulties hinted at in the theoretical disquisitions of the first part of the novel, the narrator simply gives up, stops telling. The contrast with *Escenas* is instructive, since in Jarnés' novel the difficulties stem from a surplus of narrative leads: the professor has *too many* stories in him; to his dismay, characters and incidents proliferate with bewildering diversity. One moment we are in seventeenth-century Spain, the next in a Chaplin film. *Superrealismo*, on the contrary, gives us nothing or very little. The inaugural begetting impulse soon peters out and the prenovel lapses into a fictionally unproductive encyclopedia of Alicantiana. If in *Escenas* the conflict between the author and the anthologist is drawn out to the end, in *Superrealismo* the anthologist quickly prevails.

One ought to recognize, also, that the story leads that do materialize are none too promising. When the angel appears in the third chapter, the narrator admits as much: "The angel has destroyed everything. Everything was artificial, fake, like a bad play. No more mountain hotel, no more mysterious gentleman, no more magic formula heard from the lips of a Hindu ascetic and conveyed to the novel's protagonist" (p. 29). And yet the "angel hypothesis," as he calls it, does not seem any more fruitful. As a belated epigone of the *deus ex machina* of the Greek stage, the angel is every bit as artificial, as theatrical, as the figures that had preceded him. The extravagance of the resource is almost in itself a declaration of imaginative poverty. Interestingly, moreover, *Superrealismo* is not the only piece of vanguard fiction in which an angel is called upon to reinvigorate a flagging artistic will. Ximénez de Sandoval's *Tres mujeres más equis* opens with a "novelist" who has gone hunting, both for fowl and inspiration. Not having caught either he tries one last shot in the air, and much to his surprise, a creature falls in the distance. Upon drawing near he discovers that he has shot an angel. Angel and novelist get to talking and the novelist confesses that he has been going through bad times, for his well of inspiration seems to have run dry: "I had nothing left to write. . . . Things had run out. I had to give them time so they would again yield poems and images. And even then, I feared having used them up completely."[16] But the angel comes up with an "infallible remedy." He gives the novelist a small notebook that contains "an unwritten novel" (p. 56). This prenovel contains an outline of the biography of the individual entrusted to the angel's guardianship, and to whose side the angel was headed when the novelist shot him out of the sky. The outline occupies the rest of the book.

Superrealismo and *Tres mujeres más equis* make a nearly perfect fit. Both works divide into two parts, the first of which consists of a metafictional experiment marked by the intervention of an angel. And if the novelist's creative sterility is described thus: "his eyes had clouded over and he saw life, as from within a tunnel, all full of black masses" (p. 53), Azorín's prenovel is called "the black and amorphous mass" (p. 73).[17] The two works differ in that the section of *Superrealismo* occupied by the nonnarrative

Alicantine chapters corresponds in Sandoval's book to a biographical sketch of Equis, the preprotagonist. But the essential similarity resides in the portrayal of the situation of the novelist. Written in the wake of Ortega's and others' declarations of the death or decadence of the genre, these novels exhibit an awareness of belatedness that manifests itself in a failure or enervation of narrative will, in a kind of novelist's anorexia, that engenders "agonic" texts like *Escenas* or *Superrealismo* or *Tres mujeres más equis*. When the novelist character in Ximénez's novel asserts, with an Ortegan idiom, that "things had run out," he is formulating the beginning condition of vanguard fiction as a whole.

The dearth of stories in vanguard fiction does not therefore result from a deliberate abstention on the novelists' part. It is rather an involuntary response that betrays the genre's inability to meet the narrative challenge posed by its late coming. This enervation of narrative will is perhaps the most pervasive of all the shared characteristics of the genre. Many other common features—brevity, the undivided attention to one central character, the meticulous notation of his (or hers, but almost always his) thoughts and feelings, the abundance of digression and commentary—can be regarded as ways of compensating for this central deficiency. And when stories do get told, as in *Tres mujeres más equis* or *Escenas junto a la muerte*, the storytelling context displays all sorts of quirks. Telling is simply something that does not come easily to the vanguard author, who stands at the opposite pole from Benjamin's *Erzähler*. The "uselessness" of Jarnés' paradigmatic protagonist is above all a narrative uselessness, a storytelling incompetence. The professor knows all the words; he has heard all the stories. But when it comes down to spinning a novel of his own, he is hopelessly *inútil*.

In the prologue to *La educación sentimental* a fictitious editor states that the pages that follow contain the journal of the unnamed narrator, which is now seeing the light of day because of the editor's "curiosity." As a former student of the author, the editor also provides a brief semblance, part of which runs: "How often we saw him walk up and down [*recorrer*] the classroom while we did our first literary exercises, with a taciturn slowness in his eyes, swollen by the panorama—if not by the vertigo—of his failed vocation!"[18] Like Jarnés' professor, like Azorín's surrogate, Torres Bodet's protagonist is also a novelist *manqué*, and his journal is a kind of prenovel— the novel of a novelist who cannot write novels. This explains the rather unexpected reappearance in this work of the convention of the discovered manuscript, an embarrassingly hoary device that serves here not so much to impart credibility as to excuse enervation. By pretending that the novel is true to life, the editor warns the reader not to expect too much. We are being told, in effect: *La educación* lacks the vitality, the energy, the force of an original fiction because it is only the authentic diary of a frustrated novelist. All throughout the prologue this defensive posture is maintained: do not expect novelty; do not expect vigor of expression; be ready to be "disillusioned."[19] The novel is so insignificant, in fact, that it must seek the patronage of Flaubert. Like the narrator, the text remains anonymous. Were it not for Flaubert's borrowed authority, it might never have been published. The begetting impulse is consequently displaced twice: the publication is undertaken at the request of the editor, not the author; and the account itself amounts to a juvenile exercise in the Flaubertian mode. In the scant three pages of his prologue, the editor dissembles the generic identity of the manuscript with a remarkable variety of names: he calls it *un cuaderno, un relato, un diario, un libro*; what he does not call it, of course, is a novel, for this is the one rubric his heteronymy is intended to supress. And yet the hidden name, the real name, finally slips out in the last sentence of the prologue: "the title of the *novel* by Flaubert that decidedly protects it: *La educación sentimental*" (my italics). This is as much as an admission that Torres Bodet's *Sentimental Education* aspires to be a novel but cannot bring itself to openly acknowledge it, settling instead for the "honorable poverty" of the lesser genre of the memoirs. It dares be a novel by association only, though the account of Alejandro and the narrator's friendship, as we have seen, bears out just how profound the kinship really is.

When the editor thus speaks of the "panorama—if not the vertigo—of his [the author's] failed vocation," it is not difficult to relate this professor's dizziness with that of Jarnés' own. Vertigo is the chronic complaint of the prenovelist, who always feels as if things were swirling about him, as if the ground were giving way under his feet.[20] And the reason is that his predicament is preeminently a matter of footing—he cannot find secure and solid ground from which to speak. Like the professor in the "prelude" to *Escenas*, he is not allowed to station himself—hence the incessant *recorrer* of Torres Bodet's character in the excerpt quoted in the previous paragraph. The vanguard author arrives too late at the novelist's place. By the time he gets there the edifice has been demolished: the walls are transparent, movable, in ruins; the soil has turned into air.

Placed in this context, the many appeals in vanguard fiction and vanguard-fiction criticism to the cooperation of the reader are revealed as one side-effect of the novelists' vertigo. According to Azorín, for instance, a novel like *Escenas* requires that the reader fill in the gaps; in order for the text to make sense, he must "unite what is missing and what he sees."[21] As we saw in chapter 2, statements of this kind are not uncommon. In a sense, what they do is call upon the reader to take the place of the angel. (The collaboration of novelist and angel in *Tres mujeres más equis* thus conceals a modest allegory: like the angel, the reader acts in partnership with the author to bring the work to fruition; without the reader's fortuitous mid-wifing, fictional begetting is impossible.) But such appeals, in Ximénez or Azorín as well as in Cortázar or Claude Simon, will always ring hollow. The reader, if he reads, always collaborates—as much in a novel by Balzac as in a story by Cortázar. *Escenas junto a la muerte* shows, furthermore, that authorship is not a prerogative that the novelist willingly forswears. The alleged or desired involvement of the reader in the creative act is but another symptom of enfeeblement. The novelist would complete the novel, if only he could. When in Owen's *Novela como nube* the narrator jocularly enlists the reader's help, his playful tone hides a real impotence: "I anticipate a valid objection by saying that I have deliberately dressed my story in a harlequin costume, constructed it with diverse, multi-colored pieces of prose. Only the thread of my few readers' attention can connect them, a thread that might break in the middle of my pirouette if the spectators look away. I am only a mediocre acrobat [*alambrista*]."[22] Owen's high-wire act, which undoubtedly belongs in Azorín's circus, joins the already familiar resource of putting the novelist *junto a la muerte* with an entreaty to the reader, who now has the responsibility of keeping the novelist up there, *in his place*. But Owen's helplessness is more than an act. His proleptic injunction has exactly the same function as the similarly anticipatory preface of *La educación*: it tries to conceal the novelist's vexation, one might even say his embarrassment, over the diminishment of his powers. Owen is slipping, and he knows it. By bringing the audience into the act, he attempts to shore himself up against what Azorín, evoking once again the picture of a collapsing edifice, called "the agony of the novel in ruins." But the security the novelist thereby achieves, like that of the *alambrista*, is at best precarious and wavering.

It is important to remember, nevertheless, that agony and renewal do not necessarily rule each other out. In stating that he undertook his "Nuevas Obras" because of the need to "renovate the procedure of the novel that agonizes in ruins,"[23] Azorín overlooked the underground passages, the sub-ways, that connect vanguard fiction's belatedness to its formal and thematic innovations. Agony *is* renewal. And not in the obvious sense that new forms always emerge from the wreck of the old: in vanguard fiction nothing "emerges"; the novelty resides in the wreck itself. The withering of authority that in one respect attests to a lack of vigor simultaneously produces such striking and hermeneutically exploitable effects as the double focus and decharacterization. It is not then a matter of dismissing the genre as derivative, decadent, or spurious, as is and was often done, but of measuring and mapping the territory that separates it from the forms of the canonic novel. In order to appreciate the vanguard novel one must cultivate its dialectical dependence on previous fiction, for it is the genre's own peculiar brand of imitation, of derivativeness, of (in)subordination, that defines its distinctiveness and marks its appeal.

6. The Novel as Matrass

El actor, siempre papel, no vive.
Subvive.

> [The actor, always in character, does not
> survive.
> He sub-vives.]

Antonio Espina, *Pájaro pinto*

My discussion thus far has exploited the reflexive dimension of vanguard fiction, but without directly confronting it. Although I have extracted from these works a set of congruent attitudes toward important aspects of the novel—reference, characterization, distance, and control—I have not yet attempted to study in any detail the mere presence of embedded critical speculation. I have not yet attempted, that is, to examine the impact of self-consciousness on the fabric of these novels. Of course, part of what needs to be said here has already been mentioned in the preceding chapter, since the injection of commentary into fiction is another of the stratagems whereby an author tries to refasten a loosening grip. As Jarnés made clear in comparing fiction and commentary to a medication and the instructions for its use, one of the basic functions of embedded criticism is to monitor the reader's access to the work.[1] When the novelist or one of his doubles interrupts the action to comment, his remarks have a preemptive and to some extent coercive intent. The aim, as Jarnés puts it, is "to leave nothing unsaid," to prescribe the transactions between reader and text. Behind this unrealizable desire one can glimpse the faltering performance of Owen's high-wire artist, who certainly does not want an unruly spectator to topple him from his seat. And although it might not seem so at first, such interventions are strictly consistent with calls for the reader's collaboration, for both blur the barrier between reader and author (or critic and author) in order to protect the integrity of the novel. (It goes without saying that asides to the reader are by nature always indices of self-consciousness.) Embedded commentary is both an invitation to interpret and a guide to interpretation;[2] even as it solicits response it works to constrain it.

This is part of what needs to be said, but not all. Once we have looked at another of Jarnés' works, *Locura y muerte de Nadie*, we will see that fictional self-consciousness poses problems that go well beyond the novelist's desire to dominate. My discussion will show that the intertwining of narration and commentary precipitates an unstable compound whose volatility threatens the very security it was supposed to bolster. Although self-consciousness can benefit the novelist, it can also undermine him, since it complicates his enterprise in several ways. In order to keep the high-wire act together, the novelist has now to accomplish three things: (1) maintain control over the narrative (2) maintain control over the theorizing and (3) find the proper articulation of 1 and 2, of narration and commentary. Such diverse tasks will require our *alambrista* to do also a good bit of juggling.

Of all of Jarnés' novels none has been so generously praised as *Locura y muerte de Nadie*. Generally regarded as one of his most mature and representative works, it is also (along with *Superrealismo*) probably the best-known piece of vanguard fiction, and has been the target of a number of readings.[3] The best among these (I am thinking of Ilie's and Zuleta's) have approached the novel indirectly, by way of Ortegan cultural and aesthetic theory, of which Jarnés was an exponent. *La deshumanización del arte, Ideas sobre la novela*, and *La rebelión de las masas*, all published in the years immediately preceding its appearance, have seemed the natural entranceway to the novel itself, which not only treats fictionally some of the same material as *La rebelión de las masas* but also indulges in a good deal of essayistic speculation. It has even been possible to detect distinctly Ortegan echoes in Jarnés' phrasing and vocabulary.[4]

This manner of reading *Locura y muerte* is noteworthy for the emphasis it places on the novel's capacity for mirroring what are taken to be the sad and impersonal realities of life in modern industrial society, where man has been reduced to a number, a face in the crowd, a cog in a machine. Thus, the different components of the novel are searched for their mimetic resources, and the novel as a whole is judged according to how well it has impersonated certain outstanding characteristics of the real world.[5] (Of course, strictly speaking, when one takes the novel as an illustration of Ortega's notion of the *hombre masa*, as in Ilie's study, one is not juxtaposing the novel and reality but the novel and Ortegan cultural theory, the latter providing a perhaps faithful, perhaps deceptive, image of the "real" world.)

But these readings overlook, I think, the extent to which *Locura y muerte* is steeped in the traditions of fiction. The novel exhibits, indeed exposes, a whole set of novelistic conventions as much as it mirrors reality. One of the important scenes, for example, concerns Juan Sánchez's suspicion that he is the natural son of a Count Monte Azul. To satisfy his curiosity he travels to the Monte Azul's seat in the country, where it is disclosed—by an old and trusty majordomo no less—that Juan is indeed the bastard son of the Count, a Don Juan (his Christian name) who in his younger days was given to cavorting with chorus girls, one of whom (Parisian of course) brought Juan into the world. The typicality of this episode can hardly be overlooked. Like many a fictional hero, Juan turns out to be the bastard son of an aristocrat, an orphan whose biological identity remains hidden for a large part of his life. The entire scene, set in the ancient estate, with pictures of Juan's ancestors hanging from the walls, with Juan's very cradle, covered by dust and crisscrossed by cobwebs, lying abandoned with other relics in a musty room (creaking door and all), smacks of nothing so much as of parody or stylization. Juan's family name, Monte Azul, with its punning reference to highness of birth and purity of blood, reinforces this impression. And when the butler, "chronicler" of the family and a vestige of the previous century (p. 1476), reveals Juan's origins, his account reads like something out of a *folletín*: "Some thirty years ago—I have served in this house for forty!—'this land was unspoiled. Honeysuckle climbed the walls; rosebushes lined the avenues; a vault of poplars shaded the house; haughty peacocks strolled. . . .'" (p. 1477).[6] One cannot help but concur with Arturo's assessment of Juan's discovery; as he puts it to Juan on their way back to the city: "You have a splendid past. It is an admirable novel" (p. 1483).

Even Juan's obsession with being somebody, with making someone and something of himself, is not essentially different from the impulses that drive the protagonists of the classical novel, from *Robinson Crusoe* to *Nostromo*. That is to say, even that aspect of the novel most available to naturalization as a fictionalization of Ortegan theory can be accounted for without leaving the pale of novelistic tradition. Juan's quest takes on a peculiar cast because of the historical moment when it occurs (and here Ortega may come in handy), but in its structure and overall design his dilemma resembles that of other *héroes de novela*. The biographical mode of the narrative, evident from the title, the conception of life as a career that one has to forge for oneself, the search for origins—all place the work squarely within the canonic genre. Like many another novel, *Locura y muerte* is basically a story of great expectations run aground, and this is made all the more manifest by the fact that Juan's quest is bared of all frills and accessories. In the classical novel the protagonist's search is mediated by, and objectivized in, certain external tokens: wealth, power, a high station, even a birthmark. Here no such mediation exists. Even the disclosure of his noble birth no longer profits Juan. His only token is his signature, which does no more than emptily designate the individual on whose chest it has been imprinted. In this respect too *Locura y muerte* represents stylization or parody, thus calling attention to its filiation with other novels.

Like Juan, *Locura y muerte de Nadie* descends from "noble" ancestry; like Juan, the novel is fully aware of its forebears. This awareness manifests itself clearly in the widespread use of scriptural and literary comparisons. Jarnés' language, it is true, is immensely diversified: his imagery draws on mathematics, the plastic arts, religious iconology, sports, and other areas. In sheer density, however, as well as in their incidence at certain important junctures in the novel, none of these can match those figures culled from literature or from writing. The novel has no more poignant scene than that of Juan's death. Jarnés describes it thus:

> Both men are moved. The moment calls for a dramatic flourish [*un latiguillo escénico*]. Juan gets ready.
> "Good-bye, my friend."
> "Good-bye."
> "Take care of Ma . . ."
> All of a sudden a speeding truck emerges from the shadows and cuts short his solemn flourish. In one second, with a disdainful gesture, it eliminates from the face of the earth Juan Sánchez's signature and rubric and problem.
> Like an eraser [*goma de borrar*]. (p. 1550)

The metaphors here come from two areas—the dramatic arts ("latiguillo escénico") and writing ("goma de borrar"). At the culminating moment of his life, Juan is imaged as a *dramatis persona* and as a fragment of text. He is imaged, in other words, as a *character*, in the sense both of a fictional personage and of a graphic mark. Since the substance from which fictional characters are created is the word, the two meanings complement each other and their combination exposes Juan for what he is: an imaginary construct inscribed on a page. All of the characters in *Locura y muerte* are depicted as "characters" in these two senses. The death of Juan's mother, appropriately, also consists of an erasure: "[a truck] eliminated her from the world, like an eraser" (p. 1482); Arturo sees himself as "a line of verse in an impassioned quatrain" (p. 1432) and Matilde as "a forced rhyme in this trivial love poem" (p. 1507). The romantic triangle (or quadrangle) involving Juan, Matilde, and her two lovers, Alfredo and Arturo, is a "dramatic conflict" (p. 1420) or a "complicated comedy" (pp. 1495-96). Physical setting is also portrayed in this manner. The Sánchez's living room, Arturo thinks maliciously, "is the room one finds in illustrations of novels that extol conjugal peace" (p. 1416). As one reads the novel, then, one is repeatedly alerted to the fictiveness of its personages and events.

This kind of imagery appears frequently not only in Jarnés' other novels but in vanguard fiction as a whole. Consider, to give but one additional example, the following striking portrait of one of the characters in *La educación sentimental*: "Compared to the rest of the students, who resembled—because of their number and monotony—a set of machine copies made in some office with a multigraph, he alone seemed written by hand, like those schoolbook aphorisms—mottos, practical advice, psychological maxims—that Miss González, in order to improve our course grades, reproduced on the first page of our notebooks with the angular perfection of her English lettering, invariably svelte."[7] Comparisons like these bring out clearly the two interpretive routes available to the reader of *Locura y muerte* in particular and of vanguard fiction generally. One route is to explain the metaphors as indices of dehumanization, thereby establishing once again an implicit correspondence between novel and world. In *Locura y muerte* a description similar to Torres Bodet's, Juan's depiction of his mother as "a splendid machine with which to print dozens of copies of men" (p. 1465), has been interpreted precisely in this way.[8] The references to a machine and to a process of serial duplication encourage this approach by suggesting that the metaphor illustrates these aspects of life in modern society. There is sameness and anonymity in one; there is sameness and anonymity in the other. Hence, the metaphor reflects real-life circumstances. The other route is to regard such figures as we just regarded the metaphors whereby Juan's death was represented: as indices not of dehumanization but of fictionality. To the reader who adopts this route, the choice of metaphor seems as important as the sociological point that can be inferred from it. There exist all kinds of machines that would have served just as well to convey the impression of dehumanization. That a printing press was chosen, and a meat slicer was not, would seem in itself significant, or so one would claim.

Undoubtedly both interpretive courses can be fruitfully traversed and together help to account fully for the presence of these images. A traveller on the second route would argue, however, that the "literary" reading is more consistent with vanguard fiction as a whole (not all vanguard novels are "dehumanized" in this sense; most are, however, eminently bookish), and therefore more easily relatable to other textual phenomena. This kind of imagery, instead of making stronger the nexus between the work and reality, only emphasizes the novel's nonmimetic, nonreferential, "intranscendent" dimension. The title of one of the chapters, "Textos vivos" (p. 1454), captures succinctly the ambiguous status of fictional characters in light of such self-conscious devices as scriptural comparisons: even as they create the illusion of life, they cannot help betraying their textuality.

Scriptural and literary comparisons make *Locura y muerte* a typical piece of vanguard fiction. It is also typical in another equally pertinent way. Like other vanguard novels, it combines narrative and critical discourse.[9] (In addition to the works I have discussed, one could mention *Los terribles amores de Agliberto y Celedonia* and *Teoría del zumbel*, both of which feature Pirandellian encounters between the author and his characters; *Luna de copas; Pájaro pinto;* and Mario Verdaguer's *El marido, la mujer y la sombra,* which goes one up on Pirandello—and Unamuno—by portraying a novelist who is cuckolded by his protagonist.) This hybridism, we saw in an earlier chapter, is one of the traits of the "new novel" recovered in the metalanguage. We saw also that hybridism was regarded as subversive of the integrity of a novel. Jarnés' opinion, for example, was that, touched by the critical faculty, "the novel volatilizes. It leaves our hands in search of rarefied air."[10] In a way perhaps not suspected by him, *Locura y muerte* gives proof of this incompatibility. At four different points in the novel, one of the characters, or the narrator, speculates about matters of novelistic theory and technique. In the two instances where the narrator intervenes, he pauses to comment on the characteristics of the story he is telling (pp. 1498 and 1535); in the other instances the remarks occur in conversation between the characters (pp. 1500-1504, Arturo and Juan; pp. 1510-11, Matilde and Arturo), although what is here said can—and has been—also extended to cover the novel. This speculation bears a close kinship to the phenomenon of scriptural and literary comparisons. Both function as devices that transform the novel into a statement about novelistic or aesthetic theory. Robert Scholes calls this "metafiction," which he defines as that brand of fiction that "assimilates all the perspectives of criticism into the fictional process itself."[11] Scriptural and literary comparisons and embedded theorizing are the two basic mechanisms of metafiction. The latter by its mere presence obviously adds a critical dimension to a work. Scriptural and literary comparisons also accomplish this, but indirectly, for they operate as textual signals that incite the reader to take an allegorical leap and naturalize the text as an implicit commentary on itself, or on other novels, or on fictional procedures in general (as I did in a previous chapter with *La educación sentimental*). Because of the way Jarnés pictures Juan's death, thus, one could say that the scene dramatizes not the tragedy of an unfulfilled life but the failure of an unfulfilled fiction (I will want to say something akin to this a bit later). These two strains of metafiction, which I will call discursive and narrative respectively, constitute the principal means whereby *Locura y muerte* can be said *not* to be a mimetic work, the means whereby the "real" world's hold upon it is loosened and replaced with the grip of fiction, of fictionality, of novelistic and aesthetic theory.[12] We can thus pursue our discussion of the novel by delving further into its metafictional properties.

It has been generally assumed that the theoretical and narrative sections of *Locura y muerte* are linked to each other as an abstract formulation is linked to its instantiation. A great deal of attention has been paid, in particular, to two of the sections of theoretical exposition: one in which the narrator states that the novel lacks those tense moments of high-pitched drama that one associates with conventional plots; and another, ostensibly corollary to the first, in which Arturo expounds his theory of the "novela red" or "novela poligráfica," a new form of fiction whose protagonists will be collectivities instead of individuals. Taken together these two passages have been considered the aesthetic justification of the novel, which then becomes an essay in this new fictional mode.[13] To use a metaphor Jarnés employed apropos of another metafictional work, Huxley's *Point Counter Point*: the notion of polygraphic novel is the "theoretical egg" from which springs the fictional chicken. Nevertheless, the relationship between the polygraphic novel and *Locura y muerte* is far more complex than that between precept and example, or egg and chicken. As a gloss of the novel it is at best partial, at worst inappropriate. I want to argue, in fact, that *Locura y muerte* constitutes a counterexample (a counterpoint?) to its own theorizing: it is precisely the kind of work excluded and criticized in these two passages.

There exists very little resemblance, first of all, between *Locura y muerte* and Arturo's polygraphic novel; all of the actors in Jarnés' novel are individuals, not masses, and the most differentiated of them all, the least commonplace, is Juan Sánchez—certainly *not* an embodiment of the Ortegan mass man, one of whose defining traits is his unselfconsciousness.[14] To say that Juan Sánchez is a man bestowed with a collective psyche, as Ilie does,[15] is to overlook how incomprehensible Juan's dilemma would be for the true mass man, and thus to slight its uniqueness. It is revealing that when Arturo describes the *novela poligráfica* he refers to cameramen and cameras, and not to writing and words. His choice of vocabulary is obtrusive because of the profusion of scriptural and literary comparisons in the text. Although he has all along seen his behavior and that of others in fictional and scriptive terms, Arturo abandons this lexicon when speaking about the novel. To Juan's protestation that masses lack a distinctive profile and are therefore not susceptible of novelistic treatment, he replies: "That depends on the operator that views it. On the skill and potency of his machine" (p. 1503). Earlier in the same conversation he had also resorted to a cinematic vocabulary: polygraphic novels, he says, "are novels without a unipersonal focus" (p. 1503). In order to witness the kind of spectacle Arturo envisions, it seems, one will have to go to the movies. And indeed, the one glimpse we do get of a polygraphic novel is the description of a newsreel and of a movie audience's reaction to it (in a chapter entitled "Las dos muchedumbres").

This amounts, I think, to a tacit admission that the polygraphic novel is not intended as a verbal artifact. Arturo is thinking of film, not fiction, and this sets his theory at odds with the *text* it purportedly inspires and explains. His recurrence to a lexicon so different from the novel's dominant idiom establishes an adversary, rather than a complicitous or collaborative, relationship between *Locura y muerte* and his theorizing. As in *Margarita de niebla*, filmic concepts and vocabulary tear away at the fabric of fiction. I should stress that I am not disputing that one can find stretches in the novel where Jarnés experiments with a kind of literary cinematography— the most prominent instance being the chapter I mentioned above. On the contrary, Jarnés' attempts to produce cinematic effects in pursuit of the polygraphic novel bear directly on my point, which is simply that this kind of novel is not a novel, is not even a verbal artifact, and thus is not *Locura y muerte de Nadie*. Inferable from Arturo's language is the proposition that for the novelist to compose a polygraphic novel he must go beyond his medium and recreate in words an essentially unwriteable spectacle. Matilde makes somewhat the same point when she says to Arturo: "You are obsessed with the masses. But the masses do not exist. Only a few suspicious individuals exist. I see them because I perceive details, while you only see totalities. You'd make a bad novelist. I perceive nuances. You only perceive blobs" (p. 1510). There is no reason to privilege Arturo's views over Matilde's, any more than there is to suppose that the *novela poligráfica* accounts for *Locura y muerte*.

Arturo's discussion of the polygraphic novel mainly touches upon the question of characterization. He says nothing directly of the action or plot of such a novel. Earlier in the same conversation, however, he asserts that modern life has all but eliminated opportunities for heroism and suggests that the polygraphic novel, as a faithful mimetic artifact, would also not provide a forum for great deeds. This suggestion echoes earlier remarks by the narrator in which he points out and explains the apparent lack of dramatic climaxes in *Locura y muerte*. The passage occurs immediately after Juan Sánchez has once again missed the opportunity of asserting himself by proving his wife's infidelity:

> Only an astute novelist will succeed in harmonizing the great system of forces in a dramatic situation: the opportune moment for feminine desire, for the virile impetus of lovers, the boiling point in a fit of rage, the period when all human beasts are in heat.
>
> Only a false novelist will be able to cut out from here and there unique pieces of life, combine them like liquids in a matrass, and then make them boil noisily at a predetermined moment. In this brief tale, in this fragment of Juan Sánchez's life, it has not been possible to find the characters at the high point in their lives. For some the novel came too soon; for others, not soon enough. Here they figure as they were when called to participate in this simple tale. (p. 1498)

Unlike Arturo's theory of the novel, which can only be assumed to be intended as a gloss of *Locura y muerte*, these remarks by the narrator are offered as direct and, coming from him, authoritative commentary. This makes their inappropriateness all the more striking. For although this passage is certainly cited often, not enough has been made of its dubious status as a gloss of the events in the text. Already within the quoted material difficulties begin to surface, since the speaker's attitude toward his subject—plot in the novel—wavers between approbation and reproval. The first paragraph speaks of an astute novelist; the second, even though it is only reprising the first, changes the qualifier to "false." In the first instance the contrivance of a plot in which characters coincide at emotional peaks is worded in terms loaded with favorable overtones. The narrator speaks of "harmonizing," of a "great system of forces." In the second paragraph the tone turns pejorative. The great system of forces degenerates into a mechanical combination of ingredients, and the novelist's task is presented not as a harmonizing but as a mutilation of the fabric of life. It is of course possible to explain away the about-face by reading a sarcastic edge into the narrator's compliments. I doubt, however, that there exists any linguistic basis for this explanation. One would have to say that Jarnés' reference to the astuteness of the novelist is sarcastic precisely *because* the about-face is inconsistent, and this would only beg the question. Moreover, this minor difficulty reflects larger ones in the novel.

One can note, for one thing, that *Locura y muerte* begins with a description whose overriding metaphor is that here employed to criticize a novel's mounting toward a climax. Just as in the cited passage the novelist takes characters, "unique pieces of life," and throws them into the matrass, in the opening paragraph an "invisible hand" (the novelist's) snatches passers-by from the street and places them inside the Banco Agrícola, figured as a huge boiling cauldron. Here is what happens when the turmoil inside the bank peaks: "Twelve o'clock. One hundred degrees. The huge marble and glass cauldron is boiling. The bubbles explode hurling numbers" (p. 1389). Thus the novel begins with one of those noisy explosions that the narrator subsequently claims are absent from his "simple tale." Even if the contexts in which the two images occur are dissimilar, one can still feel the incompatibility, or at least the friction, between *Locura y muerte's* theorizing and its depicted events—especially when the same image appears a third time, now in reference to the potential clash between the protagonists: "To judge by the number of characters, the tragic possibilities are few; a brief meditation on the number four reassures him about the possible conclusions, just as an examination of the substances combined in a test tube allows one to pinpoint the properties of the resulting explosive body" (p. 1430).

This friction is equally apparent at the level of plot. The novel contains adultery, fits of jealousy, blackmail, grand larceny (a "noisy operation" [p. 1539]). We have a two-timing wife (actually three-timing: melodrama to the second power) and a cuckolded husband, surreptitious love letters and secret rendezvous. Picture the scenario: Matilde, unfaithful but good at heart ("the faithful heroine" she is called in one of the chapter titles [p. 1534]), sleeps with Alfredo (his role: "the traitor in a melodrama" [p. 1438]) in order to save her husband from financial ruin. Arturo supplies the affection that she does not receive from her introverted spouse. Appropriately, Matilde and Arturo meet in a second-hand bookstore where she is perusing romantic novels (p. 1409), for Matilde's predicament is nothing if not one of those "dramas pasionales" which, according to Arturo, betray the imaginative poverty of their authors (p. 1501). And indeed, Arturo's discovery of Matilde's liaison with Alfredo did not take any great imaginative gifts to contrive. At the same bookstore he runs across a devotional book, "The Anchor of Salvation," in which he finds a memento bearing the

name of one of her relatives. He inquires about the provenance of the book
and is told that it was left there by a waiter who had found it in one of the
rooms of the Villa Juanita, a popular *casa de citas*. That night Arturo goes to
Villa Juanita and confirms his suspicions when he observes Matilde going
into one of the rooms. This is a turn of events that one associates with the
kind of literature that in Jarnés' time was called "galante," and whose
contemporary incarnations are the soap opera and the *fotonovela*. It is certainly a far cry from the sophistication of the narrator and Arturo's theorizing. A small but telling detail punctuates the conflict between the events in
the novel and the adjacent speculation. In the prologue, anticipating the
notion of a plotless, characterless novel, Jarnés states that in *Locura y muerte*
"apenas hay trances ruidosos, conflictos" (p. 1385). But in the narration
itself the word "trance" is used at least twice to describe the predicament of
the characters, once to refer to Arturo's precarious affair with Matilde
(p. 1461), and again when Arturo finds out that Matilde is Juan Sánchez's
wife (p. 1420). This scene, in addition, is also called "un profundo conflicto
dramático."

One is tempted to appropriate the image of the boiling cauldron to
represent *Locura y muerte*: an unstable mixture of theory and narrative
about to explode.[16] As Jarnés had predicted, fiction and criticism do produce
a volatile compound ever on the verge of disintegrating. The theoretical
program elaborated by Jarnés and his delegates is never realized in the text
itself, which reads much—too much for some tastes perhaps—like a typical
story of adultery and deceit, complete with all of the clichés and stereotypes
of the genre. In this sense *Locura y muerte* comprises two novels or, more
accurately, comprises one novel and a prescription for a second one, totally
different from the first. Robert Musil's characterization of his *Der Mann
ohne Eigenschaften*, a work in other ways comparable to Jarnés', applies equally
well to this novel: "What the story that makes up this novel amounts to is
that the story that was supposed to be told in it is not told."[17] One could say
also that what it amounts to is that the theory that would have justified the
story that is told is not the theory one finds in the book. The description on
the label does not match the contents of the medicine flask.

Because *Locura y muerte* self-consciously incorporates the commonplaces
of the *novela galante*, it is, in this respect also, stylization or parody. In this
instance, however, this procedure serves another purpose besides exposing
the conventions of a certain kind of fiction. The outstanding feature of the
plot of the novel such as it has been discussed above is that Juan hardly
figures in it. His marginality is repeatedly stressed in the novel, and has

been amply commented upon. What has not been stressed is that this marginality is construed within the novel as an inability to participate, not in the course of real events, but in a fictional drama. More than a man in search of a character, Juan is a character in search of a role. He is "a fanatical pursuer of his own essence" (p. 1397), but as the death scene makes clear, Juan is essentially dramatic gesture and text. His finding himself can only mean becoming part of a fictional world. The narrator puts this precisely: Juan "cannot even win the right to be an actor in the drama of his shared conjugal life" (p. 1497). Unlike Augusto Pérez, who is sometimes regarded as his immediate literary predecessor, Juan will not be satisfied until he has become a full-fledged *ente de ficción*.[18] The issue is not "life." It is rather that strange mode of being peculiar to fictional personages, and which Espina in the epigraph to this chapter defines with the coinage *subvivir*. There is "survival," living on or living over; and there is "subvival," barely living or bogus living—that equivocal existence of those who do not actually live or die. Espina's pun on *papel* (both "role" and "paper"), rendered in English by the dual meaning of "character," serves to remind us that the truck that emerges from the shadows to abort Juan's final "latiguillo escénico" resembles nothing so much as the hook that comes out of the wings to drag the unsuccessful performer offstage.

Seen in this light, Juan's ejection reprises the prelude to *Escenas junto a la muerte*, where the professor's final theatrical flourish is similarly truncated. Even if the professor's companion acts to preserve life rather than to destroy it, the two scenes have the same significance: both dramatize the collapse of a character's begetting authority. Juan differs from the professor in that he does not tell his own story. But the two characters' dilemmas are identical: like the professor, Juan finds it impossible to author his life; he cannot control his fate, his *papel*, his script. He too is besieged by unwelcome collaborators. Indeed one of the climactic episodes of *Locura y muerte* anticipates the interpretive agons of the later novel: in a last-ditch effort to assert his distinctiveness, Juan aids Alfredo in a bank theft. The newspaper accounts of the crime, however, ignore his participation. Although Juan proclaims his guilt, no one will believe him; in fact, he is taken for one of the victims. The "author" of the theft thus becomes one of the bit players in the drama—exactly the kind of distortion that bedevils the professor. And here is how Jarnés describes his protagonist: "Juan Sánchez spends his life touching his spirit, for fear of losing it in the claws of his immense restlessness. But he does not move away from the railing. His life is a succession of scenes next to the executioner" (pp. 1385-86). Change the narrative perspective of the novel, put Juan at the center of his story, and *Locura y muerte de Nadie* will metamorphose into *Escenas junto a la muerte*.

The failure of Juan's aspirations is underscored by Arturo's taking the part of the two-timed husband. It has been argued that, as part of the project of composing a polygraphic novel, Jarnés refrains from presenting a scene in which Matilde would be confronted with her unfaithfulness.[19] But the novel does contain such a scene, except that its protagonist is not Juan but Arturo—Arturo, who in the midst of his accusations thinks of himself as her husband: "I have felt for a moment that ridiculous possessiveness that a husband usually feels when he sees that his wife is coveted by someone else" (p. 1537), and who speaks of Matilde's shared affection as "a love with two sources" (p. 1537) that includes only Alfredo and himself. If we remember Jarnés' fascination with Arthurian legend (as evidenced, for example, in *Viviana y Merlín*), even Arturo's name evokes the picture of the cuckolded husband.

The contrast between Juan and Arturo brings out clearly the former's inability to perform in the *role* that properly belongs to him. Try as he may to orchestrate a scene whereby to prove his wife's infidelity, he cannot pull it off. As "tramoyista de su propia tragedia," he fails utterly (p. 1497). As he puts it, "I challenge tragedy, but tragedy does not accept" (p. 1497). Arturo, on the contrary, has tragedy—or at least melodrama—fall into his unsuspecting lap. His trajectory consists of an increasing involvement in Matilde's *ménage à trois*. Considering himself at first an ancillary part of her love life ("a sporadic member," he says, with an unintended but obvious sexual pun [p. 1422]), he eventually realizes that he can no longer regard his involvement frivolously and his initial nonchalance is replaced by deep passion (see, for example, pp. 1461 ff.). Juan's trajectory consists of a progressive disengagement from the plot of the novel, which culminates logically in his "erasure." In the end he cannot even successfully establish his complicity in the swindle of the Banco Agrícola. Thus *Locura y muerte* narrates the process by which Juan and Arturo exchange places, the process by which Arturo assumes the role of which Juan is bereft. At first an outsider, a "pure spectator" (p. 1428), Arturo eventually comes to occupy centerstage; while Juan, the original protagonist, becomes the spectator of a fiction in which he would like to, but cannot, participate. As one enters the novel, the other exits.

Another of Jarnés' works contains a character whose fate is exactly that which Juan would have wished for himself. In the epilogue to the second edition of *El profesor inútil*, Jarnés has the professor read a novel called

Transmigración. The main character of this novel-within-a-novel, Judas Tadeo Martínez del Prado, is an *indiano* who returns to Spain to marry his bride Araceli, whom he knows only through photographs. Upon arriving he discovers that the buxom woman of the pictures is not Araceli but her mother. At first angered, he soon realizes that such an occurrence has all but turned him into a novelistic character (the supposition being that such things do not happen in real life):

> Judas is going to burst into a fit of rage. . . . But while he says hello to his friends who congratulate him on such a lucky trip, he meditates, he reflects. . . . How could such a scene, full of tragic overtones, befall him, a simple fruit merchant? He begins to believe in a doubling of his being. Doesn't that pathetic situation encourage him to abandon his trivial mercantile personality and ascend to the realm of fiction? Perhaps he was destined for immortality. But so as to achieve it he must not hinder the dramatic event; he must let himself be carried to the epilogue that the gods have in store.[20]

He goes ahead with the marriage, thus becoming "an ideal entity on the road to anthologies and libraries" (p. 254). When the professor is asked about the novel, he replies: "A friend had invited me to witness a birth. I saw a character be born" (p. 254). This is the kind of birth that never does take place for Juan, who undoubtedly would have envied Martínez del Prado's fate. *Transmigración* is the novel *Locura y muerte* would have become had Juan achieved his aspirations.

We can see, then, that the two metafictional modes of *Locura y muerte* interfere with one another. As discursive metafiction the novel attempts to impersonate a revolutionary form of fiction without plot or characters. As narrative metafiction it draws attention to the conventionality (not to say triteness) of its contents. This reading of Juan's dilemma, which depends crucially on the presence of scriptural and literary comparisons, turns *Locura y muerte* into a self-conscious imitation of the *novela galante*, a genre totally alien to the sophisticated problematics of the polygraphic novel. Arturo's theorizing is subverted precisely by the kind of literature that, instead of objectively portraying the masses, caters to their tastes. For the romantic novel *is* mass literature, is one of the kinds of fiction avidly consumed by the "mass" man and woman. *Locura y muerte* wants to be highbrow stuff, and ends up in the clutches of the commonplace. Savor, if you will, the irony. Inside every *minoría selecta* there is an *hombre masa* trying to get out. Inside every Jarnés there is an Alberto Insúa filtering through. In spite of its avowed experimentalism, *Locura y muerte* does not stray far from the *folletín*, a fact that did not go entirely unacknowledged in the early reactions to the novel.[21] But what distinguishes the vanguard practitioner of a popular form, of course, is that extra reflexive twist produced by the self-conscious employment of materials that others take for granted. Jarnés' novel, with its clash of metafictional modes, provides an excellent illustration of the difference.

The opposition between the two varieties of metafiction surfaces clearly in the work's problematic stance toward the past. *Locura y muerte* as a whole attests to a rejection of the past that comes across most palpably as a devaluation of genealogy. Nowhere is this more noticeable than in Juan Sánchez's excavation of his roots, which concludes with an *auto da fe* during which all of the family mementos go up in smoke. The question is whether one's ancestors bequeath "a treasury of memories," as the majordomo thinks, or only "a heap of old junk," as Juan claims (p. 1482). The butler recognizes both the continuity of past and present in memory and the value of the past. He assumes that our ancestors' experiences flow into a familial reservoir from which succeeding generations can draw, a belief that makes him keep a family chronicle. But Juan, after the revelation that his mother was a chorus girl, views genealogy only as a burden. He would like to think that nothing ties him to his ancestors. By transforming the "treasury of memories" into a "heap of old junk," he dissolves the bond of remembrance into mere temporal anteriority. The state of his inheritance seems to corroborate his devaluation, for when one's family history can be catalogued, collected in a truck, and dumped in one's front porch, it has probably stopped signifying. Genealogy subsists as a shaping force only when progenitor and progeny issue from a common stock and persist in a common medium. A certain equality or commensurability between the living and the dead is needed for the generational segments to coalesce into a family line. The reification of genealogy, its reduction to artifacts of various sorts, suggests that the line has been broken. This is precisely what has happened to Juan's ancestry: "Juan Sánchez paces nervously up and down the living room, waiting for his inheritance. His past is coming in a truck: a succinct past, excerpted epochs, loves synthesized in a couplet, ambitions reduced to a diploma, fevers—wilted, dry, deplorable—pressed between the pages of a novel" (pp. 1484-85). All of the components of his past have been denatured: emotions, loves, ambitions are now no more than scraps of paper.

Yet it would not be accurate to say that Juan succeeds in shedding his inheritance. The past can be tampered with, diminished, even incinerated, but it cannot be suppressed entirely. In Juan's life it reasserts itself at the very end, inscribed in his final gesture, since his death simply duplicates his mother's, which had also been portrayed as an erasure. Paradoxically this effacement reinscribes him in the family circle. The erasure not only breaks up Juan's act, it also brands him as his mother's son—the one thing he wishes he weren't. It is thus not surprising that a truck kills both Juan and his mother, for the family relics had been deposited also in a truck (the same one? the "van" in the vanguard?) No matter how much Juan might want to abolish his past, he cannot. In the end the family claims him for its own.

As narrative metafiction, *Locura y muerte* displays a similarly inescapable atavism. Under this aspect the novel presents, in effect, an inventory or junk heap of superannuated novelistic motifs and devices, not least of which is Juan's search for, and subsequent rejection of, his natural parents. The novel's fictional inheritance undergoes the same modifications to which Juan's past is submitted—extraction, reduction, synthesis. Like Juan, *Locura y muerte* consumes its past, in both senses. But as in Juan's life, the past persists, and not merely as "old junk." It persists as informing remembrance, as a backdrop against which the events in the novel unfold. At one point the narrator says about Arturo: "Since in order to please the frustrated Rebeca he had of late been reading a copious lot of XIXth-century novels, he defines the strange situation of the intimate group with this vague formula: 'Tragedy is hovering over us'" (p. 1430). The narrative operates much the same as Arturo. As the scene in Juan's family estate demonstrates, the novel exhibits a similar alertness to fictional precedent. For this reason all of *Locura y muerte* has a vaguely formulaic air about it, a peculiarity already evident in the title and present as well in some of the chapter headings: "Bodegón y celos," "Nocturno y fuga," "La heroína fiel," "Remate y preludio."

In its incarnation as discursive metafiction, however, the novel positions itself very differently with respect to the past. No longer does one witness any attempt to incorporate it, however deviously or self-consciously. Because Arturo's theorizing proceeds by analogy with film, the effect is just the opposite: to render irrelevant any fictional inheritance. By modeling the polygraphic novel on a newly invented art form, one without a long and onerous history, Arturo seems to be hoping for an absolute beginning. To the extent that the polygraphic novel resembles film, it isolates itself from its literary ancestry. It places itself at the beginning, and not at the end, of history. This aim is well-suited to the forum chosen for its formulation, for the interpolation of commentary in fiction may also be seen as a means of preempting the past. Embedded commentary leads the reader to think that the work accounts for itself. Whatever guidance or explanations he may require, the work provides. Such a text posits *itself* as the principal source of intelligibility; it is, in this sense, self-begetting, since the narrator's or the characters' theorizing usurps the determining function normally reserved to history or tradition.[22]

Both because of its content and because of where it is formulated, the theory of the polygraphic novel thus stands as a kind of ultimate generic fantasy. Vanguard fiction is so nagged by belatedness that the possibility of a novel without a past, of a truly novel novel, possesses an irresistible allure. One can imagine that even someone as text-obsessed as the professor might want, in his exasperation, to exchange the *papeletas* for a clean roll of film: could one not interpret the presence of the Chaplin "film" in *Escenas* as a symptom of this very desire? Go to the movies and avoid repetition, so seems to run the slogan of the polygraphic novelist, whom film beckons with the promise of a fresh start. The screen is the vanguard novelist's *tabula rasa*. Its blankness protects him against the hazards of latecoming, assuring that every image there projected will form part of that "incipient personal melody" denied to the professor and to Juan.

For this reason, if structurally vanguard fiction oscillates between innocence and self-consciousness (the double focus), generically it oscillates between the nineteenth-century novel and film. The polygraphic novel, with its plotlessness, with its trans-individualism, with its antibiographical bias, embodies the filmic extreme. It exists as a limit concept, as a threshold whose crossing would produce a text so unfamiliar, so unfamilial, that it could no longer be regarded as a novel. Significantly, although such texts were written in the 1920s and 30s, they were not classed with the *novela nueva*.[23] The story of Juan's family romance, a skein of narrative clichés, represents the other extreme. The achievement of *Locura y muerte de Nadie* consists in juxtaposing the two available generic options. This novel too oscillates between adherence to received norms and complete disengagement from them. That the disengagement occurs only in theory (in Arturo's theory) confirms what we already knew, that vanguard fiction is never so entirely itself as when, looking back, it bemoans its lack of individuality.

Conclusion: Hermes in and out of the Subway

Vanguard fiction exists between parentheses. From its inception the genre enjoyed a subordinate, liminal status, a parenthetical placement amply documented in the hostile reaction of many reviewers. As we have already seen, these texts were insistently regarded as a deviation from the normal course of development of the modern Hispanic novel—less a "prelude" than an interlude, and less an interlude than an indecorous *carcajada*: a boisterous, momentary disruption of the serious business of novel writing. Ortega, once more: "the novel imposes an inexorable decalogue of imperatives and prohibitions. One shouldn't toy with the novel. It is perhaps the only serious thing left in the realm of poetry."[1]

The vanguard novel does not need to be told, however, that its playfulness is out of order, for it knows this full well, as it knows that a nebular, pneumatic novel—the novel of play—will be inevitably parenthesized, cordoned off and segregated from contiguous forms. But this fate does not faze the genre, which voluntarily occupies the enclosure in which others would imprison it. Indeed when critics bracket or denaturalize these novels, they are only repeating the genre's initial gesture. As in Salinas' story, vanguard fiction begins by shutting itself in a closed world, by opening parentheses and placing itself inside them. And I say "initial" not only because of "Mundo cerrado," but also because, from the first, parentheses have figured largely in my own discussion. In chapter 2 the crucial passage on volatilization depicted the pneumatic effect as an expansive, adversative parenthesis, as the "in" in (in)subordination. And even earlier, in the first chapter, my entire argument grew out of the consideration of a parenthetical remark: "The novel already knows its masters; it has learned to love them and begins to feel the need to choose them. In the beginning—one must not forget that the novel, with its present characteristics, is yesterday's genre—to say 'novel' was, implicitly, to allude to Balzac."

Consider now, in light of the foregoing, this excerpt from the initial paragraph of *El profesor inútil*, 1926 edition:

The students are away in the country. The notebooks are asleep on their desks. Today I can feel that I fully exist; I can follow beat by beat, metaphor by metaphor, the rhythm of my body, the rhythm of my soul. I have a few hours to attend to my own spectacle, to lean over the railing and observe the deepest eddies of my soul. It is the first morning of my vacation. With my back to the books, far from the curious eyes of my students, I can invent a morning. On other days, when the little tyrant that pursues me makes me see things according to the books, in every stone and in every tree I see only a name, a word from a dictionary. Today I can forget all the catalogues and create a new, beautiful nomenclature. In this seventh day when the gods rest, I will collaborate with nature's plan to renew its contours, worn down by the slow pounding of the centuries.[2]

Like "Mundo cerrado," these sentences inscribe another of those privileged, inaugural moments: the first paragraph of the first novel by the best of the vanguard novelists. And as with "Mundo cerrado," I take this beginning to be emblematic. The professor, a master of ceremony, is here officiating at the inauguration of the genre, an inauguration that consists also in opening a parenthesis. For a vacation is a parenthesis in time, a suspension of daily habit and chores. As Rafael Laffón perceptively remarked: "A vacation action: a parenthesis of action or action contradicted."[3] What Laffón should have added, though, is that this vacation involves a special sort of inactivity, for the professor intends to use the hiatus to initiate a new enterprise. He speaks of wanting to "invent," of naming, and even alludes to the Genesis account of creation. As a kind of *deus otiosus*, the professor will devote his sabbatical to the leisurely exercise of his creative powers. The title of the vignette, "Mañana de vacación," summarizes his ambition: to start afresh, to begin anew, but to do so outside of time, or better, in *his own* time. For this reason the novel opens on the morning of a new day, a different day, one freed from the usual rules and restrictions. And lest there be any doubt about the symbolism of the event, let me quote a sentence from the prologue to *Paula y Paulita*: "Freed from the oppressive impediments of centuries, Art relaxes during its vacation, without resolving to act again, to sin again."[4] The similarity in phrasing confirms that the portrait of the professor renders also the profile of the artistic moment, the genre, to which he belongs. Jarnés could just as well have named this vignette: "Mañana de vacación, or The Professor and His Class," for vanguard novels are nothing if not vacation pieces, idle fictions for the professor's days off.

A vacation, literally, is an emptying. Hence, alongside the references to creation, the opening ceremonies include several mentions of obliteration or effacement: the students' notebooks are "sleeping"; the students are out of sight; the professor has "turned his back" on his books; he is going to "forgot" everything he knows. No more books, no more students, no more classrooms—which is to say, also, no more professor. While on vacation Jarnés' protagonist intends to forget himself, to block out who he is and what he does. He is trying to obliterate precisely all those things that so bedevil the narrator of *Escenas junto a la muerte*. Thus, the professor's behavior reveals that he also feels oppressed by time, by tradition, by that cultural storehouse of memories incarnated in the church of *Escenas*. Like candidate #7, he lives with the nagging concern that nothing remains to be said because language and nature have been exhausted. His good humor is simply a cover, the other face of candidate #7's melancholy. This is the professor's crucial, if unintended, lesson: in vanguard fiction euphoria is a sign of depression, youthfulness a sign of age, vitality a sign of fatigue, levity a sign of worry. Like Proserpine, the genre leads a charmed, dual existence, oscillating between the upper- and the under-world, between the sanguine ramblings of the professor and the somber meditations of candidate #7. Vanguard novels bring us a literature of exhaustion in the register of delight.

I know of no better emblem for this condition than Batty's poster, which pictures Proserpine and Hermes (the novel and its reader) on the threshold between the subway and *la vía pública*. If one looks closely at the poster, one will notice that its title, "The Return of Persephone," is placed on either side of the two figures. One will notice, that is, that it encircles Hermes and Persephone within the arching arms of a parenthesis.

Notes

Abbreviations

C   *Contemporáneos*   RA   *Repertorio Americano*
GL   *La Gaceta Literaria*   RAv   *Revista de Avance*
MF   *Martín Fierro*   RO   *Revista de Occidente*

Introduction

1. The methodological justification and results of this approach are recorded in my "The Novel as Genres," *Genre*, 12 (1979), 269-92; and "Genre as Text," *Comparative Literature Studies*, 17 (1980), 16-25.

2. See Paul de Man, *Blindness and Insight* (New York: Oxford University Press, 1971), p. 10.

3. I use 1926 and 1934 as liminal dates because they are the years of the first and second editions of *El profesor inútil*, one of the best-known and most representative novels of the group. But since these boundaries are only markers of convenience, I have not hesitated, in some instances, to discuss texts situated just beyond them. The chronology of vanguard fiction is treated in chap. 1.

4. On the notion of interpreting relationship, see Ross Chambers, *Meaning and Meaningfulness* (Lexington, Kentucky: French Forum Publishers, 1979), p. 142.

5. Here and elsewhere I use the terms *vanguard novel* and *vanguard fiction* interchangeably, partly out of convenience, partly because, as we will see, the criticism of the time did not normally distinguish between longer and shorter fictional forms.

1. The Vanguard Novel as a Discursive Category

1. Jaime Torres Bodet, "Reflexiones sobre la novela," in *Contemporáneos. Notas de crítica* (Mexico City: Herrero, 1928), p. 12. Other page references are given in the text. Here as elsewhere all translations from the Spanish are my own.

2. *Revolution and Repetition* (Berkeley: University of California Press, 1977), p. 107.

3. The first quotation comes from Enrique Diez-Canedo, "Manuel Bueno: *Poniente solar*," *El Sol*, 29 November 1931, p. 2; the second one from Guillermo de Torre, "Veinte años de literatura española," *Nosotros*, 57 (1927), 319.

4. The other work published by "Nova novorum" was Valentín Andrés Alvarez's "farce," *Tararí* (1929). The Revista de Occidente also published Espina's *Luna de copas* (1929) and

Jarnés' *Paula y Paulita* (1929), though no longer officially under the "Nova novorum" imprint. For a thorough discussion of the *Revista de Occidente*, see Evelyne López Campillo, *La Revista de Occidente y la formación de minorías (1923-1936)* (Madrid: Taurus, 1972).

5. This sudden transatlantic leap from Madrid to Mexico City should not seem surprising, for there were close ties between the Spanish vanguard and the Contemporáneos. Writers from each group read and reviewed each other; Jaime Torres Bodet, one of the founders of *Contemporáneos*, resided for a few years in Spain, where he published several novels and became a frequent contributor to *Revista de Occidente*; Eduardo Villaseñor, a peripheral member of the Mexican group, also was published by Espasa-Calpe. These personal and literary contacts resulted in an ongoing transoceanic dialogue whose interlocutors and content I will seek to identify. For Torres Bodet's reminiscences of this period, see his *Tiempo de arena* (Mexico City: Fondo de Cultura Económica, 1955), and the interview contained in Emmanuel Carballo, *Jaime Torres Bodet* (Mexico City: Empresas Editoriales, 1968), pp. 56-57.

6. On the difficulties that beset many publishing houses in the early 30s, see José Esteban, "Editoriales y libros de España de los años 30," *Cuadernos para el diálogo*, No. 32 (December 1972), pp. 298-302.

7. Aub's repudiation of vanguard fiction is well-known; see his *Discurso de la novela española contemporánea* (Mexico City: El Colegio de México, 1945), where he describes the typical work of vanguard fiction as follows: "a minuscule work, engendered with difficulty, exquisite in the choice of ornaments, difficult to understand at first sight, decked out with ingenious and intranscendent ideas, and considered the culmination of its young author's efforts" (p. 63).

8. Ernesto Giménez Caballero, "Los contemporáneos franceses: Proust," *El Sol*, 17 June 1926, p. 2. A listing of reviews for each of the works I will be discussing can be found in the Bibliography.

9. The translated excerpt reads in part: "Livia m'apris, dernière perfidie qui veut m'attraper, me rendre prisonnier dans l'enigme tissu avec ces fils à deux couleurs: Livia, Suzanne (Suzanne, le nom de ce soir, Livia, sa meilleure amie . . . alors, inéxplicable qu'elle part lorsque l'autre arrive. . . . Peut-être . . .). Mais, non; le brouillement croît prodigieusement, j'y m'égare, j'en rénonce, à résoudre, et je me démande dans mon intérieur, à grands cris, un acier décisif qui coupera—le lâcher est impossible—ce noeud gordien." It is taken from the last story in the collection, "Livia Schubert, incompleta."

10. Corpus Barga, "La originalidad y el valor," *El Sol*, 1 October 1926, p. 1.

11. Azorín, "El arte de Pedro Salinas," *ABC*, 9 July 1926, pp. 3-4.

12. Fernando Vela, "Pedro Salinas: *Víspera del gozo*," *RO*, 13 (1926), 124-29.

13. Ibid., pp. 127 and 128 respectively.

14. Other reviewers who also defended Salinas' originality were: Enrique Diez-Canedo, "De Proust a Salinas," *El Sol*, 16 June 1926, p. 2; E. Gómez de Baquero, "Las prosas líricas de Salinas," *El Sol*, 22 July 1926, p. 1; "Pedro Salinas: *Víspera del gozo*," *Mediodía*, No. 2 (July 1926), pp. 14-15; and José Ballester, "Pedro Salinas: *Víspera del gozo*," *La Verdad*, 22 August 1926, p. 1.

15. The passage is worth quoting in full: "Diverging from its primitive narrative or historical form, the novel has enriched itself with new elements, incorporating dramatic, lyrical, psychological, and didactic materials and forms. But in a genre so vast that it resembles a continent more than a province, it happens that the cultivation and development of these elements is taking the novel away from its properly narrative nature. Trying to be so many things, the novel becomes denaturalized. It is likely that after these pleasure trips and artistic loitering the future of the novel lies in a return to its home ground. The appearance of a Balzac or a Galdós would create a sensation."

16. Ernesto Giménez Caballero, "Los profesores inútiles," *El Sol*, 23 September 1926, p. 2.

17. E. Gómez de Baquero, "Los poemas novelescos de Jarnés," *El Sol*, 29 September 1926, p. 1.

18. Juan G. Olmedilla, "Benjamín Jarnés: *El profesor inútil*," *Heraldo de Madrid*, 5 October 1926, p. 4.

19. Azorín, "Un librito de sensaciones," *ABC*, 8 October 1926, p. 3.

20. Rafael Laffón, "Benjamín Jarnés: *El profesor inútil*," *Mediodía*, No. 5 (October 1926), pp. 15-16.

21. Francisco Ayala, "Benjamín Jarnés: *El profesor inútil*," *GL*, 1 February 1927, p. 4.

22. Esteban Salazar y Chapela, "Literatura plana y literatura del espacio," *RO*, 15 (1927), 283.

23. Eduardo Mallea, "Divagación en torno a Jarnés," *MF*, 28 March 1927, n. pag.

24. Espina states in the prologue to the novel that his aim was "to bring to literature the emotions, the chiaroscuro, the corporeal irreality or the incorporeal realism of the cinema, to search for a kind of imagistic projection on the white screen of a book." *Pájaro pinto* (Madrid: Revista de Occidente, 1927).

25. Luis Bello, "Antonio Espina: *Luna de copas*," *El Sol*, 23 June 1929, p. 2.

26. R. Ledesma Ramos, "Tres libros: tres perfiles," *GL*, 1 August 1929, pp. 1-2.

27. José Gorostiza, "Antonio Espina: *Luna de copas*," *C*, 5 (1929), 157-59.

28. Esteban Salazar y Chapela, "Antonio Espina: *Luna de copas*," *RO*, 24 (1929), 384. Other page references are given in the text.

29. Guillermo de Torre ("Perfil de Antonio Espina," *GL*, 15 February 1927, p. 1) mentions that Espina's "deforming aesthetic" is reminiscent of Valle-Inclán's *esperpentos*.

30. On the cosmopolitan orientation of the *martinfierristas*, see the testimonies of two of the members of the group, Córdova Iturburu, *La revolución martinfierrista* (Buenos Aires: Ediciones Culturales Argentinas, 1962), and Eduardo González Lanuza, *Los martinfierristas* (Buenos Aires: Ediciones Culturales Argentinas, 1961). One of the most extravagant encomia of Giraudoux that I have seen appeared in this magazine. Part of it runs: "Jean Giraudoux is one of the greatest writers that the world has ever seen. There is not a single young writer alive today who has not felt Giraudoux's influence. He is great enough to be an adjective! Just as one says that a work is symbolist, cubist, dadaist, or surrealist, one can say that there exists a giraudoux genre, a giraudoux style, a giraudoux feeling. The world is divided into six parts: Europe, Asia, Africa, America, Oceania, and Giraudoux." Alberto Hidalgo, "Juan Giraudoux," *MF*, 18 June 1925, n. pag. Jarnés published an excerpt from *El profesor inútil*, "Nidia en Atocha," in *MF*, 5 October 1926.

31. Benjamín Jarnés, "Eduardo Mallea: *Cuentos para una inglesa desesperada*," *GL*, 1 May 1927, p. 4.

32. Guillermo de Torre, "Dos novelas poemáticas," *RO*, 17 (1927), 117-21. Other page references are given in the text.

33. For a thorough overview of this important movement, see Merlin H. Forster, *Los Contemporáneos: 1920-1932* (Mexico City: Ediciones de Andrea, 1964). Excerpts from *Contemporáneos* are available in two useful anthologies: Manuel Durán, *Antología de la revista "Contemporáneos"* (Mexico City: Fondo de Cultura Económica, 1973) and Edward J. Mullen, *Contemporáneos: Revista Mexicana de Cultura (1928-1931)* (Salamanca: Anaya, 1972). Outside of the novels produced by this group and of Mallea's *Cuentos para una inglesa desesperada*, there was little interest in this kind of fiction in other parts of Spanish America. It should be remembered that this was the heyday of the so-called *novela de la tierra*, exemplified by such works as *La vorágine* (1924), *Don Segundo Sombra* (1926) and *Doña Bárbara* (1929). Concha Meléndez, in her 1933 survey of "Novelas del novecientos en la América Hispana" (*RA*, 27 [1933], 329-32), names only Jaime Torres Bodet in her discussion of "la novela vanguardista." Many of the important Spanish-American journals of this time—*Amauta, Atenea, Nosotros, Sur*, for instance—showed little interest in the new fictional vogue. The three notable exceptions are *Contemporáneos, Revista de Avance*, and to a lesser extent, *Repertorio Americano* (whose principal contribution to the movement consisted in reprinting book reviews from Spanish newspapers).

34. Francisco Ayala, "Jaime Torres Bodet: *Margarita de niebla*," *RO*, 18 (1927), 133-37. This quotation and the following one occur on p. 135.

35. Esteban Salazar y Chapela, "Jaime Torres Bodet: *Margarita de niebla*," *El Sol*, 1 October 1927, p. 2.

36. Benjamín Jarnés, "Jaime Torres Bodet: *Margarita de niebla*," *GL*, 15 September 1927, p. 4.

37. "*Margarita de niebla* y Benjamín Jarnés," *Ulises*, No. 5 (December 1927), pp. 24-26. Page references are given in the text.

38. Benjamín Jarnés, "Ramón Gómez de la Serna: *La Quinta de Palmyra*," *RO*, 10 (1925), 113. Subsequent page references are given in the text.

39. Although they were not published until several years later, by this time Jarnés had already completed several of his novels. The text of *El convidado de papel* is dated 1924, that of *Paula y Paulita*, 1925-26. "El río fiel," one of the chapters of *El profesor inútil*, had already appeared in *Revista de Occidente*, and "Mañana de vacación," another segment of the novel, had appeared in *Plural*.

40. Benjamín Jarnés, "Pentagrama: Ramón," *Alfar*, No. 41 (June-July 1924), p. 8.

41. Martí Casanovas, "Jaime Torres Bodet: *Margarita de niebla*," *RA*, 16 (1928), 245; and Salazar y Chapela, "*Margarita de niebla*," p. 2.

42. Martí Casanovas, ibid.; and Ayala, "*Margarita de niebla*," p. 134.

43. Juan Marinello, "Jaime Torres Bodet: *Margarita de niebla*," *RAv*, 1 (1927), 292.

44. Martí Casanovas, p. 244.

45. Ayala, "*Margarita de niebla*," p. 136.

46. One might also include Torres Bodet's collection of stories, *Nacimiento de Venus*, not published until 1941 but written between 1928 and 1937. All but one of these stories appeared originally in *Revista de Occidente*. *Primero de enero* (Madrid: Ediciones Literatura, 1935), another novel by Torres Bodet, came on the scene a little too late to have much of a role.

47. Rubén Salazar Mallén, "Jaime Torres Bodet: *La educación sentimental*," *C*, 6 (1930), 186-88. Other page references are given in the text.

48. Jaime Torres Bodet, "Novela y nube," *C*, 2 (1928), 87-90.

49. Jaime Torres Bodet, "Las letras hispanoamericanas en 1930," *GL*, 1 January 1931, p. 7.

50. José Gorostiza, "Morfología de *La rueca de aire*," *C*, 7 (1930), 241.

51. *Frente literario*, 1, No. 1 (1934), 3.

52. Benjamín Jarnés, "José Díaz-Fernández: *El blocao*," *GL*, 1 July 1928, p. 3.

53. "An excellent student—the best qualification for becoming an exemplary teacher—of the *School for Indifferents*, founded by Jean Giraudoux, *Dama de corazones* is one of the best exercises we have seen in that school where we also got our early education." From Benjamín Jarnés, "El arte como juego" (1929), in *Ariel disperso* (Mexico City: Stylo, 1946), p. 114.

54. Benjamín Jarnés, "Nuevos prosistas mejicanos," *GL*, 1 January 1929, p. 6.

55. Benjamín Jarnés, "Prosa poética" [1930], in *Ariel disperso*, p. 164.

56. Esteban Salazar y Chapela, "Xavier Villaurrutia: *Dama de corazones*," *El Sol*, 19 August 1928, p. 2. An earlier discussion of the *narración* can be found in José Díaz Fernández's review of Joaquín Arderius' *La duquesa de Nit* (*La Voz*, 15 October 1926, p. 4). According to Díaz Fernández the narration is an increasingly popular genre (*Víspera del gozo* and *El profesor inútil* had just been published) equidistant from the novel, the novelette, and the short story, in which style substitutes for character and plot. The popularity of this "ambiguous genre," in his view, threatens the survival of the novel.

57. Though similar to his earlier works in style and content, Jarnés' novelistic output in exile falls outside the scope of this book. It has been studied by J. S. Bernstein in *Benjamín Jarnés* (New York: Twayne, 1972) and Emilia de Zuleta in *Arte y vida en la obra de Benjamín Jarnés* (Madrid: Gredos, 1977).

58. Antonio Espina, "Un libro de Benjamín Jarnés: *El convidado de papel*," *El Sol*, 30 December 1928, p. 2.

59. Carlos Fernández Cuenca, "Literatura de vanguardia: *Paula y Paulita*," *La Epoca*, 3 August 1929, p. 2.

60. Melchor Fernández Almagro, "Jarnés y su *Locura y muerte de Nadie*," *GL*, 15 December 1929, p. 3.

61. Díaz Fernández, "Una novela. Una biografía," *Luz*, 7 June 1932, p. 4; Diez-Canedo, "Homenaje a Stendhal," *El Sol*, 19 June 1932, p. 2. The quoted material comes from Díaz Fernández's review.

62. José Escofet, "Novela de vanguardia," *La Voz*, 8 December 1928, p. 1; José Gorostiza, "De Paula y Paulita," *C*, 5 (1929), 68-69; Ledesma Ramos, "Tres libros: tres perfiles," p. 2.

63. "Benjamín Jarnés: *Lo rojo y lo azul*," *Indice literario*, 1 (1932), 50-51; and Miguel Pérez Ferrero, "Homenaje a Stendhal: Sobre *Lo rojo y lo azul*," *Heraldo de Madrid*, 9 June 1932, p. 7.

64. Most notably Azorín's *Nuevas Obras*, and especially *Superrealismo*, which were regarded as applications of "the most audacious theories of vanguard art" (Antonio Espina, "Azorín: *Superrealismo*," *RO*, 28 [1930], 132). Less noticed were Juan Chabás' *Sin velas, desvelada* (1927) and *Puerto de sombra* (1928), Mario Verdaguer's *El marido, la mujer y la sombra* (1927), Francisco Ayala's *El boxeador y un angel* (1929) and Max Aub's *Geografía* (1929).

65. Referring to Valentín Andrés Alvarez's *Naufragio en la sombra* (in "Libros de España, 1930," *GL*, 1 January 1931, p. 4), Giménez Caballero states: "His novel fulfills the imagistic and pure criteria of the new 'Ulises' collection." For the sobriquet "generación de 1930," see below.

66. Miguel Angel Hernando mistakenly includes *Víspera del gozo* in this series. Some of the titles, also, are given incorrectly: *Argor sin fin, Tres mujeres más equix* [sic!], *Víspera de gozo*. In *Prosa vanguardista en la generación del 27* (Madrid: Prensa Española, 1975), p. 62.

67. Benjamín Jarnés, *Crisol*, 6 July 1931, p. 2. A couple of years earlier Jarnés had said the same thing of *Novela como nube*: "I don't know whether the book *Novela como nube* is destined to figure in the future as an 'archeological marvel' or as a volume of the 'Forgotten Classics.' I tend to think that it will not be possible to forget it soon. It captures so precisely this delicious literary moment that at least it will always be a testimony—clear, accurate—of the spirit of an artistic epoch" (*GL*, 1 January 1929, p. 6).

68. Antonio de Obregón, *Efectos navales* (Madrid: Ediciones Ulises, 1931), p. 14.

69. José Díaz Fernández, "Los libros nuevos," *El Sol*, 16 March 1930, p. 2.

70. José Díaz Fernández, "Los libros nuevos," *El Sol*, 23 November 1930, p. 2; and F. C. S., "Felipe Ximénez de Sandoval: *Tres mujeres más equis*," *El Sol*, 7 January 1931, p. 2.

71. Ramón Feria, "La novela: género efusivo, género amplio," *GL*, 1 May 1932, pp. 5-6.

72. Guillermo de Torre, "Veinte años de literatura española," *Nosotros*, 57 (1927), 320; Esteban Salazar y Chapela, "Juan Chabás: *Puerto de sombra*," *El Sol*, 12 July 1928, p. 2; Azorín, "Baroja y los jóvenes," *ABC*, 19 January 1928, p. 3; "Novelas de evasión y novelas de regreso," *Heraldo de Madrid*, 26 February 1931, p. 8.

73. Respectively in: *El Sol*, 23 November 1930, p. 2; *El Sol*, 21 September 1930, p. 2; and *Luz*, 24 January 1933, p. 3. Díaz Fernández's fullest exposition of his views on this score is *El nuevo romanticismo* (Madrid: Zeus, 1930), for a discussion of which see Pablo Gil Casado, *La novela social española*, 2nd ed. (Barcelona: Seix Barral, 1973), pp. 31-40 and 91-96; also Víctor Fuentes, "De la literatura de vanguardia a la de avanzada: en torno a José Díaz Fernández," *Papeles de Son Armadans*, 54 (1969), 243-60.

74. Carlos and Pedro Caba, "Pío Baroja y el personaje masa," *Atlántico*, No. 18 (May 1933), p. 79. See also, by the same authors, "La rehumanización del arte," *Eco*, 2, No. 9 (October 1934), n. pag., where the same passage is reproduced and glossed.

75. All three novels were published in 1934 within a few months of each other—Jarnés' in February, Obregón's in April and Gullón's in June.

76. "With the trajectory of a poem": "Ricardo Gullón: *Fin de semana*," *Noreste*, No. 7 (Summer 1934), n. pag. "Proustian narration": F. V., *Eco*, 2, No. 8 (May-June 1934), n. pag. "Poematic generation," etc.: Leopoldo Panero, "La observación y la poesía," *Literatura*, 1 (1934), 150.

77. The first quotation is from Leopoldo Panero, "La observación y la poesía," p. 150; the second from A. Ochando, "Ricardo Gullón: *Fin de semana*," *Isla*, No. 6 (1935), n. pag. Compare also the following from Guillermo de Torre's review of *Estrella de día* (*Luz*, 27 February 1934,

148

p. 10): "As an essentially poetic temperament, Torres Bodet imparts to his novelistic fabulations a captivating lyricism and grace. The filiation of this novelistic manner is well known, and there is no reason to insist on it."

78. J. López Prudencio, "Ricardo Gullón: *Fin de semana*," *ABC*, 14 October 1934, p. 8.

79. Enrique Azcoaga, "Antonio de Obregón en la vía pública," *Literatura*, 1 (1934), 106-108; Miguel Pérez Ferrero, "*Hermes en la vía pública* y la novela," *Heraldo de Madrid*, 3 May 1934, p. 7; Guillermo de Torre, "Una novela nueva: *Hermes en la vía pública*," *Luz*, 24 April 1934, p. 4; Benjamín Jarnés, "Hermes de fiesta," *RO*, 45 (1934), 93-100. The cited passages from Jarnés occur on pp. 95-96, 95, and 99 respectively.

80. Antonio de Obregón, "Benjamín Jarnés: *El profesor inútil*," *Luz*, 13 February 1934, p. 10: "It was a textbook of influences. In a provincial university I exchanged Physics, Chemistry, Biology, and the Bible for *El profesor inútil*, for literature and the new poetry."

81. Juan José Domenchina, "*El profesor inútil*," in *Crónicas de Gerardo Rivera* (Madrid: Aguilar, 1935), pp. 106-107. The quotations that follow appear on pp. 106 and 109 respectively.

82. Benjamín Jarnés, *El profesor inútil*, 2nd ed. (Madrid: Espasa-Calpe, 1934), p. 7.

83. Generic metalanguage may be said to comprise three types of information: constative, deictic, and criterial. As I state in the text, constative information identifies a class while deictic information lists its membership; criterial information, complementarily, sets forth the body of defining norms. In this chapter I have been concerned primarily with the constative and deictic components in the critical reaction to vanguard fiction. The criterial component will be treated in chapter 2. For a discussion of these concepts, see my "Genre as Text," *Comparative Literature Studies*, 17 (1980), 16-25.

84. "*La Quinta de Palmyra*," pp. 113-14.

85. Ramón Gómez de la Serna, "Sobre la novela," *Síntesis*, 3 (1929), 48. A version of this article appears also in *Ismos* (1931) under the title "Novelismo."

86. Ibid., p. 44.

87. Antonio Espina, "Benjamín Jarnés: *Libro de Esther*," *RO*, 48 (1935), 111. An often-voiced idea during this time was that the traditional novel was essentially biographical. From this some critics concluded that the true novels of the period were biographies, which were immensely popular. Thus, according to Rufino Blanco Fombona, "the current vogue of biographies—and of autobiographies, personal diaries, etc.—does not reflect a lack of interest in the novel. The novel is the biography of the unknown; biography, the novel of the famous" ("La crisis de la novela" [1930], in *El espejo de tres faces* [Santiago de Chile: Ediciones Ercilla, 1937], p. 189). Similarly, for Félix Lizaso, "the rise of the biography has coincided with the decline of the novel, so much so that one can think of a substitution." In "Boga de la biografía," *El libro y el pueblo*, 13 (1935), 73.

88. Azorín, *Crisol*, 2 November 1931, p. 2.

89. José Ortega y Gasset, "*El Obispo leproso*, novela por Gabriel Miró," in *Obras completas*, III, 545; and *Ideas sobre la novela*, ibid., p. 419.

90. This image has correlates in other criticism. Ramón's novels were also described as "poliedros" (Rafael Calleja, "Ramón Gómez de la Serna: *El torero Caracho*," *RO*, 16 [1927], 380). Ramón himself stated that he wrote in order to lose himself in the "polidreísmos del mundo y sus combinaciones libres" ("Sobre la novela," p. 45). Jarnés was said to possess "un estilo poliédrico" (José Gorostiza, "De *Paula y Paulita*," p. 69). And several years before the publication of *Escenas*, in his review of *Víspera del gozo*, Azorín was already toying with the same idea: Salinas portrays reality, says Azorín, "indirectly, as if dealing not with the species of things but with the reflection of those things in multiple mirrors" ("El arte de Pedro Salinas," p. 4). In the review of *Escenas* the multiple mirrors have been reorganized into a circus. Although he does not consider "Jarnés, letal," Leon Livingstone has studied Azorín's mirror images in "Novel and Mirror: the Eye and the I," in *Homenaje a Azorín*, ed. Carlos Mellizo (Laramie: University of Wyoming, 1973), pp. 51-73.

91. "They speak now, with apparent redundance, of the 'novelistic novel' ['*novela novelesca*']. Strictly speaking, there is no pleonasm. The 'novelistic novel' has a definite reality in

the generation and even in the degeneration of the genre. Superficially, one can say that the 'novelistic novel' is the integral story, the 'hundred-percent' narration" (Juan José Domenchina, *Crónicas de Gerardo Rivera*, p. 157). See also Melchor Fernández Almagro's review of *Locura y muerte de Nadie* (cited in note 60) and, by the same author, "Literatura nueva," *GL*, 15 November 1929, p. 3. There was also a series by this name—"La novela novelesca"—published by Editorial Siglo XX of Madrid.

92. The term "noveloide" is used by Gerardo Diego apropos of his story "Cuadrante," published in *RO*, 14 (1926), 1-24. "Pre-novela" is Azorín's well-known designation for *Super-realismo* and is discussed in the following chapter. "Ultra-novela" is Espina's name for Azorín's "pre-novela" and is also discussed in chapter 2. For "novela grande" and "novela chica," the two categories in Ramón's typology of fiction, see José Camón Aznar, *Ramón Gómez de la Serna en sus obras* (Madrid: Espasa-Calpe, 1972), pp. 299-390.

93. Michel Foucault, *L'Ordre du discours* (Paris: Gallimard, 1971), p. 54.

94. Thus, for example, Corpus Barga claims that he has "cleansed" his novel from the customary paraphernalia: "In the following manuscript the author has wanted to present a novel cleansed of facts, descriptions, scenes, the most concrete—and perhaps the barest— novel ever written in Spanish; a novel that, for the entertainment of mathematicians, could have been written in algebraic formulas." From the preface to his *Pasión y muerte. Apocalipsis* (Madrid: Ediciones Ulises, 1930).

95. "Placed in the middle of quotidian reality with no object other than to reproduce it faithfully, the novelist does the work of the chronicler, of the historian. But the historian only receives the official version while the novelist receives the most unusual confessions. According to Alain, 'History has no place for confessions.' Both history and the novel are nourished by facts, but historical facts need witnesses, while the novel disdains them. I believe only in the reality invented by the novelist, a reality far removed from that repro- duced by the historian." From Benjamín Jarnés, *Ejercicios* (Madrid: Cuadernos Literarios, 1927), pp. 77-78.

96. "The decadence of the novel is for Ortega y Gasset a question of the number of themes. We will not join him in this return to naturalism. No work of art lives off its theme. To affirm that a novel's merit depends on the novelty of its plot is to confuse merit with success. The preeminence of the accidental over the essential, of plot over art, would make *Camille* superior to *The Red and the Black*" ("Reflexiones sobre la novela," p. 9). One must note, however, that Torres Bodet's supposed refutation amounts to no more than a paraphrase of Ortega: "Subject matter does not save a work of art, and the fact that a statue is made of gold does not assure a lasting achievement. A work of art lives more from its form than from its material and owes its essential gracefulness to its structure, to its organism" (*Ideas sobre la novela*, p. 399).

97. Torres Bodet, "Reflexiones," p. 18. The previous quotation appears on p. 12.

98. Jarnés, "*La Quinta de Palmyra*," p. 113. The previous quotation appears on p. 112.

99. Jarnés, *Ejercicios*, pp. 78-79.

100. Rufino Blanco Fombona, "Personalidades contra escuelas," *El Sol*, 30 October 1927, p. 1; rpt. in *El espejo de tres faces* (Santiago de Chile: Ediciones Ercilla, 1937), p. 36.

101. The sources of the cited passages are, in order: Azorín, "El arte de Pedro Salinas," p. 3; Francisco Ayala, "*El profesor inútil*," p. 4; Jarnés, "*Margarita de niebla*," p. 4; Félix Lizaso, "Eduardo Villaseñor: *Extasis*," *RAv*, 3 (1928), 330; Rafael Laffón, "Lectura," *GL*, 15 December 1931, p. 5; "Noticias literarias," *GL*, 1 April 1931, p. 12; Antonio Espina, "Rosa Chacel: *Estación. Ida y vuelta*," *El Sol*, 4 May 1930, p. 2; Rafael Marquina, "Jaime Torres Bodet: *Proserpina rescatada*," *GL*, 1 August 1931, p. 14.

102. The sources of the cited passages are, in order: Fernández Almagro, "Literatura nueva," p. 3; Guillermo de Torre, "Dos novelas poemáticas," pp. 120-21; Hernani Rossi, "El mes de julio: *Efectos navales*," *GL*, 15 October 1931, p. 16; Espina, "*Libro de Esther*," pp. 111-12; Carlos Reyles, *Incitaciones* (Santiago de Chile: Ediciones Ercilla, 1936), p. 59.

103. *L'Ordre du discours*, p. 35.

104. Domenchina, *Crónicas de Gerardo Rivera*, pp. 247-48.

105. One might say that Domenchina crosses discourse and intercourse to produce a new entity—the textile: a (private) part of language that attests to its author's virility.

106. The first quotation comes from Manuel Gálvez, "La decadencia de la novela," *Criterio*, 4 (1929), 308; the second from José Lorenzo, "Joaquín Arderius: *Justo el Evangélico*," *Heraldo de Madrid*, 13 February 1930, p. 9.

107. "Libros y mujeres," *Luz*, 24 May 1934, p. 3; rpt. in part in *Feria del libro* (Madrid: Espasa-Calpe, 1935). These allegations were apparently not restricted to the literary arena. The *Suplemento de la Revista Blanca* for 1 February 1929 gives an account of a free-for-all that broke out at a banquet for Montero Alonso when one of the speakers started identifying different vanguard novelists by feminine names (Baturrillo, "La trifulca vanguardista," p. 5). According to the chronicler, the forces of reaction at the banquet rallied to Alberto Insúa's cry of "¡Viva la mujer española!" Juana Chabás? Paquita Ayala? Mauricia Bacarisse? Rosa Chacel?

108. "Tres novelas nuevas," *Indice literario*, 5 (1936), 1.

109. The sources of the quotations are, respectively: S. V., "Luis Villalonga: *Prometeo, novio*," *El Sol*, 23 March 1934, p. 7; J. M. A., "Antonio Botín Polanco: *Logaritmo*," *El Sol*, 28 October 1933, p. 4; and Miguel Pérez Ferrero, "Derrotero de la novela," *Cruz y raya*, No. 22 (January 1935), p. 65.

110. Although I am aware that the demise of vanguard fiction in Spain must ultimately be explained by reference to the political situation during the Second Republic, I have been interested here only in the discursive dimension of the phenomenon. But the two spheres are of course connected; indeed, the violence perpetrated against the vanguard novel is an echo, and a not unimportant one, of violence perpetrated at other levels. The relationship between politics and culture during this period has been studied by José-Carlos Mainer in *Falange y literatura* (Barcelona: Labor, 1971), and by Jean Bécarud and Evelyne López Campillo in *Los intelectuales españoles durante la Segunda República* (Madrid: Siglo XXI, 1978). See also, more generally, Guillermo Díaz-Plaja, *Estructura y sentido del novecentismo español* (Madrid: Alianza, 1975); José-Carlos Mainer, *La edad de plata (1902-1931)* (Barcelona: Los Libros de la Frontera, 1975); and Rafael Osuna, "Las revistas españolas durante la Segunda Pública," *Ideologies and Literature*, 2, No. 8 (Sept.-Oct. 1978), 47-54.

2. A Pneumatic Aesthetics

1. Enrique Diez-Canedo, "Ricardo Güiraldes: *Xaimaca*," *RO*, 4 (1924), 390.

2. Dámaso Alonso's phrase in "A un río le llamaban Carlos," one of the poems in *Hombre y Dios*.

3. Juan José Domenchina, *Crónicas de Gerardo Rivera* (Madrid: Aguilar, 1935), p. 107.

4. José Gorostiza, "Morfología de *La rueca de aire*," *C*, 7 (1930), 241.

5. See E. Gómez de Baquero, "La lírica en prosa," in *Pen Club* (Madrid: Renacimiento, 1929), pp. 351-54.

6. On the concept of isotopy, see A. J. Greimas, *Sémantique structurale* (Paris: Larousse, 1966), chap. 4; also François Rastier, "Systématique des isotopies," in *Essais de sémiotique poétique* (Paris: Larousse, 1972).

7. Jorge Mañach, "Xavier Villaurrutia: *Dama de corazones*," *RAv*, 3 (1928), 331; Ricardo Gullón, "Antonio de Obregón: *Efectos navales*," *GL*, 1 July 1931, p. 14; Enrique Azcoaga, "Novela, armonía, ritmo," *RA*, 24 (1932), 347; Max Aub, "Escala de Juan Chabás," *Verso y prosa*, 2, No. 11 (June 1928), 2.

8. Félix Lizaso, "Eduardo Villaseñor: *Extasis*," *RAv*, 3 (1928), 330; Gorostiza, "Morfología de *La rueca de aire*," p. 245; Esteban Salazar y Chapela, "Ramón Gómez de la Serna: *Chao*," *El Sol*, 7 February 1934, p. 7; Benjamín Jarnés, *Feria del libro* (Madrid: Espasa-Calpe, 1935), p. 254; Domenchina, *Crónicas de Gerardo Rivera*, p. 109.

9. Domenchina, *Crónicas de Gerardo Rivera*, p. 252.

10. Jaime Torres Bodet, "Novela y nube," *C*, 2 (1928), 87; Melchor Fernández Almagro, "Literatura nueva," *GL*, 15 November 1929, p. 3.

11. Francisco Ayala, "Benjamín Jarnés: *Paula y Paulita*," *GL*, 15 September 1929, p. 1.

12. Guillermo de Torre, "Dos novelas poemáticas," *RO*, 17 (1927), 118; Benjamín Jarnés, "Aventuras mentales" [1930], in *Ariel disperso* (Mexico City: Stylo, 1946), pp. 147-48; Rafael Marquina, "Jaime Torres Bodet: *Proserpina rescatada*," *GL*, 1 August 1931, p. 14; Benjamín Jarnés, *Feria del libro*, p. 235; Benjamín Jarnés, "Nuevos prosistas mejicanos," *GL*, 1 January 1929, p. 6.

13. R. Ledesma Miranda, "La novela y su mundo," *Eco*, No. 9 (October 1934), n. pag.; Jorge Mañach, "Benjamín Jarnés: *Paula y Paulita*," *RAv*, 4 (1929), 343; "Juan Cabezas: *Señorita O-3*," *El Sol*, 25 November 1932, p. 2.

14. Benjamín Jarnés, "Jaime Torres Bodet: *Margarita de niebla*," *GL*, 15 September 1927, p. 4; Benjamín Jarnés, "Juan Chabás: *Puerto de sombra*," *GL*, 1 July 1928, p. 3; Benjamín Jarnés, *Ejercicios* (Madrid: Cuadernos Literarios, 1927), p. 77; César M. Arconada, "Cuatro libros de jóvenes," *GL*, 15 December 1928, p. 2.

15. Gilberto Owen, "Antonio Espina: *Pájaro pinto*," *Ulises*, No. 1 (May 1927), p. 26.

16. Francisco Ayala, "Jaime Torres Bodet: *Margarita de niebla*," *RO*, 18 (1927), 135-36.

17. Antonio Espina, "George Bernanos: *Sous le soleil de Satan*," *RO*, 13 (1926), 387.

18. Benjamín Jarnés, *Feria del libro*, p. 276.

19. Hernani Rossi, "Antonio de Obregón: *Efectos navales*," *GL*, 15 October 1931, p. 16.

20. Ramón Feria, "La novela: género efusivo, género amplio," *GL*, 1 May 1932, p. 5.

21. Jarnés, "Nuevos prosistas mejicanos," *GL*, p. 6.

22. Ibid.

23. Francisco Valdés, *Letras. Notas de un lector* (Madrid: Espasa-Calpe, 1933), p. 85. The quoted excerpt appears in a review of César Arconada's *Tres cómicos del cine*. The obvious if unintended sexual overtones of Valdés' language connect with the discussion of denaturalization: to build is to erect; a building is an erection; hence, "Nada más parado," etc.

24. *Ideas sobre la novela*, in *Obras completas* (Madrid: Revista de Occidente, 1957), III, 414-15.

25. For "novela gaseiforme," see the opening paragraph of *Superrealismo*; the other phrases appear in Azorín's prologue to the excerpt of the novel that was published in *RO*, 26 (1929), 145-57. In the prologue to *El hombre perdido* (1947) Ramón labels some of his earlier novels like *El incongruente* (1922) and ¡*Rebeca*! (1936) "novelas de la nebulosa." I wonder to what extent the choice of metaphor was influenced by the paranomastic resemblance between *nebulosa* and *novela*. Only a few years after Unamuno had invented the *nivola*, another variation on the same rubric appears. One might say that the nebula is the *nivola* of the *novela vanguardista*. As part of the background of the metaphor one should mention also the great interest that existed during this time in modern cosmological theories. *Revista de Occidente* published many articles on the topic, including pieces by Lemaître, Jeans, Eddington and others. I have studied the influence of the hypothesis of the exploding universe on the poetry of Dámaso Alonso in "Cosmology and the Poem: Dámaso Alonso's 'Sueño de las dos ciervas,'" *Hispanic Review*, 46 (1978), 147-71.

26. It might have been inspired by this passage from *Ideas sobre la novela*: "We note that [Proust's works] lack a skeleton, a rigid and tense support like the wires in an umbrella. Without a backbone, the novelistic body becomes an amorphous cloud, a plasma without form, a pulp without contours" (in *Obras completas*, III, 402).

27. I employ the term "deconstruction" in its exoteric sense without intending any particular reference to Derridean usage.

28. Benjamín Jarnés, "Hermes de fiesta," *RO*, 45 (1934), 98: "Deep life is chained to a rock; epidermic life has winged feet. The former moans under the sign of Prometheus; the latter frolics under the sign of Hermes: an eternal mythology, to which we always return. Two attitudes that a man can take before reality: to stop or to keep on going, to dive into the essential or to glide merrily over mere circumstances, over the cheerful skin. An entire literary epoch has preferred the god with winged feet," etc. We recall that Jarnés had greeted the

publication of *El blocao* with the statement that vanguard art was giving way before "the sharp imperative of deep life." See also Rafael Vázquez-Zamora, "Mitología novísima," *Luz*, 4 June 1934, p. 12.

29. Benjamín Jarnés, *El profesor inútil*, 2nd ed. (Madrid: Espasa-Calpe, 1934), p. 28.

30. Antonio Espina, "José Bergamín: *El cohete y la estrella*," *RO*, 3 (1924), 125.

31. José Ortega y Gasset, "*El Obispo leproso*, novela por Gabriel Miró," in *Obras completas*, III, 545.

32. Melchor Fernández Almagro, "Jarnés y su *Locura y muerte de Nadie*," *GL*, 15 December 1929, p. 3.

33. Ayala, "*Margarita de niebla*," pp. 135-36.

34. Adolfo Salazar, "Alberto Moravia: *Los indiferentes*," *El Sol*, 8 September 1932, p. 2.

35. Antonio Espina, "*Azorín: Superrealismo*," *RO*, 28 (1930), 135.

36. Antonio Espina, "Benjamín Jarnés: *Libro de Esther*," *RO*, 48 (1935), 108.

37. Azorín, "Jarnés, letal," *Crisol*, 2 November 1931, p. 2.

38. Benjamín Jarnés, *Libro de Esther* (Madrid: Espasa-Calpe, 1935), p. 149.

39. Torres Bodet, "Reflexiones sobre la novela," *Contemporáneos. Notas de crítica* (Mexico City: Herrero, 1928), p. 18.

40. From Azorín's prologue to *Superrealismo*, in *RO*, 26 (1929), 145.

41. Benjamín Jarnés, *Feria del libro*, p. 252. This is said apropos of Mauricio Bacarisse's *Los terribles amores de Agliberto y Celedonia*, "an amphibious novel, between the sky, the earth, and the sea; half apologue, half poem; half philosophical disquisition, half fable." The review, entitled "Un mundo disperso," appeared originally in *Luz*, 22 April 1932, p. 2.

42. The sources of the cited passages are, in order: Enrique González Rojo, "Xavier Villaurrutia: *Dama de corazones*," *C*, 1 (1928), 321; Magda Portal, "Panorama intelectual de México," *RA*, 16 (1928), 158; Torres Bodet, "Novela y nube," p. 87; Lizaso, "*Extasis*," p. 330; Gorostiza, "Morfología de *La rueca de aire*," pp. 245-46; Antonio de Obregón, "Benjamín Jarnés: *El profesor inútil*," *Luz*, 13 February 1934, p. 10.

43. R. Ledesma Ramos, "Tres libros: tres perfiles," *GL*, 1 August 1929, pp. 1-2.

44. In his review of the novel, in *RO*, 28 (1930), 135-36.

45. Ibid.

46. Benjamín Jarnés, *Feria del libro*, p. 253: "In Bacarisse—as in all the members of his generation—the critical sense, which shreds and annihilates, prevails over the novelistic sense, which gathers, reconstructs, recasts, vivifies." Significantly, Jarnés sees this trait as a generational indicium.

47. Ibid., p. 252.

48. R. Ledesma Miranda, "La novela y su mundo," *Eco*, 2, No. 9 (October 1934), n. pag.; Juan Marinello, "Jaime Torres Bodet: *Margarita de niebla*," *RAv*, 1 (1927), 292; Antonio Marichalar, "Ultimo grito," *RO*, 31 (1931), 102-3; Benjamín Jarnés, "El novelista en la novela," *RO*, 42 (1933), 230. On the reflexive quality of vanguard art in general see Fernando Vela, "El arte al cubo," *RO*, 16 (1927), 79-86; Antonio Marichalar, "Síntomas literarios," *RO*, 16 (1927), 122-23; idem, "Momento crítico," *RO*, 14 (1926), 254-59; Guillén Salaya, *Parábola de la nueva literatura*, 2nd ed. (Madrid: Biblioteca Atlántico, 1931), pp. 9-13.

49. José Martínez Sotomayor, *La rueca de aire* (Mexico City: Imprenta Mundial, 1930), pp. 62-63.

3. Closed World

1. Pedro Salinas, *Víspera del gozo* (Madrid: Revista de Occidente, 1926), p. 9. Other page numbers refer to this edition.

2. *Víspera del gozo* (Madrid: Alianza, 1974), pp. 11-22.

3. *La deshumanización del arte*, in *Obras completas* (Madrid: Revista de Occidente, 1957), III,

357-58. The same image is put to a different use in *El tema de nuestro tiempo* (*Obras completas*, III, 188).

4. *Ideas sobre la novela*, in *Obras completas*, III, 410-11.

5. The different emphases of *Ideas sobre la novela* are illustrated by Ortega's different use of the metaphor of the garden. To read a novel that makes us aware of its fictive status is "like looking at a painting of a garden in a garden. The painted garden only flowers and turns green in the precinct of a room, on an anodyne wall, where it creates an imaginary day" (*Ideas*, p. 411). Here the work of art—the painted garden—acts as a simulacrum of life: there exists a *symmetrical* connection between them. In the version of the image presented in *La deshumanización*, however, there is an obvious asymmetry: no longer pictures of trees vs. trees, but a sheet of glass vs. trees. The asymmetry is intended, as the point is that life and art are not commensurable. Art belongs to a different order of being and should not be assimilated to life.

6. "The author's tactic shall be to remove the reader from his real horizon and imprison him in a hermetic and imaginary horizon created by the novel's inner world" (*Ideas*, p. 409); "In this sense I would even say that only the novelist has the ability to forget, and to make us forget, the reality that lies outside his novel" (*Ideas*, p. 411); "The novelist should, on the contrary, try to anesthetize us to reality, leaving the reader caught in the hypnosis of a virtual reality" (Ibid.); "As a divine sleepwalker, the novelist has to infect us with his fertile somnambulism" (*Ideas*, p. 413); etc.

7. Implicit in the Ortegan tenor of my discussion is the (debatable) proposition that aesthetic preoccupations are somehow less human than nonaesthetic ones. Only this belief makes possible the neat separation of "art" and "life."

8. Ortega does say that the novel should be intranscendent (*Ideas*, p. 412), but he is clearly using the term here in another sense. Intranscendence in the novel results from the reader's amnesia—he forgets that he is reading a work of fiction. Intranscendence in dehumanized art results from the opposite reaction: the spectator or reader is never allowed to forget the artificiality of the object before him.

9. Jaime Torres Bodet, *La educación sentimental* (Madrid: Espasa-Calpe, 1929), pp. 49-50. Page numbers in the text refer to this edition.

10. *Contemporáneos. Notas de crítica* (Mexico City: Herrero, 1928), pp. 128-29.

4. Decharacterization

1. *Margarita de niebla* (Mexico City: Cvltvra, 1927), p. 11. Other page numbers are given in the text.

2. *Tiempo de arena* (Mexico City: Fondo de Cultura Económica, 1955), p. 232.

3. Merlin H. Forster, "Las novelas de Jaime Torres Bodet," *La Palabra y el Hombre*, No. 34 (April-June 1965), p. 212. See also Sonja Karsen, *Jaime Torres Bodet* (New York: Twayne, 1971), pp. 70-72; and Mercedes Ruiz García, *La obra novelística de Jaime Torres Bodet* (Mexico City: Secretaría de Hacienda y Crédito Público, 1971), pp. 27-29.

4. See Ian Watt's discussion of this feature of the classical novel in *The Rise of the Novel* (Berkeley: University of California Press, 1957), pp. 19-21.

5. *El Sol*, 7 February 1934, p. 7. This passage was quoted and discussed briefly in chap. 2.

6. According to Merlin H. Forster in *Los Contemporáneos* (Mexico City: Ediciones de Andrea, 1964), p. 55, the epigraph paraphrases the beginning of the Fourth Act of the Second Part of Goethe's play. The exact reading, however, can be found in the scene of the First Part where Faust and Mephistopheles visit the witch's den. In J. Roviralta Borrell's Spanish prose translation the passage reads: "Si me muevo de este sitio, si me aventuro a acercarme, no puedo verla sino envuelta en niebla" (p. 104). Since this translation was published in 1924 by the Universidad Nacional de México, it is almost certainly Torres Bodet's source.

7. Forster (*Los Contemporáneos*, p. 43) states that the novel "has a somewhat fragmented plot." Karsen echoes this opinion (*Jaime Torres Bodet*, p. 70).

8. An excerpt from Martínez Sotomayor's *La rueca de aire* presents an imaginary reconstruction of the process whereby an album becomes a newsreel: "Ana decides to do it: she opens the prayerbook. She hurries through the pages to reach the moment of the mass. With great leaps of her fingers she skips the preliminary prayers. The pious images in the text pass in quick succession; as they superimpose, ritual acquires a galvanic mobility. She has gotten ahead of the service and quickly backtracks, making the pages jump with her thumb: the grave figures in the holy images dance. She flips the pages again: the figures dance with disorderly movements; they jump, stand, gesticulate. And the tiny castanets of the rosary crackle. Again the dance. Again the thumb flipping through the pages. The girl is surprised at having casually invented motion pictures, which lay hidden in the folds of the Mystic Rose" (*La rueca de aire* [Mexico City: Imprenta Mundial, 1930], p. 97).

9. "The Work of Art in the Age of Mechanical Reproduction," in *Illuminations*, ed. Hannah Arendt (New York: Schocken Books, 1969), pp. 217-51.

10. Jaime Torres Bodet, *Estrella de día* (Madrid: Espasa-Calpe, 1933), pp. 142-43.

11. "The Work of Art in the Age of Mechanical Reproduction," p. 246.

12. Proust's influence on Torres Bodet was sometimes mentioned in reviews of his novels, as in Miguel Pérez Ferrero, "Jaime Torres Bodet: *Estrella de día*," *Heraldo de Madrid*, 28 December 1933, p. 12; and Francisco Ayala, "Jaime Torres Bodet: *Margarita de niebla*," *RO*, 18 (1927), 136. More recently Sonja Karsen (*Jaime Torres Bodet*, pp. 69-70) has drawn attention to it. The subject still awaits, however, an adequate treatment.

13. *Primero de enero* (Madrid: Ediciones Literatura, 1935), pp. 130-31.

14. *Dama de corazones* (Mexico City: Ediciones de Ulises, 1928), p. 15.

15. A conception of character generally in keeping with the Modernist (in the European sense) aesthetic, for which see Irving Howe, "The Idea of the Modern," in *The Idea of the Modern in Literature and the Arts*, ed. Irving Howe (New York: Horizon Press, 1967), esp. pp. 33-34. Compare also D. H. Lawrence's remarks on his own characters: "You mustn't look in my novel for the old stable *ego* of character. There is another *ego*, according to which the individual is unrecognizable, and passes through, as it were, allotropic states which it needs a deeper sense than any we've been used to exercise, to discover are states of the same radically unchanged element." Lawrence here is addressing the question of intercontextual identity; his allotropic states of character are comparable to the shifting images of Margarita. For a recent discussion of the philosophical and social implications of the Modernist theory of character, see Fredric Jameson, *Fables of Aggression* (Berkeley: University of California Press, 1979), chap. 2, where the passage from Lawrence is quoted and commented.

16. "From her father—an administrator in a record-player company in Ciudad Victoria— Proserpina had inherited a gold pen, a copy of *Quo Vadis?*, a picturesque terror of mules, and a pleasing though laborious English pronunciation.

There is more. She had inherited, besides, a repertoire of four twelve-inch records in which the company had recorded, in chronological order, her grandfather's, her father's, and her mother's voices in addition to her own voice at the age of seventeen. A family custom prevented me from hearing the first three recordings. But of her own voice she sent away to Chicago for one hundred and fifty copies. And she gave them away with the same generosity with which other women distribute their pictures" (*Proserpina rescatada* [Madrid: Espasa-Calpe, 1931], pp. 34-35). Not for nothing is Proserpine's doublet Perse-phone. In *Hermes en la vía pública* the story of Hermes and Proserpine is also given a phonographic rendition: Hermes plays the part of "rey de los gramófonos," head of a record-player company. Other page references to *Proserpina rescatada* are given in the text.

17. The metaphor of the flood is also employed apropos of Proserpina: "My memories of Proserpina, on the other hand, assault me everywhere; they envelop me, they cover me, they perforate me with invisible arrows, they destroy me like a plague. They sweep me away like a flood" (p. 23). The mention of a plague makes the Biblical context of the "flood" unmistakeable.

5. From Palimpsest to Pastiche

1. "Un libro agónico," *RO*, 34 (1931), 223-28. Page references to Jarnés' novel (Madrid: Espasa-Calpe, 1931) are given in the text.

2. Ibid., p. 227.

3. "Jarnés, letal," *Crisol*, 2 November 1931, p. 2.

4. For a fine, wide-ranging analysis of the question of novelistic authority, see Edward Said, *Beginnings* (New York: Basic Books, 1975), pp. 81-188; also Patricia Tobin, *Time and the Novel* (Princeton: Princeton University Press, 1978).

5. "The Storyteller," in *Illuminations*, ed. Hannah Arendt (New York: Schocken Books, 1969), pp. 73-74.

6. *The Art of the Novel*, intro. by Richard P. Blackmur (New York: Charles Scribner's Sons, 1937), p. 322.

7. "[Mr. Lehar] compressed Proserpina's name into one syllable. He thought it too long. He reduced it to a minimum. He just called her 'Pop'" (*Proserpina rescatada* [Madrid: Espasa-Calpe, 1931], p. 89). Lehar's family problems are sketched in "Retrato de Mr. Lehar," one of the stories in *El nacimiento de Venus y otros relatos*.

8. Cf. *Félix Vargas* (Madrid: Biblioteca Nueva, 1928), p. 37: "Impossible to evoke a figure from the past with archeology; archeology is the enemy of living sensation. Saint Theresa, imprisoned by rhetoric. To throw down the wall of erudition. To recapture the past by uniting in today's sensations present and past. Saint Theresa in an automobile, with a telegram in her hand; or on the deck of an ocean liner."

9. Benjamín Jarnés, *El profesor inútil*, 2nd ed. (Madrid: Espasa-Calpe, 1934), p. 8.

10. The recurrence of images of conduction underscores the professor's mediative performance. At the post office he thinks of himself as a conducting wire (p. 91; see also pp. 92-93). When Elvira receives a love letter, it is as if she were holding an electric cable (p. 101). Elsewhere life and death are likened to the alternating current in an electrical circuit (p. 205).

11. See, for example, José María Martínez Cachero, *Las novelas de Azorín* (Madrid: Insula, 1960), pp. 221-33; and Leon Livingstone, *Tema y forma en las novelas de Azorín* (Madrid: Gredos, 1970), p. 66. Page numbers from *Superrealismo* refer to the first edition (Madrid: Espasa-Calpe, 1929).

12. "Azorín: Superrealismo," *RO*, 28 (1930), 132.

13. "Superrealismo," *RO*, 26 (1929), 145.

14. Ibid.

15. See his *Obras completas*, ed. Angel Cruz Rueda (Madrid: Aguilar, 1960), V, 14-15. Martínez Cachero explains: "*Libro de Levante* because, after the initial explorations in search of firm ground, the book becomes a heartfelt and beautiful apology for the writer's native region, evoked or seen in memories colored by a nostalgia that erases or attenuates the hard edges of an unpleasant reality, leaving only a graceful and serene image" (*Las novelas de Azorín*, p. 224).

16. *Tres mujeres más equis* (Madrid: Ediciones Ulises, 1930), p. 52. Other page references to the novel are given in the text. There is of course at least one more vanguard angel, the one who appears in Ayala's story, "El boxeador y un ángel."

17. Cf. also this excerpt from *Superrealismo*: "Angels of strength help us find the energies latent in our personalities, energies that we didn't know we had. When we say: 'I feel like someone else; I have strength I didn't have before'; when we say this, the angel at our side smiles. He's the one, the one who has made us write the book that we thought we could not write, the one who has given us the strength to endure an arduous task" (p. 50).

18. Jaime Torres Bodet, *La educación sentimental* (Madrid: Espasa-Calpe, 1929), p. 18.

19. Ibid., pp. 15-16.

20. Compare also the following observation by Jarnés apropos of *Félix Vargas*: "Elliptical,

156

sensitive, harmonious books, these last books by Azorín. Didn't his previous books already have these qualities? Yes, but his recent works have more energy, more daring, more transforming power. Before, Azorín used to see the mutable from an immutable perspective. Now he sees it from a trapeze. In this way perspectives are multiplied and enriched. It's no longer just the world that revolves about the artist, the artist—as in the cinema—also constantly changes his focus, his axis, his point of view. Before, Azorín witnessed parades of clouds; now he dives into whirlwinds." From "El gran pasmado" (1928), in *Cartas al Ebro* (Mexico City: Casa de España en México, 1940), pp. 47-48.

21. "Jarnés, letal," p. 2.

22. *Novela como nube* (Mexico City: Ediciones de Ulises, 1928), p. 64.

23. As quoted in Martínez Cachero, *Las novelas de Azorín*, p. 211.

6. The Novel as Matrass

1. "What is there to say about *Point Counter Point*? Huxley—or any of the novelists inside the novel—leaves nothing unsaid. *Point Counter Point*, like a flask of good medicine, lists its ingredients and even the way to use the drug. It tricks no one." "El novelista en la novela," *RO*, 42 (1933), 230.

2. See Ross Chambers, "Commentary in Literary Texts," in *Meaning and Meaningfulness* (Lexington, Ky.: French Forum Publishers, 1979), p. 110.

3. Joaquín de Entrambasaguas, ed., *Las mejores novelas contemporáneas*, (Barcelona: Planeta, 1961), VII, 1356-69; Paul Ilie, "Benjamín Jarnés: Aspects of the Dehumanized Novel," *PMLA*, 76 (1961), 247-53; J. S. Bernstein, *Benjamín Jarnés* (New York: Twayne, 1972), pp. 78-82; Emilia de Zuleta, *Arte y vida en la obra de Benjamín Jarnés* (Madrid: Gredos, 1977), pp. 172-92; María Pilar Martínez Latre, *La novela intelectual de Benjamín Jarnés* (Zaragoza: Institución "Fernando El Católico", 1979), passim. See also, more generally, Víctor Fuentes, "La dimensión estético-realista y la novelística de Benjamín Jarnés," *Cuadernos Hispanoamericanos*, No. 235 (1969), pp. 25-37; and, by the same author, "La narrativa española de vanguardia (1923-1931): Un ensayo de interpretación," *Romanic Review*, 63 (1972), 211-18. I will use the second, revised edition of the novel, completed by Jarnés around 1937 but not published until 1961 in Entrambasaguas' collection (VII, 1381-1564).

4. Zuleta, p. 186.

5. See, for example, Ilie's interpretation of the style of the novel as an emulation of the properties of a machine ("Aspects of the Dehumanized Novel," pp. 251-53).

6. The "literariness" of the scene is underscored by the fact that the butler is actually *reading* his account, which has been preserved in a family chronicle.

7. Jaime Torres Bodet, *La educación sentimental* (Madrid: Espasa-Calpe, 1929), p. 21.

8. Ilie, "Aspects of the Dehumanized Novel," p. 252.

9. Ramón Buckley and John Crispin have remarked briefly on this feature of vanguard fiction in their anthology, *Los vanguardistas españoles (1925-1935)* (Madrid: Alianza, 1973), pp. 14-15.

10. *Feria del libro* (Madrid: Espasa-Calpe, 1935), p. 252.

11. "Metafiction," *Iowa Review*, 1, No. 4 (Fall 1970), 106-7.

12. The concepts of discursive and narrative metafiction are discussed more fully in my "Metafiction Again," *Taller literario*, 1, No. 2 (Fall 1980), 30-38.

13. Ilie, "Aspects of the Dehumanized Novel," pp. 149-51 and Zuleta, *Benjamín Jarnés*, pp. 121 and 191.

14. E. G. de Nora makes this point in *La novela española contemporánea* (Madrid: Gredos, 1962), II, 172. See also Zuleta, p. 182.

15. "Aspects of the Dehumanized Novel," p. 250.

16. When the novel first appeared, José Díaz Fernández labeled it "una novela química" (*El Sol*, 24 November 1929, p. 2).

17. As quoted in John Fletcher and Malcolm Bradbury, "The Introverted Novel," in *Modernism*, ed. M. Bradbury and J. McFarlane (New York: Penguin Books, 1976), p. 410.

18. In this respect *Niebla* and *Locura y muerte de Nadie* hardly resemble each other; if anything, Unamuno's novel exerted an influence *à rebours*, for Jarnés has taken a metaphysical problem and turned it into an aesthetic one. Paul Ilie makes a similar observation regarding *Teoría del zumbel* in *The Surrealist Mode in Spanish Literature* (Ann Arbor: University of Michigan Press, 1968), p. 157.

19. Ilie, "Aspects of the Dehumanized Novel," p. 249.

20. *El profesor inútil*, 2nd ed. (Madrid: Espasa-Calpe, 1934), p. 252. Other page references are given in the text. The title of the interpolated tale was probably suggested by Ortega, who in *Ideas sobre la novela* praises fiction's enveloping power thus: "¡Sublime, benigno poder que multiplica nuestra existencia, que nos liberta y pluraliza, que nos enriquece con generosas transmigraciones!" *Obras completas* (Madrid: Revista de Occidente, 1957), III, 410.

21. See Melchor Fernández Almagro, "Jarnés y su *Locura y muerte de Nadie*," *GL*, 15 December 1929, p. 3.

22. A recent study of metafiction by Steven G. Kellman is appropriately titled, *The Self-Begetting Novel* (New York: Columbia University Press, 1980).

23. One example is Luis Cardoza y Aragón's *Maelstrom* (Paris: Excelsior, 1926), subtitled "Films telescopiados."

Conclusion: Hermes in and out of the Subway

1. *Obras completas* (Madrid: Revista de Occidente, 1957), III, 545.

2. *El profesor inútil* (Madrid: Revista de Occidente, 1926), p. 11.

3. *Mediodía*, No. 5 (October 1926), p. 16.

4. *Paula y Paulita* (Madrid: Revista de Occidente, 1929), p. 14.

Bibliography

The first section of the bibliography lists works of vanguard fiction. As usual, my criterion has been whether, at the time a work was first published, it was considered part of the *novela nueva*. This determination, of course, was not always easy to make, since about some novels a consensus did not exist. The roster of novels may thus be incomplete, but I believe that such a list is nevertheless necessary if one is to form some idea of the contours of the genre. (The one deliberate omission is that of Ramón Gómez de la Serna, who is discussed in passing in the text, but whose output is too large and multifarious to be treated here.) After each novel I have ennumerated the reviews I have seen; for omnibus reviews an entry appears under each of the novels discussed. In listing the novels I have only mentioned editions published during the years that concern me.

The second section contains selected criticism pertinent to the vanguard novel from the period under study (excluding the book reviews given in the first section). The third section brings together magazines and newspapers cited.

I. Novels

Andrés Alvarez, Valentín. *Sentimental dancing*. Madrid: Artes de la Ilustración, 1925.
REVIEWS
César A. Comet, *Alfar*, No. 53 (October 1925), p. 26.
Enrique Diez-Canedo, *El Sol*, 16 June 1925, p. 2.
Augusto de Moncada, *La Revista Blanca*, No. 53 (August 1925), p. 19.
————. *Naufragio en la sombra*. Madrid: Ediciones Ulises, 1930.
REVIEWS
Azorín, *Crítica de los años cercanos* (Madrid: Taurus, 1967), pp. 63-66. Review orig. pub. in 1930.
José Díaz Fernández, *El Sol*, 8 June 1930, p. 2.
Ernesto Giménez Caballero, *GL*, 1 January 1931, pp. 2-5.
J. López Prudencio, *ABC*, 13 June 1930, p. 11.
J. López Prudencio, *ABC*, 29 August 1930, p. 7.
Aub, Max. *Geografía*. Madrid: Cuadernos Literarios, 1929.
REVIEWS
César Arconada, *GL*, 15 July 1929, p. 3.

———. *Fábula verde*. Valencia: n.p., 1932.
REVIEWS
Enrique Azcoaga, *Hoja literaria*, March 1933, p. 11.
Juan Chabás, *RO*, 39 (1933), 103-05.
Indice literario, 2 (1933), 90-91.
Benjamín Jarnés, *Libro de Esther* (Madrid: Espasa-Calpe, 1935), pp. 174-76.
Ayala, Francisco. *El boxeador y un ángel*. Madrid: Cuadernos Literarios, 1929.
REVIEWS
Antonio Espina, *El Sol*, 24 March 1929, p. 2. Rpt. in *RA*, 19 (1929), 73; and *La Voz Nueva*, No. 29 (April 1929), n. pag.
Miguel Pérez Ferrero, *GL*, 15 March 1929, p. 3.
———. *Cazador en el alba*. Madrid: Ediciones Ulises, 1930.
REVIEWS
J. López Prudencio, *ABC*, 26 February 1931, p. 16.
Jorge Rubio, *GL*, 15 March 1931, p. 14.
Esteban Salazar y Chapela, *El Sol*, 14 March 1931, p. 2.
Azorín. *Félix Vargas*. Madrid: Biblioteca Nueva, 1928.
REVIEWS
Enrique Diez-Canedo, *El Sol*, 23 December 1928, p. 2.
F. S.-O., *ABC*, 19 December 1928, p. 7.
Antonio Espina, *RO*, 23 (1929), 114-18.
E. Gómez de Baquero, *La Voz*, 24 December 1928, p. 1.
Benjamín Jarnés, *Cartas al Ebro* (Mexico City: La Casa de España en México, 1940), pp. 43-48. Review orig. pub. in 1928.
———. *Superrealismo*. Madrid: Biblioteca Nueva, 1929.
REVIEWS
José Díaz Fernández, *El Sol*, 5 January 1930, p. 2.
Enrique Diez-Canedo, *El Sol*, 5 March 1930, p. 2.
Antonio Espina, *RO*, 28 (1930), 131-36.
Bacarisse, Mauricio. *Los terribles amores de Agliberto y Celedonia*. Madrid: Espasa-Calpe, 1931.
REVIEWS
Benjamín Jarnés, *Luz*, 22 April 1932, p. 2. Rpt. in *Feria del libro* (Madrid: Espasa-Calpe, 1935), pp. 251-54.
J. López Prudencio, *ABC*, 10 April 1932, p. 6.
Eugenio Montes, *El Sol*, 19 February 1932, p. 2.
Barga, Corpus [pseud. of Andrés García de la Barga]. *Pasión y muerte. Apocalipsis.* Madrid: Ediciones Ulises, 1930.
REVIEWS
José Díaz Fernández, *El Sol*, 23 March 1930, p. 2.
Ernesto Giménez Caballero, *GL*, 1 January 1931, pp. 2-5.
Abraham Polanco, *El Sol*, 11 April 1930, p. 2.
Botín Polanco, Antonio. *Virazón*. Madrid: Espasa-Calpe, 1931.
REVIEWS
Félix Centeno, *Crisol*, 27 August 1931, p. 2.
F. M. N., *El Sol*, 19 August 1931, p. 2.

J. López Prudencio, *ABC*, 16 August 1931, p. 24.

———. *Logaritmo*. Madrid: Espasa-Calpe, 1933.

REVIEWS

Indice literario, 2 (1933), 211.

J. M. A., *El Sol*, 28 October 1933, p. 4.

J. López Prudencio, *ABC*, 10 December 1933, p. 19.

Cabezas, Juan A. *Señorita O-3*. Madrid: Oriente, 1932.

REVIEWS

Indice literario, 1 (1932), 78.

Eduardo de Ontañón, *Luz*, 10 May 1933, p. 2.

El Sol, 25 November 1932, p. 2.

Chabás, Juan. *Sin velas, desvelada*. Barcelona: G. Gili, 1927.

REVIEWS

Max Aub, *GL*, 15 June 1927, p. 4.

Melchor Fernández Almagro, *RO*, 16 (1927), 389-91.

Rafael Marquina, *Heraldo de Madrid*, 18 October 1927, p. 7.

Esteban Salazar y Chapela, *El Sol*, 25 June 1927, p. 2.

———. *Puerto de sombra*. Madrid: Caro Raggio, 1928.

REVIEWS

Max Aub, *Verso y prosa*, 2, No. 11 (June 1928), 2.

Benjamín Jarnés, *GL*, 1 July 1928, p. 3.

Rafael Marquina, *Heraldo de Madrid*, 14 August 1928, p. 7.

Esteban Salazar y Chapela, *El Sol*, 12 July 1928, p. 2.

———. *Agor sin fin*. Madrid: Ediciones Ulises, 1930.

REVIEWS

José Díaz Fernández, *El Sol*, 21 September 1930, p. 2.

Ernesto Giménez Cabellero, *GL*, 1 January 1931, pp. 2-5.

J. López Prudencio, *ABC*, 29 October 1930, p. 7.

Chacel, Rosa. *Estación. Ida y vuelta*. Madrid: Ediciones Ulises, 1930.

REVIEWS

José Díaz Fernández, *El Sol*, 16 March 1930, p. 2.

Antonio Espina, *El Sol*, 4 May 1930, p. 2.

Ernesto Giménez Caballero, *GL*, 1 January 1931, pp. 2-5.

Espina, Antonio. *Pájaro pinto*. Madrid: Revista de Occidente, 1927.

REVIEWS

José Bergamín, *Verso y prosa*, 1, No. 3 (May 1927), 4.

Ernesto Giménez Caballero, *El Sol*, 11 February 1927, p. 2.

Heraldo de Madrid, 25 January 1927, p. 4.

Heraldo de Madrid, 1 March 1927, p. 4.

Gilberto Owen, *Ulises*, No. 1 (May 1927), pp. 26-27.

Esteban Salazar y Chapela, *RO*, 15 (1927), 280-86.

Guillermo de Torre, *GL*, 15 February 1927, p. 1.

———. *Luna de copas*. Madrid: Revista de Occidente, 1929.

REVIEWS

Luis Bello, *El Sol*, 23 June 1929, p. 2.

José Gorostiza, *C*, 5 (1929), 157-59.

R. Ledesma Ramos, *GL*, 1 August 1929, pp. 1-2.

J. López Prudencio, *ABC*, 26 July 1929, p. 7.

Esteban Salazar y Chapela, *RO*, 24 (1929), 383-88.

Gullón, Ricardo. *Fin de semana*. Madrid: Ediciones Literatura, 1934.

REVIEWS

F. V., *Eco*, 2, No. 8 (May-June 1934), n. pag.

Pedro García Carrera, *Gaceta de arte*, No. 30 (September-October 1934), p. 4.

J. M. A., *El Sol*, 8 June 1934, p. 7.

J. López Prudencio, *ABC*, 14 October 1934, p. 8.

Noreste, No. 7 (Summer 1934), n. pag.

A. Ochando, *Isla*, No. 6 (1935), n. pag.

Leopoldo Panero, *Literatura*, 1 (1934), 150.

Jarnés, Benjamín. *El profesor inútil*. Madrid: Revista de Occidente, 1926. 2nd ed.: Madrid: Espasa-Calpe, 1934.

REVIEWS OF THE FIRST EDITION

Francisco Ayala, *GL*, 1 February 1927, p. 4.

Azorín, *ABC*, 8 October 1926, p. 3.

Enrique Diez-Canedo, *El Sol*, 9 September 1926, p. 2.

Gerardo Gasset Neyra, *El Imparcial*, 24 October 1926, p. 6.

Ernesto Giménez Caballero, *El Sol*, 23 September 1926, p. 2.

E. Gómez de Baquero, *El Sol*, 29 September 1926, p. 1.

Antonio Herrero, *Sagitario*, 2 (1927), 251-53.

Rafael Laffón, *Mediodía*, No. 5 (October 1926), pp. 15-16.

J. López Prudencio, *ABC*, 27 November 1926, pp. 12-13.

Eduardo Mallea, *MF*, 28 March 1927, n. pag.

Juan G. Olmedilla, *Heraldo de Madrid*, 5 October 1926, p. 4.

Esteban Salazar y Chapela, *RO*, 15 (1927), 280-86.

REVIEWS OF THE SECOND EDITION

Enrique Azcoaga, *Luz*, 20 April 1934, pp. 8-9.

Juan José Domenchina, *Crónicas de Gerardo Rivera* (Madrid: M. Aguilar, 1935), pp. 106-10.

Indice literario, 3 (1934), 21-24.

Antonio de Obregón, *Luz*, 13 February 1934, p. 10. Rpt. in *RA*, 28 (1934), 288.

Miguel Pérez Ferrero, *Heraldo de Madrid*, 15 February 1934, p. 6.

Esteban Salazar y Chapela, *El Sol*, 28 February 1934, p. 2.

————. *El convidado de papel*. Madrid: Historia Nueva, 1928. 2nd edition: Madrid: Espasa-Calpe, 1935.

REVIEWS

César Arconada, *GL*, 15 December 1928, p. 2.

José Escofet, *La Voz*, 8 December 1928, p. 1.

Antonio Espina, *El Sol*, 30 December 1928, p. 2. Rpt. in *RA*, 18 (1929), 101.

Ernesto Giménez Caballero, *GL*, 15 January 1929, p. 3.

J. López Prudencio, *ABC*, 16 January 1929, p. 7.

Rafael Marquina, *Heraldo de Madrid*, 11 December 1928, p. 7.

————. *Paula y Paulita*. Madrid: Revista de Occidente, 1929.

REVIEWS

Francisco Ayala, *GL*, 15 September 1929, p. 1.

Juan Chabás, *Amauta*, No. 28 (January 1930), pp. 21-24.

Carlos Fernández Cuenca, *La Epoca*, 3 August 1929, p. 2.

José Gorostiza, *C*, 5 (1929), 68-69.

R. Ledesma Ramos, *GL*, 1 August 1929, pp. 1-2.

J. López Prudencio, *ABC*, 7 August 1929, p. 7.

Jorge Mañach, *RAv*, 4 (1929), 343.

————. *Locura y muerte de Nadie*. Madrid: Oriente, 1929.

REVIEWS

José Díaz Fernández, *El Sol*, 24 November 1929, p. 2.

Enrique Diez-Canedo, *El Sol*, 8 December 1929, p. 2.

Melchor Fernández Almagro, *GL*, 15 December 1929, p. 3.

J. López Prudencio, *ABC*, 27 November 1929, p. 7.

————. *Teoría del zumbel*. Madrid: Espasa-Calpe, 1930.

REVIEWS

Luis Bello, *El Sol*, 10 June 1930, p. 2.

José Díaz Fernández, *El Sol*, 8 June 1930, p. 2.

Heraldo de Madrid, 5 June 1930, p. 9.

J. López Prudencio, *ABC*, 4 July 1930, p. 7.

Fernando del Rivero, *El Imparcial*, 15 June 1930, p. 8.

Jorge Rubio, *GL*, 1 September 1930, p. 15.

————. *Viviana y Merlín*. Madrid: Ediciones Ulises, 1930. 2nd edition: Madrid: Espasa-Calpe, 1936

REVIEWS

José Díaz Fernández, *El Sol*, 3 August 1930, p. 2.

Rafael Gil, *Popular Film*, 6 August 1936, n. pag.

Ernesto Giménez Caballero, *GL*, 1 January 1931, pp. 2-5.

J. López Prudencio, *ABC*, 5 September 1930, p. 7.

Jorge Rubio, *GL*, 1 September 1930, p. 15.

————. *Escenas junto a la muerte*. Madrid: Espasa-Calpe, 1931.

REVIEWS

Enrique Azcoaga, *RA*, 24 (1932), 345, 347.

Azorín, *Crisol*, 2 November 1931, p. 2.

José Díaz Fernández, *Crisol*, 24 October 1931, p. 2.

GL, 1 April 1931, pp. 11-12.

J. López Prudencio, *ABC*, 14 February 1932, p. 6.

Agustín Miranda Junco, *RO*, 34 (1931), 223-28.

————. *Lo rojo y lo azul*. Madrid: Espasa-Calpe, 1932.

REVIEWS

José Díaz Fernández, *Luz*, 7 June 1932, p. 4.

Enrique Diez-Canedo, *El Sol*, 19 June 1932, p. 2.

Indice literario, 1 (1932), 50-52.

J. López Prudencio, *ABC*, 10 July 1932, p. 17.

Miguel Pérez Ferrero, *Heraldo de Madrid*, 9 June 1932, p. 7.

RA, 25 (1932), 63.

Mallea, Eduardo. *Cuentos para una inglesa desesperada*. Buenos Aires: Gleizer, 1926.

REVIEWS

F. E. G., *Nosotros*, 55 (1927), 421.

Jacobo Fijman, *MF*, 12 December 1926, n. pag.

Benjamín Jarnés, *GL*, 1 May 1927, p. 4.

Víctor A. Nigou, *Sagitario*, 2 (1927), 260-65.

Guillermo de Torre, *RO*, 17 (1927), 117-21.

Martínez Sotomayor, José. *La rueca de aire*. Mexico City: Imprenta Mundial, 1930.

REVIEWS

José Gorostiza, *C*, 7 (1930), 240-48. Rpt. in *La Voz Nueva*, No. 43 (October 1930), n. pag.

Benjamín Jarnés, *Ariel disperso* (Mexico City: Stylo, 1946), pp. 163-64. Review orig. pub. in 1930.

Obregón, Antonio de. *Efectos navales*. Madrid: Ediciones Ulises, 1931.

REVIEWS

Fernando Beltrán, *El Sol*, 4 September 1931, p. 2.

Ricardo Gullón, *GL*, 1 July 1931, p. 14.

Benjamín Jarnés, *Crisol*, 6 July 1931, p. 2.

Rafael Laffón, *GL*, 15 December 1931, p. 5.

Miguel Pérez Ferrero, *Heraldo de Madrid*, 16 July 1931, p. 8.

Hernani Rossi, *GL*, 15 October 1931, p. 16.

————. *Hermes en la vía pública*. Madrid: Espasa-Calpe, 1934.

REVIEWS

Enrique Azcoaga, *Literatura*, 1 (1934), 106-8.

Indice literario, 3 (1934), 54-56.

Benjamín Jarnés, *RO*, 45 (1934), 93-100. Rpt. in part in *Feria del libro* (Madrid: Espasa-Calpe, 1935), pp. 254-57.

J. López Prudencio, *ABC*, 17 June 1934, p. 11.

P. Pérez Clotet, *Isla*, No. 6 (1935), n. pag.

Miguel Pérez Ferrero, *Heraldo de Madrid*, 3 May 1934, p. 7.

El Sol, 27 April 1934, p. 7.

Guillermo de Torre, *Luz*, 24 April 1934, p. 4.

Rafael Vázquez-Zamora, *Luz*, 4 June 1934, p. 12.

Owen, Gilberto. *Novela como nube*. Mexico City: Ediciones de Ulises, 1928.

REVIEWS

Benjamín Jarnés, *GL*, 1 January 1929, p. 6. Rpt. in *Ariel disperso* (Mexico City: Stylo, 1946), pp. 88-90.

Jaime Torres Bodet, *C*, 2 (1928), 87-90.

Salinas, Pedro. *Víspera del gozo*. Madrid: Revista de Occidente, 1926.

REVIEWS

Azorín, *ABC*, 9 July 1926, pp. 3-4. Rpt. in *RA*, 13 (1926), 112.

José Ballester, *La Verdad*, 22 August 1926, p. 1.

Corpus Barga, *El Sol*, 1 October 1926, p. 1.

Enrique Diez-Canedo, *El Sol*, 16 June 1926, p. 2.

Melchor Fernández Almagro, *Cosmópolis*, 3, No. 18 (May 1929), 72-73.

Ernesto Giménez Caballero, *El Sol*, 17 June 1926, p. 2.

E. Gómez de Baquero, *El Sol*, 22 July 1926, p. 1.

Heraldo de Madrid, 10 August 1926, p. 4.

Mediodía, No. 2 (July 1926), pp. 14-15.

Juan G. Olmedilla, *Heraldo de Madrid*, 14 September 1926, p. 4.

Fernando Vela, *RO*, 13 (1926), 124-29.

Torres Bodet, Jaime. *Margarita de niebla*. Mexico City: Cvltvra, 1927.

REVIEWS

Francisco Ayala, *RO*, 18 (1927), 133-37.

Martí Casanovas, *RA*, 16 (1928), 244-45.

Benjamín Jarnés, *GL*, 15 September 1927, p. 4. Rpt. in *Ariel disperso* (Mexico City: Stylo, 1946), pp. 46-49.

Julio Jiménez Rueda, *RA*, 15 (1927), 185.

Juan Marinello, *RAv*, 1 (1927), 292.

Esteban Salazar y Chapela, *El Sol*, 1 October 1927, p. 2.

―――. *La educación sentimental*. Madrid: Espasa-Calpe, 1929.

REVIEWS

Benjamín Jarnés, *Ariel disperso* (Mexico City: Stylo, 1946), 167-70. Review orig. pub. in 1930.

Lino Novás Calvo, *RAv*, 5 (1930), 157.

Rubén Salazar Mallén, *C*, 6 (1930), 186-88.

―――. *Proserpina rescatada*. Madrid: Espasa-Calpe, 1931.

REVIEWS

Antonio Acevedo Escobedo, *RA*, 24 (1932), 8, 16.

Benjamín Jarnés, *RA*, 24 (1932), 8, 16. Rpt. in *Ariel disperso* (Mexico City: Stylo, 1946), pp. 208-13.

Rafael Marquina, *GL*, 1 August 1931, p. 14.

Agustín Miranda Junco, *RO*, 33 (1931), 246-48.

E. Ruiz de la Serna, *Heraldo de Madrid*, 30 July 1931, p. 8.

―――. *Estrella de día*. Madrid: Espasa-Calpe, 1933.

REVIEWS

Ricardo Gullón, *Literatura*, 1 (1934), 69-70.

Miguel Pérez Ferrero, *Heraldo de Madrid*, 28 December 1933, p. 12.

Guillermo de Torre, *Luz*, 27 February 1934, p. 10.

Verdaguer, Mario. *El marido, la mujer y la sombra*. Barcelona: Lux, 1927.

REVIEWS

Antonio Ballesteros de Martos, *El Sol*, 5 May 1927, p. 2.

GL, 1 May 1927, p. 3.

Benjamín Jarnés, *RO*, 16 (1927), 220-24. Rpt. in part in *Rúbricas* (Madrid: Biblioteca Atlántico, 1931), pp. 162-66.

Villaseñor, Eduardo. *Extasis*. Madrid: Espasa-Calpe, 1928.

REVIEWS

Benjamín Jarnés, *Ariel disperso* (Mexico City: Stylo, 1946), pp. 147-48. Review orig. pub. in 1930.

Félix Lizaso, *RAv*, 3 (1928), 330.

Bernardo Ortiz de Montellano, *C*, 1 (1928), 207-9.

Villaurrutia, Xavier. *Dama de corazones*. Mexico City: Ediciones de Ulises, 1928.

REVIEWS

Enrique González Rojo, *C*, 1 (1928), 319-21.

Celestino Gorostiza, *La Voz Nueva*, No. 21 (August 1928), n. pag.

Benjamín Jarnés, *GL*, 1 January 1929, p. 6.

Benjamín Jarnés, *Ariel disperso* (Mexico City: Stylo, 1946), pp. 112-14. Review orig. pub. in 1929.

Jorge Mañach, *RAv*, 3 (1928), 331.

Esteban Salazar y Chapela, *El Sol*, 19 August 1928, p. 2.

Ximénez de Sandoval, Felipe. *Tres mujeres más equis*. Madrid: Ediciones Ulises, 1930.
    REVIEWS
    José Díaz Fernández, *El Sol*, 23 November 1930, p. 2.
    F. C. S., *El Sol*, 7 January 1931, p. 2.

II. Criticism

Azorín. "Baroja y los jóvenes." *ABC*, 19 January 1928, p. 3.

————. "Literatura española. Superación." *ABC*, 20 March 1929, p. 3.

Baturrillo. "La trifulca vanguardista." *Suplemento de la Revista Blanca*, 1 February 1929, p. 5.

Blanco Fombona, Rufino. "Personalidades contra escuelas." *El Sol*, 30 October 1927, p. 1.

————. *El espejo de tres faces*. Santiago de Chile: Ediciones Ercilla, 1937.

Caba, Carlos and Pedro. "Pío Baroja y el personaje masa." *Atlántico*, No. 18 (May 1933), pp. 79-81.

————. "La rehumanización del arte." *Eco*, 2, No. 9 (October 1934), n. pag.

Calleja, Rafael. "Ramón Gómez de la Serna: *El torero Caracho*." *RO*, 16 (1927), 378-85.

Chabás, Juan. "Horizonte de novela." *Heraldo de Madrid*, 19 February 1931, p. 9.

Díaz Fernández, José. "Joaquín Arderius: *La duquesa de Nit*." *La Voz*, 15 October 1926, p. 4.

————. *El nuevo romanticismo*. Madrid: Zeus, 1930.

————. "Samuel Ros: *El hombre de los medios abrazos*." *Luz*, 24 January 1933, p. 3.

Diez-Canedo, Enrique. "Ricardo Güiraldes: *Xaimaca*." *RO*, 4 (1924), 389-92.

————. "Manuel Bueno: *Poniente Solar*." *El Sol*, 29 November 1931, p. 2.

Domenchina, Juan José. *Crónicas de Gerardo Rivera*. Madrid: M. Aguilar, 1935.

Espina, Antonio. "José Bergamín: *El cohete y la estrella*." *RO*, 3 (1924), 125-27.

————. "George Bernanos: *Sous le soleil de Satan*." *RO*, 13 (1926), 386-90.

————. "La cinegrafía en la novela moderna." *El Sol*, 8 July 1928, p. 1.

————. "Benjamín Jarnés: *Libro de Esther*." *RO*, 48 (1935), 106-12.

Feria, Ramón. "La novela: género efusivo, género amplio." *GL*, 1 May 1932, pp. 5-6.

Fernández Almagro, Melchor. "Literatura nueva." *GL*, 15 November 1929, p. 3.

"Francisco Ayala." *GL*, 15 November 1929, p. 1.

Gálvez, Manuel. "La decadencia de la novela." *Criterio*, 4 (1929), 308-9.

Giménez Caballero, Ernesto. "Proust en español, por Pedro Salinas." *El Sol*, 14 June 1926, p. 2.

————. "Cartel de la nueva literatura." *GL*, 15 April 1928, p. 7.

Gómez de Baquero, E. *Pen Club*. Madrid: Renacimiento, 1929.

Gómez de la Serna, Ramón. "Sobre la novela." *Síntesis*, 3 (1929), 43-48.

Hidalgo, Alberto. "Juan Giraudoux." *MF*, 18 June 1925, n. pag.

Izaro, J. de. "Decadencia del esteticismo." *El Sol*, 16 September 1932, p. 2.

Jarnés, Benjamín. "Pentagrama: Ramón." *Alfar*, No. 41 (June-July 1924), pp. 6-8.

——. "Ramón Gómez de la Serna: *La Quinta de Palmyra*." *RO*, 10 (1925), 112-17.

——. *Ejercicios*. Madrid: Cuadernos Literarios, 1927.

——. "José Díaz Fernández: *El blocao*." *GL*, 1 July 1928, p. 3.

——. *Rúbricas*. Madrid: Biblioteca Atlántico, 1931.

——. "El novelista en la novela." *RO*, 42 (1933), 230-33.

——. "Libros y mujeres." *Luz*, 24 May 1934, p. 3.

——. *Feria del libro*. Madrid: Espasa-Calpe, 1935.

——. *Cartas al Ebro*. Mexico City: La Casa de España en México, 1940. (Articles and reviews from the 1920s and 30s.)

——. *Ariel disperso*. Mexico City: Stylo, 1946. (Reviews published between 1925 and 1935.)

Ledesma Miranda, R. "La novela y su mundo." *Eco*, 2, No. 9 (October 1934), n. pag.

Lizaso, Félix. "Boga de la biografía." *El Libro y el Pueblo*, 13 (1935), 69-83, 140-46.

López Prudencio, J. "Libros y notas literarias de 1926." *ABC*, 2 January 1927, pp. 6-7.

Lorenzo, José. "Joaquín Arderius: *Justo el Evangélico*." *Heraldo de Madrid*, 13 February 1930, p. 9.

"*Margarita de niebla* y Benjamín Jarnés." *Ulises*, No. 5 (December 1927), pp. 24-26.

Marichalar, Antonio. "Momento crítico." *RO*, 14 (1926), 254-59.

——. "Síntomas literarios." *RO*, 16 (1927), 122-23.

——. "Ultimo grito." *RO*, 31 (1931), 101-7.

——. "Musarañas (El ámbito de la novela)." *RO*, 43 (1934), 304-17.

Meléndez, Concha. "Novelas del novecientos en la América Hispana." *RA*, 27 (1933), 329-32.

"Novelas de evasión y novelas de regreso." *Heraldo de Madrid*, 26 February 1931, p. 8.

Ortega y Gasset, José. *La deshumanización del arte e Ideas sobre la novela* [1925]. In *Obras completas*. Vol. III. Madrid: Revista de Occidente, 1957.

Panero, Leopoldo. "Sobre la novela. Circunstancia y misterio." *El Sol*, 13 January 1932, p. 2.

Pérez Ferrero, Miguel. "Del poema en prosa a la novela de última hora." *Heraldo de Madrid*, 23 October 1930, p. 8.

——. "Los escritores frente al mar." *Heraldo de Madrid*, 16 August 1934, p. 6.

——. "Derrotero de la novela." *Cruz y raya*, No. 22 (January 1935), pp. 47-67.

"La Pesca y la Flecha." *Ulises*, No. 2 (June 1927), pp. 25-26.

Portal, Magda. "Panorama intelectual de México." *RA*, 16 (1928), 157-58.

Reyles, Carlos. *Incitaciones*. Santiago de Chile: Ediciones Ercilla, 1936.

Romero Mendoza, P. *Azorín*. Madrid: C. I. A. P., 1933.

Rubio, Jorge. "Los valores eternos de la novela." *GL*, 1 September 1931, p. 8.

Salaya, Guillén. *Parábola de la nueva literatura*. 2nd ed. Madrid: Biblioteca Atlántico, 1931.

Salazar, Adolfo. "Alberto Moravia: *Los indiferentes*." *El Sol*, 8 September 1932, p. 2.

Salazar y Chapela, Esteban. "A buena política, mejor literatura." *El Sol*, 26 April 1931, p. 2.

168

_____. "Ramón Gómez de la Serna: *Chao*." *El Sol*, 7 February 1934, p. 7.

Sánchez, Luis Alberto. "Evasión y superación." *GL*, 1 August 1931, p. 1.

Serna, José S. "¿La novela se va?" *Heraldo de Madrid*, 27 July 1933, p. 13.

Torre, Guillermo de. "Veinte años de literatura española." *Nosotros*, 57 (1927), 315-22.

Torres Bodet, Jaime. *Contemporáneos. Notas de crítica*. Mexico City: Herrero, 1928.

_____. "Itinerario de la costumbre." *RAv*, 5 (1930), 146-48.

_____. "Las letras hispanoamericanas en 1930," *GL*, 1 January 1931, p. 7.

"Tres novelas nuevas." *Indice literario*, 5 (1936), 1-6.

Valdés, Francisco. *Letras. Notas de un lector*. Madrid: Espasa-Calpe, 1933.

Vela, Fernando. "El arte al cubo." *RO*, 16 (1927), 79-86.

_____. "Literatura fonográfica." *La Voz Nueva*, No. 33 (August 1929), n. pag.

III. Magazines and Newspapers Cited

ABC (Madrid)

Alfar (Vigo-Montevideo)

Amauta (Lima)

Atenea (Santiago de Chile)

Atlántico (Madrid)

Contemporáneos (Mexico)

Cosmópolis (Madrid)

Crisol (Madrid)

Criterio (Buenos Aires)

Cruz y Raya (Madrid)

Eco (Madrid)

La Epoca (Madrid)

Frente Literario (Madrid)

Gaceta de arte (Santa Cruz de Tenerife)

La Gaceta Literaria (Madrid)

Heraldo de Madrid (Madrid)

Hoja literaria (Madrid)

El Imparcial (Madrid)

Indice literario (Madrid)

Isla (Cadiz)

El Libro y el Pueblo (Mexico)

Literatura (Madrid)

Luz (Madrid)

Martín Fierro (Buenos Aires)

Mediodía (Sevilla)

Noreste (Zaragoza)

Nosotros (Buenos Aires)

Plural (Madrid)

Popular Film (Barcelona)

La Revista Blanca (Barcelona)

Repertorio Americano (San José de Costa Rica)

Revista de Avance (La Habana)

Revista de Occidente (Madrid)

Sagitario (La Plata, Argentina)

Síntesis (Buenos Aires)

El Sol (Madrid)

Sur (Buenos Aires)

Ulises (Mexico)

La Vanguardia (Barcelona)

La Verdad (Murcia)

Verso y prosa (Murcia)

La Voz (Madrid)

La Voz Nueva (Mexico)

Index

Gustavo Pérez Firmat is Assistant Professor of Romance Languages, Duke University. A native of Cuba, he has published many articles on Hispanic fiction.

Books of related interest

Languages of Revolt
Dada and Surrealist Literature and Film
Inez Hedges

Lorca's New York Poetry
Social Injustice, Dark Love, Lost Faith
Richard L. Predmore

Accommodating the Chaos
Samuel Beckett's Nonrelational Art
J. E. Dearlove

The Circle of Eros
Sexuality in the Work of William Dean Howells
Elizabeth Stevens Prioleau

Modernismo in Chilean Literature
The Second Period
John M. Fein

Duke University Press
Durham, North Carolina 27708